W9-BOM-946

Tools for Structured Design

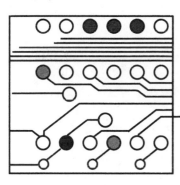

Tools for Structured Design

An Introduction to Programming Logic
Fourth Edition

Marilyn Bohl
Executive Vice President and Chief Technology Officer
Dynasty Technologies, Inc.

Maria Rynn
Northern Virginia Community College

Prentice Hall

Upper Saddle River, New Jersey   Columbus, Ohio

Library of Congress Cataloging-in-Publication Data

Bohl, Marilyn.
    Tools for structured design : an introduction to programming logic
/ Marilyn Bohl, Maria Rynn. — 4th ed.
        p.   cm.
    Includes index.
    ISBN 0-13-626466-2
    1. Structured programming.   I. Rynn, Maria   II. Title.
    QA76.6.B63   1998
    005.1'2—dc21   97-3743
                                                                                CIP

Editor: Charles E. Stewart, Jr.
Production Manager: Deidra M. Schwartz
Marketing Manager: Debbie Yarnell
Design Coordinator: Karrie M. Converse
Production Supervision: Custom Editorial Productions, Inc.
Cover Designer: Karrie M. Converse
Cover art/photo: © 1997 PhotoDisc, Inc.
Text Designer: Custom Editorial Productions, Inc.

This book was set in Times Roman by Custom Editorial Productions, Inc. and was printed and bound by Courier/Kendallville, Inc. The cover was printed by Phoenix Color Corp.

©1998, 1993 by Prentice-Hall, Inc.
Upper Saddle River, New Jersey 07458

All rights reserved. No part of this book may be reproduced, in any form or by any means, without permission in writing from the publisher.

Earlier edition © 1989 by Macmillan Publishing Company.

Acknowledgments
    Figure 2–14 reprinted by permission from GX 20-8021-2, flowcharting worksheet by International Business Machines Corporation.
    Figure 2–17 reprintd by permission from GS20-8020-1-U/MO10, flowcharting template by International Business Machines Corporation.

Printed in the United States of America

10   9   8

ISBN   0-13-626466-2

Prentice-Hall International (UK) Limited, *London*
Prentice-Hall of Australia Pty. Limited, *Sydney*
Prentice-Hall Canada Inc., *Toronto*
Prentice-Hall Hispanoamericana, S.A., *Mexico*
Prentice-Hall of India Private Limited, *New Delhi*
Prentice-Hall of Japan, Inc., *Tokyo*
Pearson Education Asia Pte. Ltd., *Singapore*
Editora Prentice-Hall do Brasil, Ltda., *Rio de Janeiro*

Preface

Tools for Structured Design: An Introduction to Programming Logic, Fourth Edition, is a textbook that teaches program design in a well-thought-out, language-independent manner. This text assumes no previous programming background. It can be used as a main text in a programming logic class or as a supplement in any beginning programming class.

Our approach is to start with simple concepts and build upon these concepts as new topics are introduced. We use a sequential, step-by-step approach that introduces, by way of example, only one new concept at a time. Sample problems are included throughout the chapters to illustrate the use of program design tools in practical situations. Enrichment sections are included in many of the chapters to illustrate the program design concepts in Basic and Visual Basic. Exercises are given at the end of each chapter to help you apply what you are learning.

Our objective is to analyze a problem and express its solution in such a way that the computer can be directed to follow the problem-solving procedure. With simple language and frequent examples, this book explains how to understand and how to use important problem-solving tools. We begin with system and program flowcharts. Flowcharting guidelines approved and published by the American National Standards Institute (ANSI) and its international counterpart, the International Standards Organization (ISO), are explained and applied to solution planning. Emphasis is placed on maintaining an overall structure in program design. We show how to use pseudocode as an alternative or supplement to flowcharting in planning the logic of a well-structured program. We analyze techniques of top-down, modular program development by describing how to read and how to develop structure charts that show the hierarchical relationships of modules within a program.

Upon completion, the solution or program design should be verified using some of the techniques we recommend. The purpose of verification is to detect and eliminate errors as early in program development as possible. Design documentation in flowchart, pseudocode, or other form of design language is also useful in subsequent program coding and program checkout. Much of the necessary documentation is created as an integral part of the program development process.

Enrichment sections are included in many of the chapters to illustrate some of the sample problems in the programming languages Basic and Visual Basic. Basic is used to illustrate how the design of a program can be implemented using a procedural approach. Visual Basic is used to illustrate how the design of a program can be implemented using an event-driven approach. It is important to note that our approach to teaching program design remains language-independent. All program design concepts are covered prior to the enrichment sections in each chapter. The enrichment sections are optional and are included as a supplement to further illustrate some of these concepts.

The fourth edition of this book offers the same pedagogical features as the third edition. Each chapter includes objectives and a list of key terms. The fourth edition also includes an index and is supported by an Instructor's Guide. The Instructor's Guide contains the same objectives and key term lists as the textbook. The Instructor's Guide also includes suggested teaching strategies, a list of transparency masters identified by number and title, and the transparency masters themselves. Solutions to all the end-of-chapter exercises are also included. A disk containing the source code for all the Basic and Visual Basic examples included in the enrichment sections of the text is available to instructors.

The text is organized into three parts as follows:

The first part (Chapters 1 through 9) introduces the theory of structured programming and includes a chapter on each control structure as well as a chapter on array fundamentals. Chapter 9 has been added to this edition to introduce object-oriented design and programming. These chapters should be covered in sequence.

The second part (Chapters 10 through 12) illustrates several more complex applications, building on material previously introduced. These chapters can be covered in any order after Chapters 1 through 9 are completed.

The final part (Appendices A through C) contains general reference material, including solutions to selected end-of-chapter exercises.

The specific content of each chapter and appendix follows.

Chapter 1 describes the system development life cycle and how program design fits with it. Computer-assisted software engineering (CASE) tools are introduced in this chapter and are referred to throughout the book, where appropriate, to increase your awareness of current tools and trends in the industry. The history of structured programming is also introduced in this chapter. Several nontechnical examples illustrate the basic control structures to give you a sense of what structured programming entails. The concepts of event-driven programming and graphical user interfaces are also introduced in this chapter.

Chapter 2 introduces the SIMPLE SEQUENCE control structure. Chapter 3 introduces the IFTHENELSE control structure and teaches simple, sequential, and nested IFs. Chapter 4, focusing on header record logic, and Chapter 5, focusing on trailer record logic, illustrate the DOWHILE control structure, but introduce different techniques for loop control. Chapter 5 also includes a discussion of automatic end-of-file processing and multiple-heading logic.

Chapter 6 introduces the CASE control structure. Chapter 7 introduces the DOUNTIL control structure. Chapter 8 introduces one- and two-dimensional arrays with many short simple examples. Chapter 9 is a new chapter that introduces concepts of object-oriented program design. Psuedocode examples are used to illustrate object-oriented design concepts such as classes, data members, methods, encapsulation, driver programs, overloading, inheritance, and polymorphism.

Chapter 10 concentrates on more advanced array applications such as searching (both sequential and binary) and sorting. Chapter 11 illustrates the design of a sequential master file update program. Chapter 12 covers control-break processing.

Appendix A contains ANSI-approved symbols for program flowcharting, and Appendix B summarizes the basic control patterns of structured programming. Appendices A and B should be referred to whenever you arc in doubt about which symbols to use in flowcharts. Responses to selected end-of-chapter exercises are provided in Appendix C to help you evaluate your understanding of the material.

Acknowledgments

This book would not exist today if it were not for the hard work of many people. We would first like to thank Charles E. Stewart, executive editor, and his assistant Kathleen Linsner, for all their help in putting this book together. We would also like to thank Jim Reidel and Louise Sette for their support and assistance during the production of this manuscript.

Maria Rynn would also like to thank her two dearest friends, Laurie McCullough and Steve Drasner, for their continuing support and advice throughout this revision. Finally, she wishes to thank her husband, Tedd, for his constant encouragement, patience, and loving support during this endeavor.

We hope that all who use this book will find that it provides a clear, systematic, and direct approach to problem solving. We welcome your comments and suggestions.

Marilyn Bohl
Maria Rynn

Contents

Tools for Structured Design

1 Introduction to Structured Design

Objectives

Upon completion of this chapter you should be able to

- Name and identify the six steps in the system development life cycle.
- Define a computer-based information system.
- State four objectives of computer-assisted software engineering (CASE) and give examples of CASE tools.
- Name and identify the five steps in the program development cycle.
- Name and identify some of the tools and methodologies used in the design of well-structured programs.
- Define what is meant by a graphical user interface (GUI).
- Distinguish between procedural languages and fourth-generation languages.
- Define what is meant by event-driven programming.
- Distinguish between syntax errors and logic errors in a program.
- Distinguish between unit testing and system testing.
- Name some forms of documentation needed in a computer-based information system.
- Name the three basic control structures of structured programming.

Introduction

We live today in a business world. Goods and services are bought and sold, distributed, produced, and created worldwide at incredible rates. Some businesses are international conglomerates; others are small mom-and-pop shops. The success of any business depends, for the most part, on how well the business is run. Every business uses one or more systems to produce its end products. A **system** is a combination of people, equipment, and procedures that work together to perform a specific function. A system can be manually operated or computer-assisted. A **computer-based information system** is a system in which some of the procedures are performed by a computer. Since desktop computers have become widely accessible, even small businesses are using computers or are looking into converting their manual systems to computer-based ones. Such a conversion is not an easy task, but it can be simplified by following a series of well-defined steps.

System Development Life Cycle

The **system development life cycle (SDLC)** (Figure 1–1) is a series of well-defined steps that should be followed when a system is created or changed. The SDLC represents the big picture of what happens during system creation or modification. In this chapter we outline the steps in the SDLC and identify the ones on which this book focuses.

Analyze the Current System

Assume the owners of a local stationery store have decided to computerize the store's ordering and inventory control procedures. By doing so they hope to know the quantities of inventory in stock at any time, what products are selling the best, when to reorder to avoid being out of stock, and so on. Where might they begin? All aspects of the current system need to be studied carefully. This is usually done with the help of an information system professional, known as a **system analyst.** The analyst studies every aspect of the existing system to get a clear understanding of what things are done and how. He or she also attempts to identify any problems associated with the system.

There are several ways the analyst can go about this task, but the most effective technique is to talk to users of the system. The **users** are people who are directly involved with the system in their day-to-day activities. (In our example, the store buyer, the clerks, and so on are users.) They are the ones who can most clearly define each system function and any problems associated with that function.

Define the New System Requirements

Once the existing system is understood, the requirements of the new or changed system are defined in the second step of the SDLC. The analyst should specify what needs to be done, not how to do it. These requirements should state which changes are necessary to eliminate the problems identified in the initial analysis. For example, concerning the required system outputs, the analyst might ask: What types of reports are required? What information should each report contain? How should the reports be formatted? What headings, spacing, and so on should be used? If users of the system will interact directly with it, the analyst may need to define screen formats for video display terminals or desktop computers.

In addition to input and output requirements, all storage and processing requirements must be defined. For example, what files will be needed? What data should be contained in those files? After all the requirements are worked out by the analyst, he or she prepares a report outlining these

---

**Figure 1–1
System Development
Life Cycle (SDLC)**

1. Analyze the current system
2. Define the new system requirements
3. Design the new system
4. Develop the new system
5. Implement the new system
6. Evaluate the new system

requirements for management. Management can then decide whether or not to proceed. If the decision is yes, the next step of the SDLC can begin.

Design the New System

In the third step of the SDLC, either the analyst or a coworker known as a **system designer** uses the requirements defined in the preceding step as a basis for designing the new or modified system. He or she determines how the system will be constructed. Any of several tools may be used to illustrate the system design.

One such tool is a **system flowchart,** which is a graphic representation detailing all of the programs within a system and how they interrelate. For each program, the system flowchart shows all the major inputs and outputs. Figure 1–2 illustrates a system flowchart for a payroll system. Each symbol in the system flowchart has a special meaning. These symbols will be discussed in more detail in Chapter 2.

In this example the data on time sheets is entered into a payroll program, together with data from the payroll master file. (Master files will be discussed in Chapter 6 and Chapter 11.) The payroll program produces two reports and the actual paychecks. This example shows what data the program needs to begin its processing and what output the program actually produces. No detail is given as to how the program actually works. This will be done when the new system is developed.

Many additional tools are used in the design of a system. These tools are very important but are more appropriately discussed in a system analysis and design textbook. This text will focus on program development tools.

In recent years much emphasis has been placed on automating the tasks of system development. The goals underlying such automation are to gain

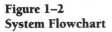

Figure 1–2
System Flowchart

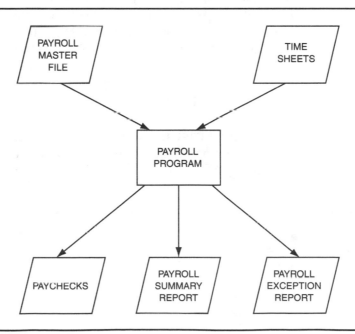

more control over the processes of system development (to avoid large budget overruns; to avoid projects that are months or years late or never completed at all); to improve programmer productivity (especially in businesses with too few trained people to do all the necessary system development); to make the programmer's job easier (manual drawing of system flowcharts, for example, can be very tedious); and to improve program quality (a program that is used to direct airplanes in flight or to maintain a hospital's patient life-support system must be right). The term **computer-assisted software engineering,** or **CASE,** has been coined to refer to the automation of tools, methods, and procedures for system development. The widespread availability of desktop computers has accelerated the trend toward the use of CASE. For example, Intersolv's Excelerator Series for Analysis and Design and Popkin's System Architect are desktop-computer–based tools used by system analysts and designers to create and maintain system flowcharts and other design tools. By increasing your basic analysis and design skills through study of this book, you can enable yourself to make effective use of the ever-increasing array of CASE tools in the marketplace.

Develop the New System

In the fourth step of the SDLC, each of the programs called for in the system design is constructed. For example, the details of the payroll program shown in the system flowchart in Figure 1–2 will be specified. This development stage is composed of a series of well-defined steps called the **program development cycle (PDC)** (see Figure 1–3). The steps of the PDC are carried out by a **programmer.** A description of the types of activities in each step follows.

Review the Program Requirements In the first step of the program development cycle, the programmer reviews the requirements defined in the second step of the SDLC. If anything is unclear at this point, the programmer asks for more information from the system analyst who wrote the original requirement, from the system designer, or even from a future user of the program (such as the store buyer). The programmer must not make unfounded assumptions. It is just as useless to solve the wrong problem correctly as it is to solve the right problem incorrectly.

Develop the Program Logic In this step the actual processing steps within each program in the system are developed. We shall focus on this step throughout this book. Just as there are tools to use in the design of a

**Figure 1–3
Program Development
Cycle (PDC)**

1. Review the input, processing, output, and storage requirements
2. Develop the logic for the program
3. Write the program using a programming language
4. Test and debug the program
5. Complete the program documentation

system, there are tools to use in the design of a program. Two common tools discussed in detail in this book are **program flowcharts** and **pseudocode.** Like system flowcharts, program flowcharts contain standard symbols. These symbols graphically depict the problem-solving logic within a program. Pseudocode consists of English-language statements that describe the processing steps of a program in paragraph form. Figure 1–4 illustrates both a program flowchart and pseudocode to compute and print an employee's paycheck.

Another important program design tool is the **hierarchy chart,** or **structure chart.** Structure charts are used in program design to show the relationships among parts of a program. Each program part is called a **module,** and the process of breaking down a program into parts or modules is called **modularization.** Figure 1–5 illustrates a structure chart for a payroll program.

In this example, the payroll program is subdivided into three major modules. Each module is identified by a name and a number. Module B010 (compute pay) is further subdivided into three modules. Notice that

**Figure 1–4
Program Flowchart and
Pseudocode**

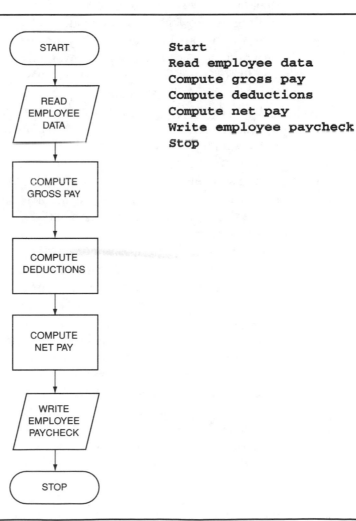

**Figure 1–5
Structure Chart**

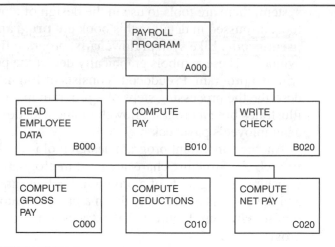

descending levels on the structure chart represent modules of greater detail or refinement.

There are many ways to divide a program into modules. Some are better than others. We will explore modularization in more detail in Chapter 4.

Program flowcharts, pseudocode, and structure charts are very useful tools during program design. They also provide handy references during program modification. Some are available in automated forms, allowing you to construct diagrams like flowcharts or structure charts using a computer and a CASE tool instead of pencil and paper.

Once the design of a program has been completed, it should be reviewed by a small group of programmers and analysts. In this way, potential problems that might have gone unnoticed by the person who designed the program surface early in the program development cycle. (It is always easier to find someone else's error than to locate your own.) The goal of the review is to ensure that high-quality software is produced. A good program is one that is reliable, producing what it is expected to produce. In other words, it works!

Another characteristic of high-quality software is ease of use. As a user, you want programs to be **user-friendly.** For example, assume you are about to use a program to compute the average of a series of numbers. You load the program into the computer and execute it. You watch the screen, and a question mark (?) appears (see Figure 1–6). What should you do? It's not clear whether you should type in all the numbers or only one number at a time. If you type in all the numbers, should they be separated by spaces or commas? You cannot tell from the screen. Now, suppose you load and execute another program to compute an average. This time a message on the screen tells you exactly what to do (see Figure 1–7). Which program would you rather use? Which one is user-friendly?

Both Figure 1–6 and Figure 1–7 are examples of what is called a **graphical user interface,** or **GUI.** Graphical user interfaces make it easier for the user to interact with the computer. They present information in an easy-to-use point-and-click fashion. For example, once the user enters a number in the box in Figure 1–7, the user can simply click the OK button using some type of pointing device. Common pointing devices include mice and track

Figure 1–6
Sample Input Screen
(Unfriendly)

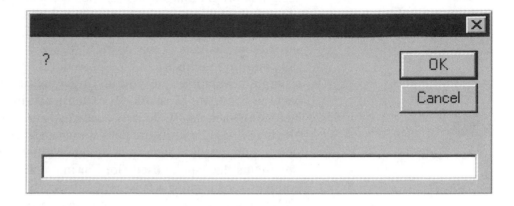

Figure 1–7
Sample Input Screen
(User-Friendly)

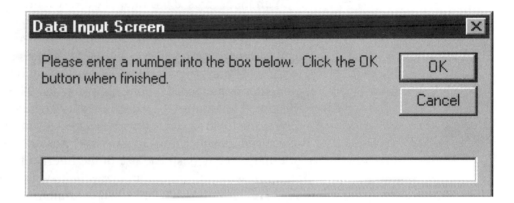

balls. Thus, a GUI minimizes the amount of typing required by presenting the user with choices from which desired options can be selected by point-and-click actions.

What about ease of use from a programmer's point of view? Although a programmer does not use a program in the same sense that a user does, he or she must be able to understand the steps in the design if modifications are required. Consider a program that handles income tax calculations based on current tax laws. What happens when some of those laws change? The program will have to be modified to reflect those changes. In all probability, the person modifying the program will not be the one who wrote it originally, so the program logic must be clear and easy to follow. This textbook discusses methodologies that are used to design reliable, well-written programs.

Write the Program After the program logic has been developed, it must be expressed in a programming-language form. The selection of the language depends on the type of application and on the software development tools available. In the past, most business applications were written in COBOL, since it is oriented to business use. Now, more structured languages such as Pascal and C are used more frequently because they contain language elements that closely parallel the structures used in program design. A programmer who uses these **procedure-oriented languages** codes the specific steps in the problem-solving process. Programming examples in Basic, a simple-to-use procedural language, are illustrated in subsequent chapters of this book.

In addition to this traditional procedural approach, another approach to program development using **fourth-generation languages (4GLs)** has become common. Most 4GLs are **nonprocedural languages;** a programmer using such a 4GL defines what needs to be done, not how. For example, many popular software packages (word processors, electronic spreadsheets, and database managers, to name a few) contain programming statements that can be used alone or in combination (macros and programs) to accomplish a task more efficiently. Even personal computer (PC) users will find that a strong base in programming logic can be a tremendous help when using a particular package to implement decision-making activities.

With the increased use of applications containing graphical user interfaces, visual languages such as Visual Basic and Visual C++ have become popular. These languages support the concept of **event-driven programming.** An event-driven program is one that is designed to respond to actions that occur when the program is executing. The actions can be initiated by the computer or by the user. For example, when the user clicks the OK button illustrated in Figure 1–7, a click event is triggered. The programmer must design the logic associated with that click event. We will see many examples of event-driven programs in the Visual Basic examples later in this book.

Finally, the widespread use of the Internet has been accompanied by rapid growth in the use of a relatively new programming language known as "Java." Java is often described as similar to C++, but without some of C++'s complex programming constructs.

Thus, programming logic is an essential skill in computer-related jobs. Some users write programs using conventional or event-driven programming languages; some use popular packages as tools; and some use previously written programs as applications. This is not to say that anyone can program. Training in program design and the use of the tools is necessary. The amount of detailed logic that users need differs according to what they do. Many of the CASE tools include basic tutorials and **online help systems** designed to help users, analysts, designers, and programmers use the applications and tools effectively (see Figure 1–8).

Test and Debug the Program In this step the program is checked for errors **(bugs)** and tested with sample data to see if actual results produced by the program match expected results. There are two main categories of errors that may exist in a program: syntax errors and logic errors. **Syntax errors** occur when the programmer does not follow the rules of the language he or she is using. For example, many statements in C must end with semicolons. If the programmer forgets to enter a semicolon, he or she makes a syntax error. Such errors are usually easy to find and eliminate. A **logic error** occurs when a step in the program logic is incorrect. For example, an averaging program will produce the wrong answer if the sum of the numbers to be averaged is divided by a number other than the total count of

Figure 1–8
Online Help Screen

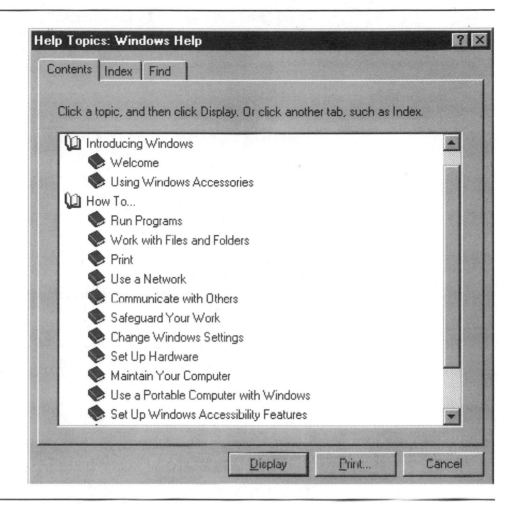

numbers. Such errors are not always easy to detect. The programmer may need to go back and review the logic created in the second step of the program development cycle in order to locate the error.

The program must also be tested thoroughly with computer help using simple data. Every possible condition should be tested, if feasible. For example, if a payroll program computes an employee's pay at time and a half for all hours worked over 40, the program should be tested using data values that are less than 40 hours, exactly 40 hours, and more than 40 hours. The program also should be designed to handle input data that is invalid. For example, an hours value that is less than 0 in the payroll example should be detected and noted in an error message or on an input exception report.

The programs that make up a system should first be tested individually to make sure that each works correctly. This is called **unit testing.** Then the programs should be tested together as a system, either entirely or in part. This is called **system testing,** or **integration.** The more thorough the unit testing is, the more likely the integration will proceed successfully. All too often, the unit testing is not adequate and the integration of the system components (programs) becomes a tedious, time-consuming sequence of do's and redo's.

Complete the Program Documentation Documentation is an ongoing process that occurs throughout the program development cycle. A technical reference needs to be created for programmers who may need to modify one or more of the programs. User guides need to be created to tell users how to use and operate the system. Some of the documentation may be in hard copy (printed) form; other documentation may be provided as online help for convenient reference by users. One cannot overemphasize the importance of good documentation. It is a tremendous help during program development and a vital aid during program modification.

Implement the New System

After the program development cycle is completed, the new system is implemented. Users are trained, and operating procedures are defined. The system documentation is reviewed, revised as necessary, and prepared in its final form. Any of several implementation strategies may be employed: The new system may be run concurrently with the existing (old) system; the new system may completely replace the old system; or the new system may be phased in gradually. The specifics of each strategy are beyond the scope of this book, but you should be aware that they exist.

Evaluate the New System

In the sixth step of the SDLC, the new system is evaluated to determine if it is meeting the required objectives. If some of the objectives are not being met, parts of the system may have to be modified. In any case, a system evaluation report should be prepared for management. It is likely to serve as one input to a subsequent system development life cycle.

Structured Programming

As stated earlier, this text will focus on the second step of the program development cycle, developing the program logic. There are many ways to solve a problem, particularly a complex one. There are usually many correct solutions; however, some are more desirable than others. In this text we will adhere to the principles of a methodology called **structured programming,** a technique that has proven to be very effective in solving problems as well as in modifying solutions. We will also look at another approach called **object-oriented programming.** Object-oriented programming bases the design of an application around the data to be manipulated. We will discuss object-oriented programming in more detail in Chapter 9. It suffices to say at this point that good program design incorporates both structured programming design principles and object-oriented design principles. We will now turn our attention to structured programming.

Structured programming is the ability to express a problem solution using only three basic patterns of logic. These patterns are referred to as **control structures.** The patterns are based on the computer's ability to execute instructions in a step-by-step, sequential manner; its ability to make decisions; and its ability to repeat instructions. The theoretical framework for this approach is usually traced to a paper by C. Bohm and G. Jacopini, initially published in Italian in 1965, then republished in English in 1966.[1] Their "structure theorem," which appears in that paper, is generally accepted as a proof of the claim that the three structures are sufficient for programming. In addition, as early as 1965, Professor E.W. Dijkstra of the Netherlands insisted that programs using definite structuring were easier to write, read, and verify.[2] There is a vast amount of literature documenting numerous program development projects in which this does, indeed, appear to be the case.

The following sections will use familiar examples to illustrate the three patterns of structured programming. They should give you a sense of how each structure works. The next several chapters will teach you how to use each structure to solve specific, well-defined problems.

Basic Control Structures

The three patterns referred to in the previous sections are called the SIMPLE SEQUENCE control structure, the IFTHENELSE control structure, and the DOWHILE control structure.

SIMPLE SEQUENCE Control Structure The **SIMPLE SEQUENCE control structure** represents the computer's ability to execute instructions in a step-by-step, sequential manner. A simple example not involving the computer can be used to illustrate this concept. The sequential steps in Figure 1–9 represent directions you might give a friend to get to your house. The steps must be followed in a sequential manner. If not, your friend might never find your house.

IFTHENELSE Control Structure The **IFTHENELSE control structure** represents the computer's ability to make a decision. Let us modify the above example to illustrate this concept. Suppose the left turn at the fork is blocked at certain times. You will need to provide alternative directions to your friend. You will also need to include the original directions (since they

**Figure 1–9
Simple Sequence:
An Example**

1. Proceed down Main Street for two miles.
2. Turn left on Ocean Drive.
3. Proceed on Ocean Drive for three blocks, to the fork.
4. At the fork, take Swan Street to the left.
5. Proceed two blocks.
6. House is second on the left (246 Swan Street).

---

[1]C. Bohm and G. Jacopini, "Flow Diagrams, Turing Machines and Language with Only Two Formation Rules," *Communications of the ACM* 9,5 (May 1966): 366–71.

[2]Among Dijkstra's writings on the subject are "GOTO Statement Considered Harmful," Letter to the Editor, *Communications of the ACM* 11,3 (March 1968): 147–48; "The Structure of the Multiprogramming System," *Communications of the ACM* 11,5 (May 1968): 341–46; and "Structured Programming," in J.N. Buxton and B. Randell, eds., *Software Engineering Techniques* (NATO Scientific Affairs Division: Brussels 39, Belgium, April 1970): 84–88.

**Figure 1–10
IFTHENELSE:
An Example**

1. Proceed down Main Street for two miles.
2. Turn left on Ocean Drive.
3. Proceed on Ocean Drive for three blocks, to the fork.
4. IF left turn at fork is blocked THEN
    Take right turn at fork onto Eagle Street.
    Proceed five blocks.
    Turn left at Clifton Avenue.
    Proceed three blocks.
    Turn left at Circle Drive.
    Proceed two blocks.
    Turn left at Swan Street.
    House is fourth on the right (246 Swan Street).
ELSE
    At the fork, take Swan Street to the left.
    Proceed two blocks.
    House is second on the left (246 Swan Street).
ENDIF

are shorter) to use if the left turn at the fork is not blocked. Notice how the directions in Figure 1–10 incorporate decision-making logic.

Notice that if the road is blocked there are eight separate instructions to follow. If the road is not blocked there are three instructions. Both sequences of instructions are included since you don't know whether or not the road will be blocked. However, your friend will follow only one of the sequences. Although this example is nontechnical, we have included the keywords and indentation that identify an IFTHENELSE control structure. You will learn more about this control structure in Chapter 3.

DOWHILE Control Structure The **DOWHILE control structure** represents the computer's ability to repeat a series of instructions. A series of repeated instructions is called a **loop.** Let us look at a different example to illustrate this concept. Consider the simple instructions on the back of a shampoo bottle (listed in Figure 1–11). Although these instructions are simple enough for us to understand, a computer would get confused. First of all, the second instruction says to "Rinse," but "Rinse" what? Also, the third instruction says to "Repeat." Clearly, we know to repeat the process from the beginning. However, we need to specify to the computer which steps it should repeat. Figure 1–12 gives a new version of these instructions.

These new instructions clarify some unknowns, but the computer would still have trouble. Can you see why? Every time the computer got to Step 3, it would begin again at Step 1, just as the instructions say. This is

**Figure 1–11
DOWHILE: Example 1**

Wash hair
Rinse
Repeat

**Figure 1–12
DOWHILE: Example 2**

1. Wash hair
2. Rinse hair
3. Repeat from Step 1

an example of an **infinite loop:** There is no way out. The computer would theoretically execute forever. In common practice, this would not actually happen. A special program would intercept the program execution and issue an error message indicating that too much time had passed since the program began executing.

Every loop must include a statement that defines how many times to execute the loop steps or under what condition to continue or to stop the looping process. In this example, we could indicate that the steps be performed two times, or that the steps be performed as long as the hair is not clean. Consider our example one more time (see Figure 1–13). We have included the keywords and indentation that identify a DOWHILE control structure. The two indented steps represent what needs to be done, and the first statement (DOWHILE) specifies the condition necessary to continue processing. We will explore DOWHILE loops in more detail in Chapters 4 and 5.

**Figure 1–13
DOWHILE: Example 3**

```
DOWHILE hair is not clean
    Wash hair
    Rinse hair
ENDDO
```

Key Terms

system
computer-based
    information system
system development life
    cycle (SDLC)
system analyst
user
system designer
system flowchart
computer-assisted
    software engineering
    (CASE)
program development
    cycle (PDC)
programmer
program flowchart
pseudocode

hierarchy (structure)
    chart
module
modularization
user-friendly
graphical user
    interface (GUI)
procedure-oriented
    language
fourth-generation
    languages (4GLs)
nonprocedural language
event-driven
    programming
online help system
bug
syntax error

logic error
unit testing
system testing
    (integration)
structured
    programming
object-oriented
    programming
control structure
SIMPLE SEQUENCE
    control structure
IFTHENELSE control
    structure
DOWHILE control
    structure
loop
infinite loop

Exercises

1. Name the steps in the system development life cycle.

2. Name the steps in the program development cycle.

3. **(a)** What does the acronym CASE stand for?
    (b) List four major objectives of CASE technologies.

4. What are the characteristics of a high-quality program?

5. (a) What does it mean to say that a program is user-friendly?
   (b) Give an example of a user-friendly program.
   (c) Give an example of a program that is not user-friendly.

6. What is a graphical user interface?

7. What does it mean to say that a language is procedure-oriented?

8. (a) Give an example of a procedure-oriented language.
   (b) Give an example of a visual language.

9. What is meant by event-driven programming?

10. (a) What is the difference between a syntax error and a logic error?
    (b) Give an example of each type of error.

11. What is the difference between unit testing and system testing?

12. Give some examples of documentation.

13. Name the three basic control structures of structured programming.

SIMPLE SEQUENCE
Control Structure

Objectives

Upon completion of this chapter you should be able to

- Define an algorithm.
- Name the characteristics of an algorithm.
- Name the four parts, in order, of a data hierarchy.
- Identify, and use in program design, the SIMPLE SEQUENCE control structure.
- Define the terms *information processing* and *information processing system.*
- Distinguish between a program flowchart and a system flowchart.
- Identify, and use in program design, the terminal interrupt, general I/O, and process program flowcharting symbols.
- Distinguish between a variable and a constant.
- Identify, and use in program design, variables, constants, and assignment statements.
- Distinguish between input and output, and explain why input and output steps are needed in program design.
- Perform a procedure execution of a simple algorithm.

Introduction

A computer is an extremely powerful, fast machine. In less than a second, it can perform difficult calculations that otherwise would take days, months, or years to perform. Yet a computer has no magical power; it is only a tool. It cannot devise a plan or decide to act. It can do only what it is told, in exactly the way it is told. We can direct the computer to do what we want by specifying our needs in a discrete step-by-step manner. Specifically, we must develop an **algorithm,** which is a step-by-step procedure to solve a problem.

A computer cannot act independently; it has no intelligence of its own. For this reason, any algorithm that we use to direct it must be set up to identify all aspects of a processing situation and to present, in detail, all steps to be performed.

The algorithm must

- Use only operations from a given set of basic operations
- Produce the problem solution, or answer, in a finite number of such operations

The concept of "a given set of basic operations" is important because the computer can perform only certain operations; its capabilities are planned very carefully by hardware designers who lay out specifications that direct subsequent construction of the machine. The concept of "a finite number of such operations" is important because each operation performed by a computer takes a certain amount of time (say, from one-millionth to one-billionth of a second, depending on the machine architecture). If an unlimited number of steps is required, it is not possible, even using the fastest computer available, to obtain the solution in a finite amount of time.

The term *algorithm* may be new to you, but most of us use numerous algorithms daily. For example, we adopt routine procedures, or algorithms, for getting up in the morning, fixing meals, going to work, and so on. A typical wake-up algorithm is shown in Figure 2–1.

Figure 2–1 is an example of a **program flowchart.** It may also be called a **block diagram,** or **logic diagram.** Very simply, a program flowchart is a

Figure 2–1
Wake-Up Algorithm

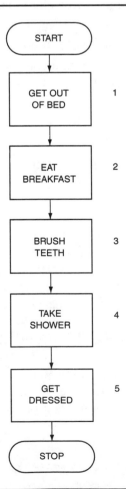

picture of an algorithm. Each step in this algorithm is defined in a rectangle, the symbol used to indicate a specific process. The rectangle represents the **process symbol.** Every algorithm must have one entry point (START) and one exit point (STOP). These are indicated by the ellipsis symbols, called **terminal interrupt symbols.**

All symbols on a program flowchart are connected by flowlines, which may or may not have arrowheads. The arrowheads show the direction of flow. They can be omitted when the flow is from top to bottom or left to right, but are otherwise required. Program flowcharts are usually easier to read when arrowheads are used.

Notice that the flowchart in Figure 2–1 has five steps, all processed one after another. The flowchart illustrates the first of the three basic control structures used to develop algorithms. As you may recall from Chapter 1, this structure is called the **SIMPLE SEQUENCE control structure.** It is the simplest and most frequently used of the three basic control structures.

In common practice, the algorithm shown in Figure 2–1 is carried out somewhat informally. The person who executes the algorithm may even be unaware that he or she is following an algorithm. In other situations, however, algorithms are more formally defined. For example, business operations within a company are firmly established—uniform accounting procedures must be followed; inventory must be tightly controlled; manufacturing volumes must be correlated with both distribution and sales; and so on.

All of these business applications involve some form of paperwork. The term **information processing** is really another name for paperwork. It is a series of planned actions and operations upon data to achieve a desired result. The methods and devices that achieve the result form an **information processing system.** Regardless of the kind of data processed or the methods and devices used, all information processing systems involve at least three basic elements:

- The source data, or input, entering the system
- The orderly, planned processing within the system
- The end result, or output, from the system

Data Hierarchy

Before we look at our first formal algorithm, we will discuss some terms associated with the structure of the data processed by algorithms. The four terms, **file, record, field,** and **character,** make up what is known as the **data hierarchy.** This hierarchy defines how data is structured for use in the algorithms that we will explore.

FILE
: A file is a collection of related data or facts. For example, payroll facts for *all* the employees in a company form a payroll file. All the data in Figure 2–2 represent a payroll file.

RECORD
: A record is a collection of data, or facts, about a single entity in the file. For example, payroll facts for a *single* employee in a company form a payroll

**Figure 2–2
Data Hierarchy**

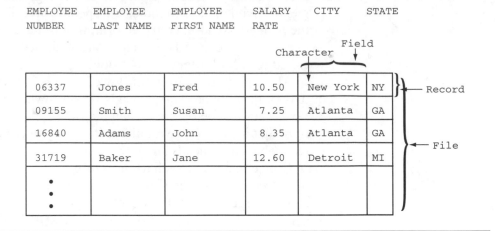

record. Each line in Figure 2–2 represents one payroll record.

FIELD A field is any single piece of data, or fact, about a single entity (record) in a file. For example, an employee number might be one of the fields in a payroll record. The employee number 06337 represents a field in the first payroll record in Figure 2–2.

CHARACTER A character is a letter (A–Z, a–z), number (0–9), or special character (for example, . or ? or %, and so on). For example, in Figure 2–2 the employee number contains all numeric characters, the employee last name contains all alphabetic characters, and the salary rate contains both numeric characters and a special character.

Sales Application Example

Consider the sales operations of a large department store. A sales manager delegates responsibilities to supervisors in various departments. Each supervisor submits a weekly sales report that is checked against inventory changes and then used as the basis for figuring commissions. Each supervisor is confronted with the task, or problem, of preparing the weekly sales report for his or her department. In some stores, each supervisor may be asked to develop his or her own procedure. In other stores, the sales manager develops a detailed set of instructions for each supervisor. In either case, the supervisor starts with the sales data available (the input), thinks about the weekly sales report that is needed (the output), and plans how to prepare the report on the basis of the sales data (the process).

Sales Application System Flowchart

Before a program flowchart is developed to solve a problem, a **system flowchart** is often created to show more general information about the application. A system flowchart illustrating the basic inputs, processes, and outputs for the sales program needed for this application is shown in Figure 2–3.

The leftmost symbol on the system flowchart is the **general input/output (I/O) symbol;** that is, the parallelogram. It always represents either input (data available for processing) or output (processed data, or information, available to users or for additional processing). Since this symbol can be used for both input and output, it appears twice on the flowchart.

The rectangular symbol appears again in Figure 2–3. Here it is a general-purpose symbol indicating, collectively, all the processing steps within the sales program. When this symbol appears on a system flowchart, it represents an action or a series of actions performed by the central processing unit (CPU)—the carrying out of an algorithm expressed in a computer-program form.

One important function of a flowchart is to aid in problem analysis and solution planning; another is to aid the problem solver in communicating ideas to others. To help standardize such communication, the American National Standards Institute (ANSI) has coordinated the development of a standard set of flowcharting symbols and associated meanings. We shall use many of these symbols in the flowcharts in this book. Their shapes and meanings are summarized in Appendix A.

Thus, a system flowchart shows the data, flow of work, and workstations within an information-processing system. In this book we shall deal with simple problems requiring only one computer program for their solution. A system flowchart may show the flow of work through several programs, each having several inputs and outputs, but such systems are beyond the scope of this book.

Sales Application Program Flowchart

Although a system flowchart is very helpful in showing the inputs, major processing functions, and outputs of an information-processing system, it gives only a limited amount of detail about how the computer performs the specific processing steps. The system flowchart in Figure 2–3 shows that a program for computing a weekly sales report is to be written and executed. It doesn't show which mathematical operations are needed or the order in which the operations must be performed. To provide this detailed information, we construct a program flowchart.

In the program flowchart, the detailed steps needed to process the data about one person's sales must be specified. It is sometimes helpful to work backward. In this flowchart, for example, we should first decide what we need to know to compute a salesperson's pay. Usually, a salesperson's pay is determined in part by how much he or she has sold in a given week. In

**Figure 2–3
Sales Problem
(System Flowchart)**

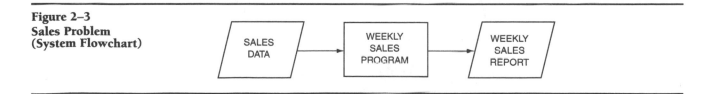

this example, the sales will be divided into two categories: those items sold at regular price, and those sold at a reduced or sale price. Each person will be paid a base amount as well as a percentage of his or her weekly sales. This percentage (commission) will be 6 percent on the sales of regular-priced items and 3 percent on the sales of sale-priced items.

Here is a representative sequence of instructions to solve this problem:

1. Input the two weekly sales totals for any employee.
2. Compute the regular commission by multiplying the regular sales amount by 6 percent.
3. Compute the sales commission by multiplying the reduced sales amount by 3 percent.
4. Compute the total pay due: $200.00 (base pay) + regular commission + sales commission.
5. Output the total pay on the payroll report.

These instructions can also be expressed pictorially, whereby the steps to be followed can be seen at a glance. A program flowchart of the required steps is shown in Figure 2–4.

Figure 2–4
Sales Problem (Program Flowchart)

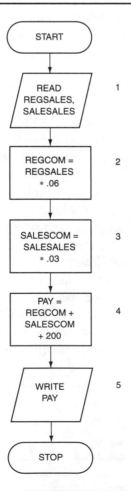

We have just traced the first two major parts of any problem-solving task:

- Defining the problem to be solved
- Developing a solution algorithm—steps to be taken to solve the problem

The five steps on the flowchart in Figure 2–4 correspond to Steps 1 through 5 of the written procedure. Notice, however, the use of the general I/O symbol in Steps 1 and 5. It is important to understand that, before the pay can be computed, the sales data must be known to the computer. We get this data into the computer in an **input** step (notice the I/O symbol). This is almost always one of the first steps in an algorithm. Typically, the word *READ* is used to indicate input, but a word such as *ENTER*, *GET*, or *INPUT* can also be used.

In Step 1 the word *READ* is followed by the words *REGSALES* and *SALESALES*. These words are names for variables. **Variables** are data items whose values may change, or vary, during processing. We create **variable names** to represent, or refer to, these data items. One common mistake is to put the specific data right in the program, as follows:

```
READ
$1000,
$3000
```

This step may lead the reader to believe that the salesperson sold $1000 worth of regular items and $3000 worth of sale items. These numbers, although correct for one employee, are likely to need changing each time the program is run, since each employee's sales data is likely to differ. This problem is handled by the use of variables. The variable names are place-holders for the specific data values. The value of a variable can change each time a program is run, or even within one run of the same program. Think of a mailbox. The address (variable name) is always the same, but the mail (content) is different every day.

When a variable is used in conjunction with a READ statement, we can assume that the value of the variable is now known to the computer; this is called a **defined value.** The use of variables helps to ensure that the program is **data independent,** which means that the program will perform the required processing steps on any set of input data. Figure 2–5 shows a snapshot of the computer's memory at this point. We will refer to the figure as a memory diagram. On the left is a list of all the variable names referenced in the algorithm. The boxes on the right represent the actual values that these variable names refer to in the computer's memory. At this point REGSALES and SALESALES represent values that were input in Step 1. Actually, these two amounts can be any numbers equal to the values of whatever was sold. In our example, we will assume that the regular sales amount (REGSALES) was $1000.00 and the reduced sales amount (SALESALES) was $3000.00. Only the values of REGSALES and SALESALES are defined to the computer at this point.

In Step 2, the regular commission is computed. Since this step involves arithmetic, it is represented by a process symbol, not by an I/O symbol. In this step we are illustrating the use of a very important fundamental

**Figure 2–5
Sales Problem—Memory
Diagram 1**

REGSALES	1000
SALESALES	3000
REGCOM	
SALESCOM	
PAY	

statement—the **assignment statement.** This statement is very commonly used when describing computer processing. An assignment statement must adhere to the following rules of formation:

1. Only a single variable name may appear to the left of the **assignment symbol,** which in our example is =.

2. Only a single variable name, constant, or expression may appear to the right of the =.

3. Everything to the right of the = must be known (defined) to the computer.

Step 2 uses an assignment statement to compute the commission on the regular sales. Since the percentage is always 6 percent, the .06 can be used in the statement. The .06 is an example of a **constant,** a value that never changes. Since .06 is a constant, it can be placed in computer storage when the program itself is placed in computer storage. Therefore it does not have to be input during processing. The times sign (∗) is defined because it refers to a basic arithmetic operation the computer can perform. The asterisk symbol is used to show multiplication because the traditional times sign, ×, may be confused with the variable name X. The only other item to the right of the = is the variable name REGSALES. Since the value of this variable was previously input (Step 1), it is also known at this time. Since everything is defined to the right of the =, the computer can now do the calculation and assign the result to the variable on the left of the =. When carrying out an assignment statement, the computer operates on everything defined to the right of the = first. In this example, $1000 is multiplied by .06, and the result, $60, is assigned to the variable name REGCOM. REGCOM is now known or defined to the computer (see Figure 2–6).

Step 3 computes the commission on the sales items (remember 3 percent). Can you see that everything to the right of the = is defined to the computer? SALESALES is multiplied by .03, and the result is assigned to SALESCOM (see Figure 2–7).

Step 4 then adds the two computed commissions to the base pay of $200 to come up with the salesperson's total pay. Notice that the base pay is a constant—all salespeople get at least $200. In this assignment statement, values for the two variables on the right were not input but are still defined to the computer. Any variable that is the result of a computation

**Figure 2–6
Sales Problem—Memory
Diagram 2**

REGSALES	1000
SALESALES	3000
REGCOM	60
SALESCOM	
PAY	

**Figure 2–7
Sales Problem—Memory
Diagram 3**

REGSALES	1000
SALESALES	3000
REGCOM	60
SALESCOM	90
PAY	

(left side) in a previous step is defined and can be used in subsequent steps. As a result of Step 4, the variable name PAY is now defined and has a value of $350 (see Figure 2–8).

At this point, the pay for a single employee has been computed, but it is still inside the computer. Normally we want to see that pay on a piece of paper. If so, it must be output from the computer to a printer. We show this operation in Step 5, again using an I/O symbol, with the word *WRITE* indicating **output.** Words such as *OUTPUT*, *PRINT*, or *DISPLAY* can also be used. The current value of a variable can be output, provided it has been defined, either by being input or by being computed. We see here that PAY was computed in Step 4.

Throughout this process, several variable names have been introduced. Usually, variable names are chosen by the programmer. It is a wise idea to choose descriptive names, like SALES, instead of S. Descriptive variable names make the algorithm (in flowchart form and later in programming-language form) much more self-documenting and easier to read.

**Figure 2–8
Sales Problem—Memory
Diagram 4**

REGSALES	1000
SALESALES	3000
REGCOM	60
SALESCOM	90
PAY	350

Design Verification

When the programmer is satisfied that all processing steps have been identified and provided for, the solution algorithm should be verified. The objective is to prevent errors from occurring, or, if some have already occurred, to detect and eliminate them as soon as possible. In the past, a major portion of a programmer's time was spent, not in program design and coding, but rather in debugging and testing. Today, many computer professionals insist that this need not be the case: A program can be written correctly, so that it executes properly the first time it is run. A careful, early verification of the program design, or solution algorithm, is an essential step in achieving this objective.

Under one approach to verification of design, the design documentation is distributed to selected reviewers, who are asked to study it and respond within a set time. Every reviewer is directed to note, individually, any required changes, additions, and deletions. This approach is known as an **informal design review.**

Another approach is the use of **structured walkthroughs.** At this point in algorithm development, the walkthrough is a **formal design review.** Here, the design documentation is made available to from two to four people selected to serve as members of a review team. After they have had time to prepare, these reviewers meet together with the program designer and a moderator for an established period, usually about two hours. Each reviewer is expected to have studied the design documentation and is asked to comment on its completeness, accuracy, and general quality. Then the moderator "walks" the group through each step of the documentation, covering any points raised by the review team.

How does one start when reviewing a solution algorithm set forth in a program flowchart or other form of design documentation? Some reviewers, individually or in groups, find that one effective approach is to pretend to be the computer. Representative values for all types of input are selected: (1) data that is normally expected; (2) valid but slightly abnormal data (e.g., minimum and maximum values allowable); and (3) invalid data. The individual or group follows the problem-solving logic step by step to process the input and determine what output will be produced. If the output matches predetermined correct results, the logic within the solution algorithm is upheld. Pretending to be the computer in this way is called **simulation, procedure execution,** or **desk checking.** While tracing the problem-solving logic, each reviewer must be careful not to make any assumptions. The computer can do only what it is told; it is unable to make assumptions.

Sample Problem 2.1 (Temperature Conversion Problem)

Problem:

The International Broadcasting Company wants a computer program that will accept a temperature reading expressed in Fahrenheit degrees as input, convert the value to Celsius degrees, and provide both the Fahrenheit value and the Celsius value as output for its hourly weather report.

Solution:

The system flowchart for this application is shown at the left in Figure 2–9. A program flowchart representation of the solution algorithm, showing how the problem is to be solved, is given at the right.

The terminal interrupt symbol containing START identifies the beginning of the program. First, the Fahrenheit value (FARENHT) is read as input. Figure 2–10 shows a memory diagram assuming an input value of 77 degrees.

In the next step, a familiar mathematical formula is executed to convert this value from Fahrenheit to Celsius. This formula contains three constants (32, 5, and 9) and several mathematical operators. The computer evaluates mathematical expressions in a specific order. All multiplication and division operations are evaluated first, in a left-to-right order. Next, all addition and subtraction operations are evaluated, again from left to right. We can place parentheses around part of an expression if we want the computer to evaluate that part first. If there are several sets of parentheses, the innermost parentheses are evaluated first. Figure 2–11 shows how two expressions,

Figure 2–9
Temperature Conversion Problem

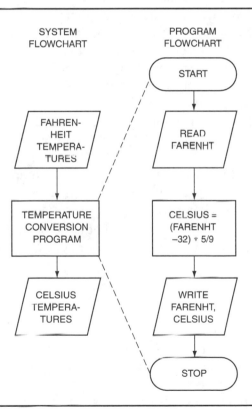

Figure 2–10
Temperature Conversion Problem—Memory Diagram 1

FARENHT	77
CELSIUS	

Figure 2–11
Expression Evaluation

Expression—no parentheses	Expression—with parentheses
$3 + 5 * 2 - 8 / 4$	$(3 + 5) * 2 - 8 / 4$
$3 + 10 - 8 / 4$	$8 * 2 - 8 / 4$
$3 + 10 - 2$	$16 - 8 / 4$
$13 - 2$	$16 - 2$
11	14

Figure 2–12
Temperature Conversion Problem—Memory Diagram 2

FARENHT	77
CELSIUS	25

one with parentheses and one without parentheses, are evaluated. Notice that the results are different.

In Sample Problem 2.1, parentheses are placed around the expression FARENHT – 32 since the subtraction needs to be done before the multiplication. Without the parentheses, first the 32 would have been multiplied by 5, then that result would have been divided by 9, and then that result would have been subtracted from the current value of the variable FARENHT. This sequence of operations, however, would have produced an incorrect result.

Figure 2–12 shows a memory diagram after the value of CELSIUS has been computed correctly.

The two temperatures, FARENHT and CELSIUS, are then written as output. Notice that the value of the variable FARENHT is not computed in the algorithm. However, since it is input, it is known to the computer (look again at Figure 2–10). At this point the computer provides two numbers as output without identifying them. In Chapter 3 we will discuss how to label output values. Finally, program execution is terminated.

When this simple sequence of basic operations is executed by the computer, it will provide the solution to this temperature conversion problem.

Sample Problem 2.2 (Billing Problem)

Problem:

A major department store needs a program to prepare a monthly bill for each customer. For simplicity, let us assume that each customer purchases (at most) one type of item each month. For each purchase, there will be four input values: customer name, item, quantity purchased, and price. The output will be the customer's monthly bill after a 10 percent discount is taken before taxes, and a 5 percent sales tax is added.

Solution:

The system flowchart to represent this billing problem appears in Figure 2–13. The program flowchart for the billing program to provide the solution appears in Figure 2–14.

Figure 2–13
Billing Problem
(System Flowchart)

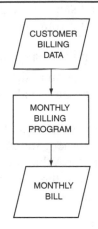

Figure 2–14
Billing Problem
(Program Flowchart)

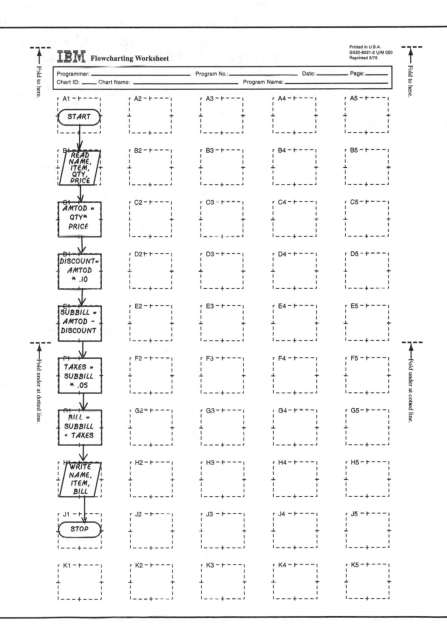

Four values are input in the first step on the program flowchart. Figure 2–15 shows a memory diagram after four specific values have been read during processing.

Notice that both AMTOD and DISCOUNT must be defined before they can be used on the right-hand side of an assignment statement. The next two steps on the flowchart compute these values. The results are illustrated in Figure 2–16.

What other variables must also be defined? Desk check the solution algorithm to verify that each assignment statement operates only on values that are well defined to the computer. What are the names of the variables that are input? What are the names of the variables that are output? What constants are used in this algorithm? (See Exercise 11 at the end of the chapter.)

Before you go on to the exercises, give some thought to the following questions. Think about why we used constants to represent the discount percent (.10) and the tax percent (.05). Could we have represented this data by variables instead? (See Exercise 12.) Also, why do you think the billing data wasn't constant? Can you think of some general criteria that might

Figure 2–15
Billing Problem—Memory Diagram 1

NAME	MR. JOHN LEE
ITEM	SCARF
QTY	2
PRICE	19.50
AMTOD	
DISCOUNT	
SUBBILL	
TAXES	
BILL	

Figure 2–16
Billing Problem—Memory Diagram 2

NAME	MR. JOHN LEE
ITEM	SCARF
QTY	2
PRICE	19.50
AMTOD	39.00
DISCOUNT	3.90
SUBBILL	
TAXES	
BILL	

determine when data used in a program should be constant and when it should be allowed to vary; that is, to be represented by variables?

Finally, think about the following questions. What happens within the computer during the stages of input? processing? output? Do you think each stage is necessary in every algorithm? We'll answer many of these questions, and more, in future chapters.

Flowcharting Tools

The program flowchart in Figure 2–14 is superimposed on a **flowcharting worksheet.** Forms of this type are designed to assist programmers in placing symbols on flowcharts. In full size, the 11-by-16$\frac{1}{2}$-inch worksheet provides an arrangement of 50 blocks with alphabetic and numeric coordinates: The 10 horizontal rows are lettered from top to bottom—*A* to *K*; the 5 vertical rows are numbered from left to right—1 to 5. The blocks are aids for squaring up flowlines, maintaining uniform spacing between symbols, and providing coordinates (for example, *A*1 and *K*3) that can be referred to elsewhere on the flowchart. The worksheet itself is usually printed in light-blue ink so that its guidelines do not appear on photographic copies of the flowchart.

Another tool usually provided for the programmer's use is a **flowcharting template.** The template is a plastic or metallic card containing flowcharting symbols as cutout forms. The programmer can easily trace the outlines of the symbols needed for both system and program flowcharts. For example, a flowcharting template made available by IBM is shown in Figure 2–17. The flowcharting symbols on this template generally comply with the American National Standards Institute (ANSI) and International Standards Organization (ISO) recommendations summarized in Appendix A. Use of such templates is not only convenient, but also encourages uniformity in flowcharting, which in turn provides for better communication between the programmer and others who refer to the programmer's flowcharts.

Figure 2–17
Flowcharting Template

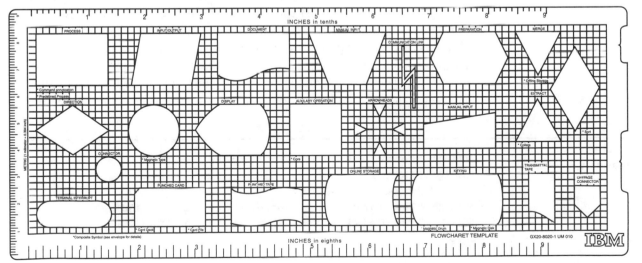

In recent years, software vendors have developed numerous CASE tools that can be used to construct and modify system and program flowcharts. These CASE tools can save the analyst and programmer many hours of work and, consequently, have become quite popular.

Enrichment (Basic)

Basic is a procedural programming language that is relatively simple to use. This section, as well as the other Basic sections in subsequent chapters, does not attempt to teach you how to program. These sections are simply illustrations of some of the program design examples in this book. As you read through these Basic examples, you should get a sense of what actually is involved in the creation and execution of a Basic program.

Figure 2–18 illustrates a listing of the program that solves the Temperature Conversion problem (Figure 2–9). Each step on the program flowchart is shown as a separate line in the listing. In Basic there are several ways in which data can be input. In this example, we use the *Input* statement, which will request a Fahrenheit temperature from the user when the program is executed. Note that this Input statement is preceded by a *Print* statement. The Print statement outputs directions to the user that specify what input is needed. Remember our discussion of user-friendly programs in Chapter 1. We have also included two additional Print statements, one for each temperature value. We have added identifying labels to make the output clearer. Text enclosed in double quotes will be printed out exactly as entered. The text is a *character-string constant.* The Basic language requires that character-string constants be enclosed in double quotes. Some programming languages require that character-string constants be enclosed in single quotes, and some programming languages accept either double quotes or single quotes. (We'll learn more about character-string constants in Chapter 3.) The *End* statement is used in Basic to stop the execution of the program.

Figure 2–19 illustrates the output that will be produced when the program is executed. When the Input statement is executed, a question mark is presented to the user, indicating that the computer is waiting for input. After the user enters a temperature, program execution continues and two lines of output are written, one for each temperature value. Note that in Figure 2–18 a blank space is included in each character-string constant prior to the ending quote. We include a blank space in each character-string constant to ensure that at least one blank space will be output between the label and the temperature value. If the temperature value is positive, the computer

**Figure 2–18
Temperature Conversion
Problem (Basic List)**

```
PRINT "Enter a Fahrenheit temperature"
INPUT FARENHT
CELSIUS=(FARENHT-32)*5/9
PRINT "The Fahrenheit temperature is "; FARENHT
PRINT "The Celsius temperature is "; CELSIUS
END
```

Figure 2–19
Temperature Conversion
Problem (Basic Run)

```
Enter a Fahrenheit temperature
? 212
The Fahrenheit temperature is   212
The Celsius temperature is   100
```

outputs an additional blank space instead of a plus (+) sign. However, if the temperature value is negative, the computer outputs a minus (–) sign to the left of the temperature value. Thus, positive temperature values will be preceded by two blank spaces, while negative temperature values will be preceded by one blank space as shown below:

The Fahrenheit temperature is 45   (positive value)

The Fahrenheit temperature is –45   (negative value)

Enrichment (Visual Basic)

Windows is a program that creates a graphical user interface on the screen while managing all the applications running on a computer. Visual Basic is used to create applications that will run in the Windows programming environment. Visual Basic is an event-driven programming language that incorporates graphical user interface design and programming that is similar to Basic. This section, as well as the other Visual Basic sections in subsequent chapters, does not attempt to teach you how to program. These sections are simply illustrations of some of the program design examples in this book. As you read through these Visual Basic examples, you should get a sense of what is actually involved in the creation and execution of a Visual Basic program.

Figure 2–20 illustrates the graphical interface for the Temperature Conversion problem (Figure 2–9). In Visual Basic, the interface is created by the programmer by placing *objects* or *controls* on the screen. In this example, five objects are created—three *labels,* one *text box,* and one *command button.* The two labels "Fahrenheit Temperature" and "Celsius Temperature" are used to identify other controls. A text box is created to accept user input. In this example, the empty rectangle below the "Fahrenheit Temperature" label is the text box. This is the area where the user will enter the temperature. Next to the text box is another empty rectangle. Although this rectangle looks exactly like a text box, it is actually another label control. Label controls should be used for items that are output only. Since the Celsius temperature is not an input, using a text box would be inappropriate for holding the Celsius value. Text boxes give the user the ability to enter data; labels do not. Thus, labels are used either to identify other controls or to display items that are output only. The other control on the screen is a command button called Convert. When the user clicks the Convert button, a *click event* is generated and the Fahrenheit temperature in the text box is converted to a Celsius amount and displayed in the label. The programmer must create the program that will be executed when the click event occurs.

Figure 2–20
Temperature Conversion
Problem (Visual Basic—
Screen 1)

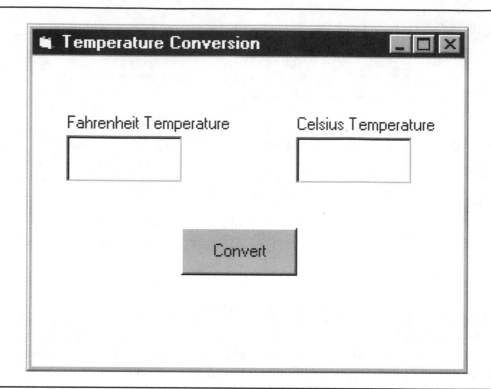

Figure 2–21 illustrates the screen after the user has entered a Fahrenheit value, and Figure 2–22 illustrates the screen after the user has clicked the Convert button.

Figure 2–21
Temperature Conversion
Problem (Visual Basic—
Screen 2)

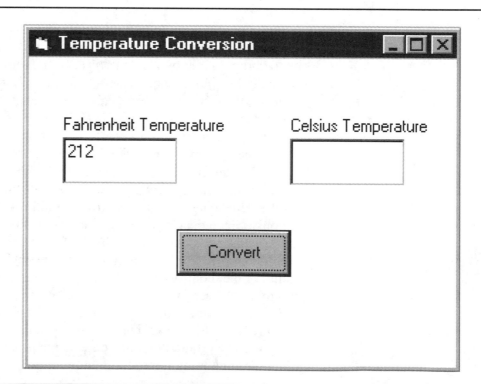

Figure 2–22
Temperature Conversion
Problem (Visual Basic—
Screen 3)

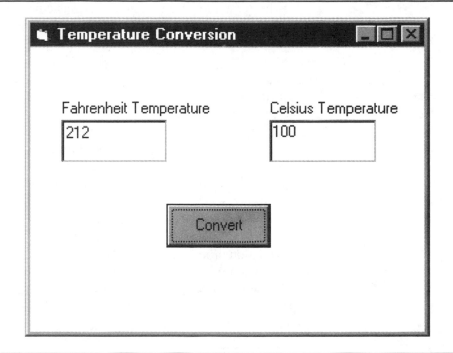

Figure 2–23 illustrates the program that is associated with the click event. In Visual Basic each event is written as a separate small program called a *Sub* (short for Subprogram). The name of the Sub is identified by the name of the control (cmd_CONVERT) followed by an underscore and the name of the event (click). Each control has a unique name as defined by the programmer. Standard naming conventions dictate that command buttons begin with *cmd,* labels with *lbl,* and text boxes with *txt.* The rest of the name can be chosen by the programmer, but should be descriptive of the control's function. Note that this segment of code contains one assignment statement that parallels the statement in the design. The only difference is that the variable names are replaced by the control names.

In Visual Basic each control has a set of characteristics called *properties.* For example, the *caption* property of a label control determines what will be displayed in that label. Similarly, the *text* property of the text box control determines what will be displayed in the text box. For example, the label that will hold the Celsius temperature (lbl_CELSIUS) contains a blank caption when the program begins. Once the program in Figure 2–23 is executed, the caption of lbl_CELSIUS is replaced with the computed Celsius value. The formula to compute this value must access the text property of the Fahrenheit temperature control (txt_FAHRENHEIT). The notation that is used to specify a property of a given control is:

controlname.property

Figure 2–23
Temperature Conversion
Problem (Visual Basic —
cmd_CONVERT_Click

```
Private Sub cmd_CONVERT_Click()
    lbl_CELSIUS.Caption=(txt_FAHRENHEIT.Text-32)*5/9
End Sub
```

It is important to note that in Visual Basic programs, variable names in design are often replaced by control names and properties in code.

Key Terms

algorithm
program flowchart
block diagram
logic diagram
process symbol
terminal interrupt
  symbol
SIMPLE SEQUENCE
  control structure
information processing
information-processing
  system
file
record

field
character
data hierarchy
system flowchart
general input/output
  (I/O) symbol
input
variables
variable names
defined value
data independent
assignment statement
assignment symbol
constant

output
informal design
  review
structured
  walkthrough
formal design review
simulation
procedure execution
desk checking
flowcharting
  worksheet
flowcharting template

Exercises

1. What is an algorithm?

2. State in your own words the two required characteristics of an algorithm. Explain why each is necessary.

3. (a) What is an information-processing system?
   (b) Name three basic elements involved in an information-processing system of any type.

4. (a) Name the four terms (highest to lowest) associated with the data hierarchy.
   (b) Give an example to illustrate each of these terms.

5. Name the fields in the payroll records shown in Figure 2–2.

6. Distinguish between system flowcharts and program flowcharts, showing how they are similar and how they differ.

7. (a) What is the normal, or assumed, direction of flow on both system and program flowcharts?
   (b) What must the designer do to indicate when the normal direction of flow is not adhered to on a particular path on a flowchart?

8. (a) How has the work of the American National Standards Institute (ANSI) affected flowcharting?
   (b) Why is this work important?

9. Evaluate the following expressions:
   (a) $7 + 4 - 6 * 5 * 2 = 50$
   (b) $10/2 - 8 + 41 * 3 = 114$

(c) $(7 + 2) - 6/3 * 2/2$ ≠ *1*

(d) $8 * (6 + (4 + 2)/3) - 2 * 2 - 1$ ≃ **59**

10. Look at the flowchart in Figure 2–4. On the basis of this flowchart, what are the total wages for an employee if the employee's sales of regular items are $1,430.00 and his sales of sale items are $820.00? *813.40*

11. Look at the flowchart in Figure 2–14. On the basis of this flowchart, answer the following questions:
    (a) For what variables are values read as input? *Name, item, Qty, Price*
    (b) What variables' values are output? *Name, item, Bill*
    (c) What constants are used? *Discount + Taxes*
    (d) Simulate the execution of this algorithm, assuming the values shown below are read as input for the first four variables named.

NAME	MRS. A.B. WALLACE
ITEM	BLOUSE
QTY	3
PRICE	49.95
AMTOD	*149.85*
DISCOUNT	*14.99*
SUBBILL	
TAXES	
BILL	

What values should the computer provide as output?

12. Redo Sample Problem 2.2, allowing the discount rate and the tax rate to vary. Provide the two rates as input at the beginning of the algorithm.

13. The computer is to read values for regular hours, overtime hours, and hourly wage rate for one employee from an employee time sheet. Payment for regular hours is to be computed as rate times hours. Payment for overtime hours is to be computed at time and a half, or 1.5 times rate times hours. The computer is to compute and output the total pay for the employee for the week. Construct a program flowchart for this application.

14. Draw a program flowchart for a program that will accept one number as input. Assume this number represents some amount of yards. Compute the corresponding values of feet and inches, and output all three values—that is, yards, feet, and inches.

15. Draw a program flowchart for a program that will compute the average of five grades. Input the five grades and output the average.

16. Draw a program flowchart for a program that will compute the area and perimeter of a rectangle. The input will contain the length and the

width of the rectangle. The output will contain the length, width, area, and perimeter of the rectangle.

17. Repeat Exercise 16, but now find the area and circumference of a circle rather than the area and perimeter of a rectangle. Assume that one value, the diameter of the circle, is provided as input. Output the diameter, area, and circumference of the circle.

3 IFTHENELSE Control Structure

Objectives

Upon completion of this chapter you should be able to

- Identify, and use in program design, the IFTHENELSE control structure.
- Identify, and use in program design, the decision and connector program flowcharting symbols.
- Use pseudocode as a tool in program design.
- Identify, and use in program design, the null ELSE pattern.
- Identify, and use in program design, the sequential IFTHENELSE pattern.
- Identify, and use in program design, the nested IFTHENELSE pattern.
- Distinguish between the logic represented by a sequential IFTHENELSE pattern and the logic represented by a nested IFTHENELSE pattern.

Introduction

The programs discussed in Chapter 2 were very straightforward. Each program directed the computer to accept some input, perform one or more calculations, and then provide written output. The computer was directed to follow a SIMPLE SEQUENCE control structure and, accordingly, the steps were carried out in a sequential manner.

In many cases, however, it may be desirable to vary the sequence of processing steps carried out within a solution algorithm. For example, the computer may need to handle different kinds of input data or respond to different situations that arise during processing. Event-driven programs often have to deal with a wide range of possibilities. To do so, we want to take advantage of the computer's logical decision-making capabilities.

Billing Example

Refer again to the task of preparing monthly statements to be mailed to the customers of a large department store (Sample Problem 2.2). Let us modify the problem slightly by stating that only customers whose bills exceed $200 (before taxes) are to receive a discount. A flowchart of an algorithm to solve this problem is shown in Figure 3–1. The diamond-shaped symbol in the flowchart is a **decision symbol.** It indicates that, at a particular point in processing, a choice between two alternative paths, or sequences of instructions, is to be made.

Figure 3-1
Billing Problem (Flowchart)

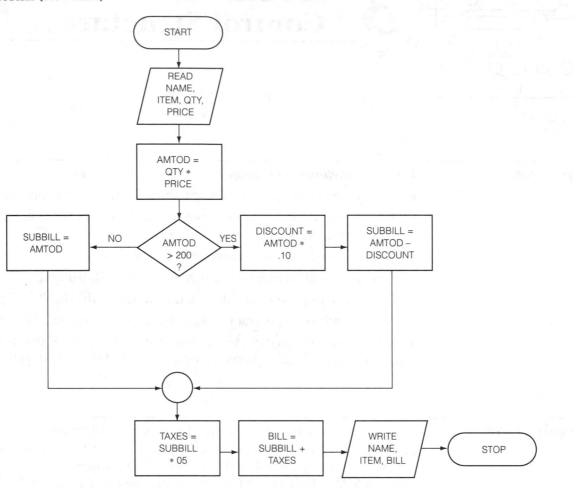

The computer reads the data and multiplies quantity by price. Then the result of the multiply operation is tested: Is the amount owed (AMTOD) greater than (>) $200? Obviously, the question can be answered in either of two ways—yes or no. If the amount owed is not greater than $200, then the "NO" path is taken and the computer sets the variable named SUBBILL to the original amount owed. No discount is computed in this case. On the other hand, if the amount owed is greater than $200, the "YES" path is taken. It is composed of two steps. First the actual discount (DISCOUNT) is computed (in this example the discount multiplier is 10 percent). DISCOUNT is then deducted from the amount owed, and again the result is placed in the variable named SUBBILL. Notice that there are two assignment statements beginning with "SUBBILL ="; however, only one of them will actually be executed by the computer. This decision point in the algorithm is called a **conditional branch.**

Notice that the test responses (yes or no) are clearly indicated on the flowlines from the decision symbol. This documentation is necessary to make the flowchart easier to understand. Programming errors are less likely to occur when the solution algorithm is expressed again in computer-program form.

Pseudocode

A flowchart is one way of expressing the decision-making logic in this solution algorithm, but there are other ways as well. One very common technique is the use of an informal language known as **pseudocode.** We can use pseudocode to express the same decision-making logic, as shown in Figure 3–2.

Whereas flowcharts express algorithms pictorially, pseudocode is a text form of representation. Pseudocode is similar to some high-level programming languages (e.g., Pascal and C), but it does not require that we follow strict rules as we would if actually writing a program. When using pseudocode, it is acceptable to use English words and mathematical symbols as we have in the flowchart. The pseudocode presents the solution algorithm in an easy-to-read, top-to-bottom fashion. For emphasis and clarity, the keywords IF, THEN, ELSE, and ENDIF are written in uppercase letters. The THEN and ELSE clauses are indented a few positions. The keywords ELSE and ENDIF are aligned at the left margin with the keyword IF to show that they are part of the same decision-making step.

IFTHENELSE Control Structure

Recall that in Chapter 2 we stated that the SIMPLE SEQUENCE pattern was basic to the design of an algorithm and one of the three basic control structures. Here we see another basic control structure, the **IFTHENELSE control structure.** Its general form is shown in Figure 3–3.

First, condition p is tested. If p is true, then statement c is executed and statement d is skipped. Otherwise (else), statement d is executed and c is skipped. Control then passes to the next processing step.

Figure 3–2
Pseudocode—Introduction

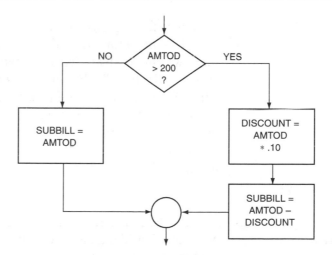

```
IF amount owed is greater than $200 THEN
     multiply amount owed by .10 to get discount
     subtract discount from amount owed to get subbill
ELSE
     set subbill equal to amount owed
ENDIF
```

Figure 3–3
IFTHENELSE—Generic

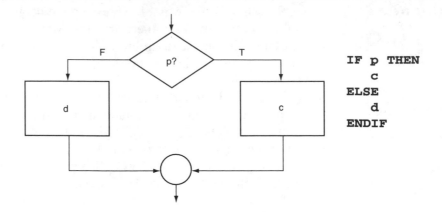

```
IF p THEN
     c
ELSE
     d
ENDIF
```

Figure 3–4
Billing Problem
(Pseudocode)

```
Start
Read NAME, ITEM, QTY, PRICE
AMTOD = QTY * PRICE
IF AMTOD > 200 THEN
    DISCOUNT = AMTOD * .10
     SUBBILL = AMTOD - DISCOUNT
ELSE
     SUBBILL = AMTOD
ENDIF
TAXES = SUBBILL * .05
BILL = SUBBILL + TAXES
Write NAME, ITEM, BILL
Stop
```

Before leaving this figure we should note that a small, circular symbol called a **connector symbol** is used in representing the decision-making logic within the IFTHENELSE pattern. It acts as a collector, emphasizing that the IFTHENELSE pattern has only one entry point and one exit point. When a connector symbol is used in this manner, it always has two flow-lines entering and one exiting. A well-structured program requires that both decision paths join together in a common exit point. Figure 3–4 shows the pseudocode for the entire algorithm shown in flowchart form in Figure 3–1.

Time Card Example

Now let's consider another variation of the IFTHENELSE structure. Assume we have been given the following problem statement: An employee time card containing employee number, name, and hours worked is to be read as input. If the employee has worked more than 40 hours, his or her number, name, and hours worked are to be printed on a weekly overtime report provided as output. If the employee has not worked more than 40 hours, no print action is required.

A program flowchart representation of the algorithm to solve this problem is given at the left in Figure 3–5. The same algorithm is expressed in pseudocode form at the right.

This algorithm introduces one new idea: the *no-function condition,* usually called a **null ELSE.** When the tested condition of the IFTHENELSE pattern (HOURS > 40, in this case) is true, we follow the "yes" path. When the tested condition is not true, no special alternative action is required. Thus the "no" path goes directly to the connector symbol closing the IFTHENELSE. In pseudocode, the no-function condition is represented by enclosing the keyword ELSE in parentheses. It is followed immediately by the keyword ENDIF.

As a system designer or programmer, you may choose to use either program flowcharts or pseudocode, or both, in developing an algorithm. Flowcharts are a good learning tool and are usually easier for the beginner; remember the old saying—"A picture is worth a thousand words." Pseudocode, however, is faster to write, and may be a more suitable tool when working on complex problems.

Another advantage of pseudocode is that it can be created using any of several available CASE tools. It can also be included as comments in program coding or as part of the prologue for a program. Once entered, pseudocode can be updated easily with computer help whenever the logic of the program is changed. We shall continue to use both program flowcharts and pseudocode as we study the basic patterns of well-structured algorithms; both techniques offer certain advantages to system designers and programmers.

**Figure 3–5
Time Card Problem**

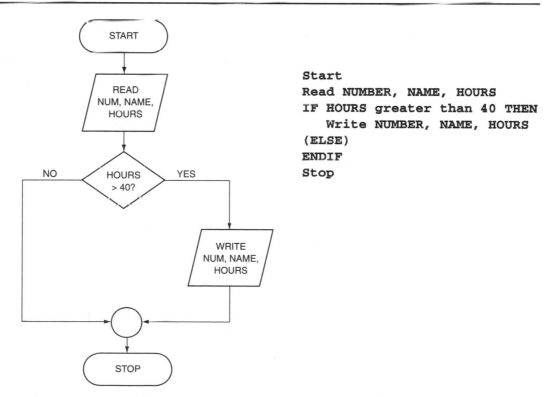

```
Start
Read NUMBER, NAME, HOURS
IF HOURS greater than 40 THEN
    Write NUMBER, NAME, HOURS
(ELSE)
ENDIF
Stop
```

Sample Problem 3.1 (Payroll Problem)

Problem:

Compute the pay for an employee, assuming that name, Social Security number, hours worked, and hourly rate are input. The output will be the name, Social Security number, and pay for the employee. Regular pay will be computed as hours (up through 40) times rate, and overtime pay will be computed at time and a half (1.5 times hours times rate) for all the hours worked over 40.

Solution:

A solution to this problem is shown in both flowchart form (Figure 3–6) and pseudocode form (Figure 3–7).

We see here numerous examples of the SIMPLE SEQUENCE control structure and one example of the IFTHENELSE control structure. Once the employee data is input, the value of the variable HOURS, which is now defined, can be tested to determine if the employee did, in fact, work

Figure 3–6
Payroll Problem (Flowchart)

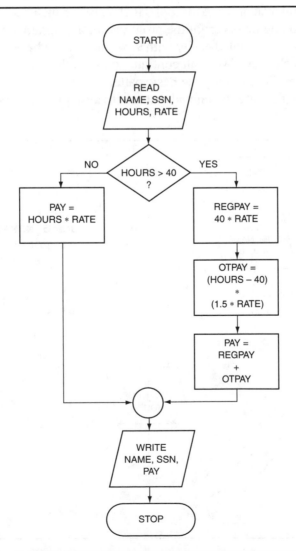

Figure 3–7
Payroll Problem
(Pseudocode)

```
Start
Read NAME, SSN, HOURS, RATE
IF HOURS > 40 THEN
    REGPAY = 40 * RATE
    OTPAY = (HOURS - 40) * (1.5 * RATE)
    PAY = REGPAY + OTPAY
ELSE
    PAY = HOURS * RATE
ENDIF
Write NAME, SSN, PAY
Stop
```

overtime (i.e., is HOURS greater than 40?). If not, the pay is computed normally (HOURS × RATE). However, if the employee did work overtime, we break the computation for pay down into three parts. First we compute the pay received for the first 40 hours (REGPAY). In this path, we know the employee worked at least 40 hours. Next, we compute the overtime pay (OTPAY); that is, the pay received for all hours over 40 (HOURS − 40), remembering to multiply the rate by 1.5 to get the time-and-a-half rate. In the last step along the "yes" path of the IFTHENELSE, the two previously computed amounts are added to determine the total pay. The WRITE statement that follows the connector will be executed, regardless of the way the pay was computed. This statement follows the IFTHENELSE structure; therefore, it is not contained within the IFTHENELSE logic. This is indicated in the pseudocode by placing the WRITE statement on the line below the keyword ENDIF. The ENDIF, in pseudocode, is equivalent to the connector on the flowchart.

Sample Problem 3.2 (Finding the Smallest Number)

Problem:

Now that we have seen how a single IFTHENELSE structure works, let us look at a problem that combines several IF statements. Figure 3–8 shows the flowchart representation and Figure 3–9 shows the pseudocode representation of an algorithm to find the smallest of four numbers.

Solution:

The four numbers are input as values for the variables N1, N2, N3, and N4. One additional variable is needed; it is identified by the name SMALL. We assume the first number (N1) is the smallest number and assign its value to the variable SMALL. All the other numbers, N2, N3, and N4, are compared one by one to the current value of SMALL. If any is, in fact, smaller than SMALL, then the variable SMALL is assigned the value of that number. In this way, SMALL always holds the value currently thought to be the smallest value.

Note the use of the three IFTHENELSE statements. After the first test is made (N2 < SMALL), the appropriate path is taken. The second test is made, and again, an appropriate path is taken. The third test is then made.

Figure 3–8
Finding the Smallest
Number (Flowchart)

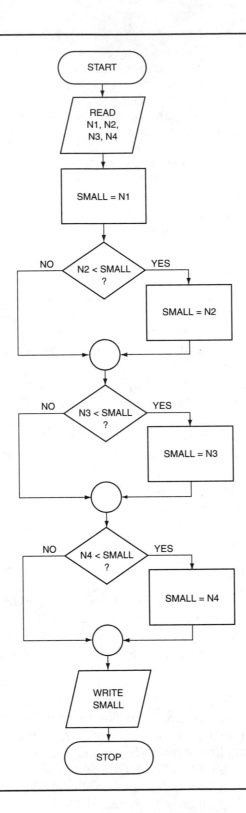

After its "yes" or "no" path is executed, the smallest value is output. It is important to see that all three IFTHENELSE statements are executed, regardless of the outcomes of previous tests. This makes sense, since each number in the group must be checked. This is an example of a **sequential IFTHENELSE pattern;** that is, all the tests are always made one after

Figure 3–9
Finding the Smallest
Number (Pseudocode)

```
Start
Read N1, N2, N3, N4
SMALL = N1
IF N2 < SMALL THEN
    SMALL = N2
(ELSE)
ENDIF
IF N3 < SMALL THEN
    SMALL = N3
(ELSE)
ENDIF
IF N4 < SMALL THEN
    SMALL = N4
(ELSE)
ENDIF
Write SMALL
Stop
```

another. Note that in the pseudocode in Figure 3–9 we see three ENDIFs. The second IF test is placed immediately following the first ENDIF, and the third IF test immediately follows the second ENDIF. Note also that, in this example, all three IF statements contain a null ELSE path. Do you see why?

Sample Problem 3.3 (Bank Problem)

Problem:

Let us look at another problem using several IFTHENELSE structures. In this example the **nested IFTHENELSE pattern** will be illustrated. Like the sequential IF pattern, the nested IF pattern utilizes several IFs but the logic behind the pattern is quite different. Consider the following problem: Assume we want to compute the new balance in a customer's bank account. The input will be the customer's name, account number, previous balance, transaction amount, and a code indicating whether the transaction was a deposit (code of 1) or withdrawal (code of 2). For simplicity, each input record will describe only one transaction. The output will contain the customer's name, account number, previous balance, and new balance.

Solution:

A solution to this problem is shown in both flowchart and pseudocode forms in Figures 3–10 and 3–11.

After the customer data is input, the code must be checked for a value of 1 or 2 to determine whether to add or subtract the transaction amount from the old balance. The first IF statement checks if the code is 1, which would indicate a deposit. If it is, the new balance is computed by adding the transaction amount; in other words, a deposit is credited. The second IF statement determines if the code is 2, which would indicate a withdrawal. If it is, the transaction amount is subtracted from the old balance. The second

Figure 3–10
Bank Problem (Flowchart)

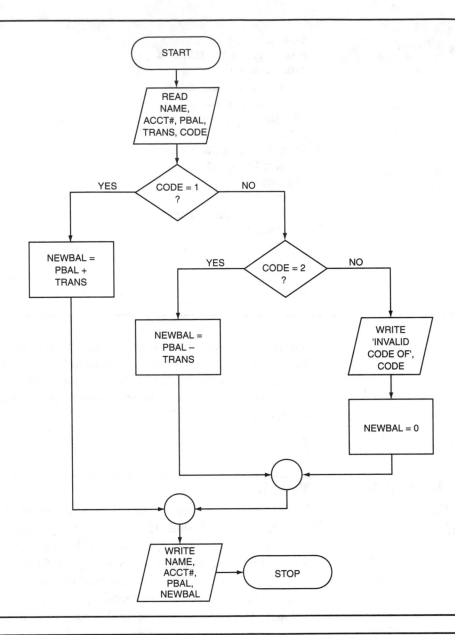

Figure 3–11
Bank Problem (Pseudocode)

```
Start
Read NAME, ACCT#, PBAL, TRANS, CODE
IF CODE = 1 THEN
    NEWBAL = PBAL + TRANS
ELSE
    IF CODE = 2 THEN
        NEWBAL = PBAL - TRANS
    ELSE
        Write 'Invalid code of', CODE
        NEWBAL = 0
    ENDIF
ENDIF
Write NAME, ACCT#, PBAL, NEWBAL
Stop
```

test is made only if the first test is not true. (It is not necessary to test for a code of 2 if we already know the code is 1.)

According to the logic of this nested IFTHENELSE pattern, each test is made only if the preceding test is not true. (On the other hand, in a sequential IFTHENELSE pattern, all tests are made in all cases.) The entire second IFTHENELSE is totally contained within the first IFTHENELSE; that is, the CODE = 2 test is actually a statement in the false path of the CODE = 1 test. Notice also that we indicate the exit point of each IFTHENELSE with a separate connector, thus giving us two connectors on the flowchart. This is shown by two consecutive ENDIFs within the pseudocode.

The nesting of each additional nested IFTHENELSE is indicated by additional indentation within the pseudocode. It is important to ensure that every IFTHENELSE has its own ending point (ENDIF), and that the words IF, ELSE, and ENDIF are aligned at the left at a uniform indentation. The statements within the IF statement's "true" and "false" paths are further indented.

Finally, in our current example, notice what will happen if both tests fail; that is, if the code is neither 1 nor 2. In this case, we assume that the code was keyed incorrectly, and we write a statement that instructs the computer to output an error message. The information within the single quotes is a **character-string constant** that will be output. The current value of the variable named CODE will also be output. (What do you think would have happened if we had also included the variable name CODE within the quotes?)

The second WRITE statement in this example is not contained within either of the IF statements. It is placed after both connectors—so it will be executed regardless of the value of the code. Therefore, the new balance (NEWBAL) will be printed even if the code was invalid. We assign a value of 0 to NEWBAL after writing the error message, so that this value of 0 will be written as output. (What would have happened if we had not?) Note that two lines of output will be printed if the code is invalid.

Sample Problem 3.4 (Sales Problem)	**Problem:** Let us now consider a more complex problem illustrating the nested IFTHENELSE pattern. Assume we want to determine the commission received by a salesperson. The commission rate is based on two factors, the amount of sales and the class to which the salesperson belongs. The input will be the salesperson's name, number, sales amount, and class. The output will be the salesperson's name, number, and commission. The commission rate will be based on the following criteria:

CLASS = 1	If sales is equal to or less than $1000, the rate is 6 percent.
	If sales is greater than $1000 but less than $2000, the rate is 7 percent.
	If sales is $2000 or greater, the rate is 10 percent.

CLASS = 2	If sales is less than $1000, the rate is 4 percent.
	If sales is $1000 or greater, the rate is 6 percent.
CLASS = 3	The rate is 4.5 percent for all sales amounts.
CLASS = 4	The rate is 5 percent for all sales amounts.
CLASS = any other value	Output an appropriate error message.

Solution:

A solution to this problem is shown in both flowchart and pseudocode forms in Figures 3–12 and 3–13.

After the sales data is input, the class must be checked for a value of 1, 2, 3, or 4 to determine the appropriate commission rate. The first IF statement determines if the class is 1. If so, another test is made to determine the value of sales. If SALES is less than or equal to 1000, 6 percent is assigned to the rate. If SALES is not less than or equal to 1000, it is checked again to determine if it is less than 2000. If so, 7 percent is assigned to the rate. Note that we did not have to check whether SALES was greater than 1000. Do you see why? Finally, if SALES is not less than 2000 (meaning that SALES is greater than or equal to 2000), 10 percent is assigned to the rate.

If the class is not 1, we check for 2. If so, the sales must also be tested. If SALES is less than 1000, 4 percent is assigned to the rate; otherwise, 6 percent is assigned to the rate. If the class is not 2, we check for 3. In this case 4.5 percent is assigned to the rate regardless of the value of SALES. Therefore, the sales amount does not have to be tested. If the class is not 3, we check for 4. In this case 5 percent is assigned to the rate, regardless of the value of SALES. Note again that the sales amount does not have to be tested. Finally, if the class is not 4, we output an error message. We also assign a value of 0 to the rate (for the same reason we assigned a value of 0 to NEWBAL in Sample Problem 3.3). At this point, the rate has been given the proper value for all possible values of SALES and CLASS. We can now compute the commission based on this rate, and output the salesperson information.

Notice on the flowchart that each IFTHENELSE structure has an associated connector. Similarly, the pseudocode indicates the keyword ENDIF for each IFTHENELSE. There are several levels of nested IFTHENELSE structures in this example. The pseudocode shows the nesting very clearly by the indentation. Make sure you understand what statements belong to each IFTHENELSE and how each IFTHENELSE structure begins and ends.

It is important to understand how a nested IFTHENELSE pattern differs from a sequential IFTHENELSE pattern. In the latter, all tests are always made in all cases. In the nested pattern, subsequent tests are made depending upon the outcome of a previous test. In the nested pattern it is probable that many of the tests will be skipped. Do you see why the nested IFTHENELSE structure was more appropriate for this problem? What would happen if we had tested CLASS using a series of sequential IF statements? (See Exercise 17.) We will see additional examples of the nested IFTHENELSE pattern in later chapters.

Figure 3–12
Sales Problem (Flowchart)

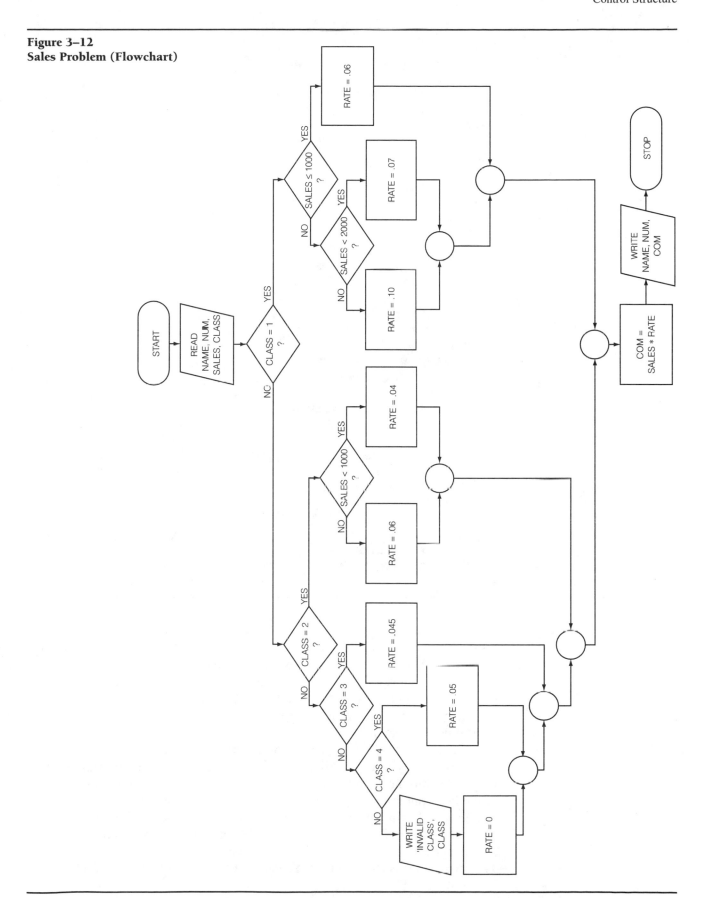

Figure 3–13
Sales Problem (Pseudocode)

```
Start
Read NAME, NUM, SALES, CLASS
IF CLASS = 1 THEN
   IF SALES ≤ 1000 THEN
      RATE = .06
   ELSE
      IF SALES < 2000 THEN
         RATE = .07
      ELSE
         RATE = .10
      ENDIF
   ENDIF
ELSE
   IF CLASS = 2 THEN
      IF SALES < 1000 THEN
         RATE = .04
      ELSE
         RATE = .06
      ENDIF
   ELSE
      IF CLASS = 3 THEN
         RATE = .045
      ELSE
         IF CLASS = 4 THEN
            RATE = .05
         ELSE
            Write 'INVALID CLASS', CLASS
            RATE = 0
         ENDIF
      ENDIF
   ENDIF
ENDIF
COM = SALES * RATE
Write NAME, NUM, COM
STOP
```

Enrichment (Basic)

Figure 3–14 illustrates a listing of a program that solves the Sales Problem (Figures 3–12 and 3–13). In this example we use the Input statement, which will request a name, number, sales, and class from the user when the program is executed. Note that this Input statement is preceded by a Print statement. The Print statement outputs directions to the user that specify what input is needed. Note that the variable name for the salesperson name is NAME$. In Basic, variables that hold non-numeric data must be represented by names ending with a $. As you can see, the Basic program is very similar to the pseudocode in Figure 3–13. Identifying text was added in the last Print statement to make the output more readable.

Figure 3–15 illustrates the output that will be produced when the program is executed. There are eight possible paths that the program can follow, depending on the input values of the variables SALES and CLASS. This program was executed eight separate times to show what output will

Figure 3–14
Sales Problem (Basic List)

```
PRINT "Enter the salesperson name, number, amount of sales and class"
INPUT NAME$, NUMBER, SALES, CLASS
IF CLASS = 1 THEN
        IF SALES <= 1000 THEN
                RATE = .06
        ELSE
                IF SALES < 2000 THEN
                        RATE = .07
                ELSE
                        RATE = .1
                END IF
        END IF
ELSE
        IF CLASS = 2 THEN
                IF SALES < 1000 THEN
                        RATE = .04
                ELSE
                        RATE = .06
                END IF
        ELSE
                IF CLASS = 3 THEN
                        RATE = .045
                ELSE
                        IF CLASS = 4 THEN
                                RATE = .05
                        ELSE
                                PRINT "Invalid Class",CLASS
                                RATE = 0
                        END IF
                END IF
        END IF
END IF
COMMISSION = SALES * RATE
PRINT "Name is "; NAME$; "  Number is "; NUMBER; " Commission is "; COMMISSION
END
```

be produced with varying values for the variables SALES and CLASS. Note that the last example prints two lines of output when CLASS is invalid. You should always test a program with data that corresponds to every possible path within the program. This type of testing will ensure that the program will be reliable. Note that blank spaces were positioned in the character-string constants shown in Figure 3–14 to ensure that the output fields are spaced appropriately.

Enrichment (Visual Basic)

Figure 3–16 illustrates the graphical user interface for the Sales Problem (Figure 3–12 and Figure 3–13). In this example, three text boxes are

Figure 3–15
Sales Problem (Basic Run)

```
Enter the salesperson name, number, amount of sales and class
?James,555,1000,1
Name is James   Number is   555   Commission is   60

Enter the salesperson name, number, amount of sales and class
?John,321,1500,1
Name is John   Number is   321   Commission is   105

Enter the salesperson name, number, amount of sales and class
?Steve,246,3000,1
Name is Steve   Number is   246   Commission is   300

Enter the salesperson name, number, amount of sales and class
?Kate,642,500,2
Name is Kate   Number is   642   Commission is   20

Enter the salesperson name, number, amount of sales and class
?Tom,678,1000,2
Name is Tom   Number is   678   Commission is   60

Enter the salesperson name, number, amount of sales and class
?Joan,111,1000,3
Name is Joan   Number is   111   Commission is   45

Enter the salesperson name, number, amount of sales and class
?Ted,222,5000,4
Name is Ted   Number is   222   Commission is   250

Enter the salesperson name, number, amount of sales and class
?Harry,333,1200,5
Invalid Class 5
Name is Harry   Number is   333   Commission is   0
```

created to accept user input. A label is created to hold the computed commission. A new control called an *option button* will be used to accept the user input for the class. Four option buttons are created with captions representing the names of the classes. Two command buttons are created, one to compute the commission and one to end execution of the program.

Figure 3–17 illustrates the screen after the user has entered the input values. Note that in this example the user clicked the first option button to indicate that the salesperson belongs to class 1. The small circle becomes darkened when the option button is selected. It is important to note, at this point, that option buttons should only be used to represent values that are mutually exclusive. Only one option can be selected, or darkened, at once. If the user selects the second button, then the second small circle will be darkened, rather than the first. Since each salesperson can be associated with only one class, option buttons are a reasonable choice in this example.

Figure 3–18 illustrates the screen after the user has clicked the Compute Commission button. The value for the commission is displayed in the label.

Figure 3–16
Sales Problem (Visual Basic—Screen 1)

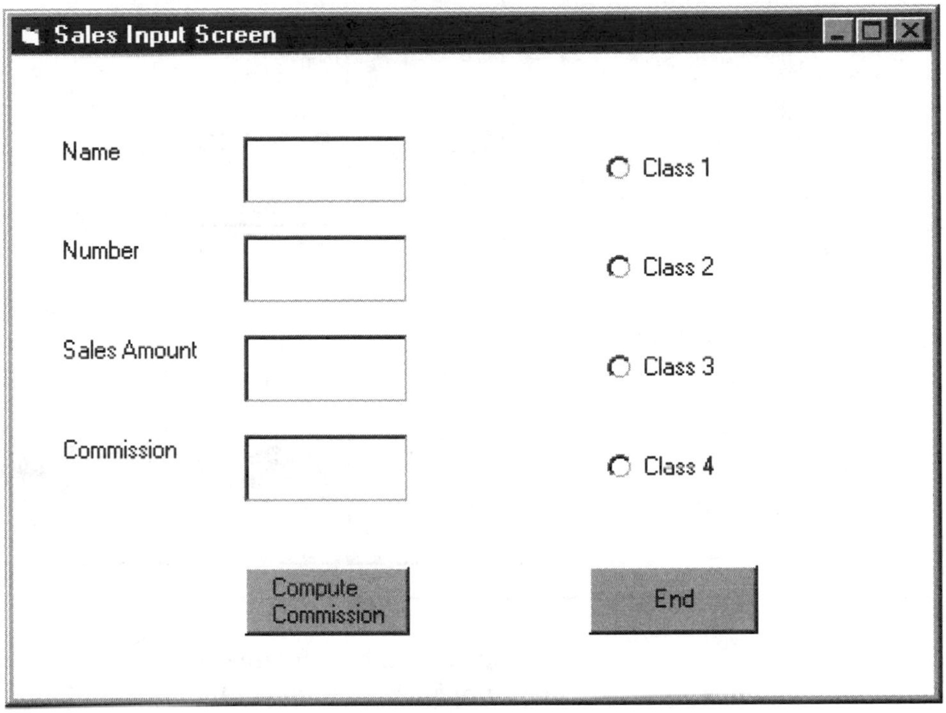

Figure 3–17
Sales Problem (Visual Basic—Screen 2)

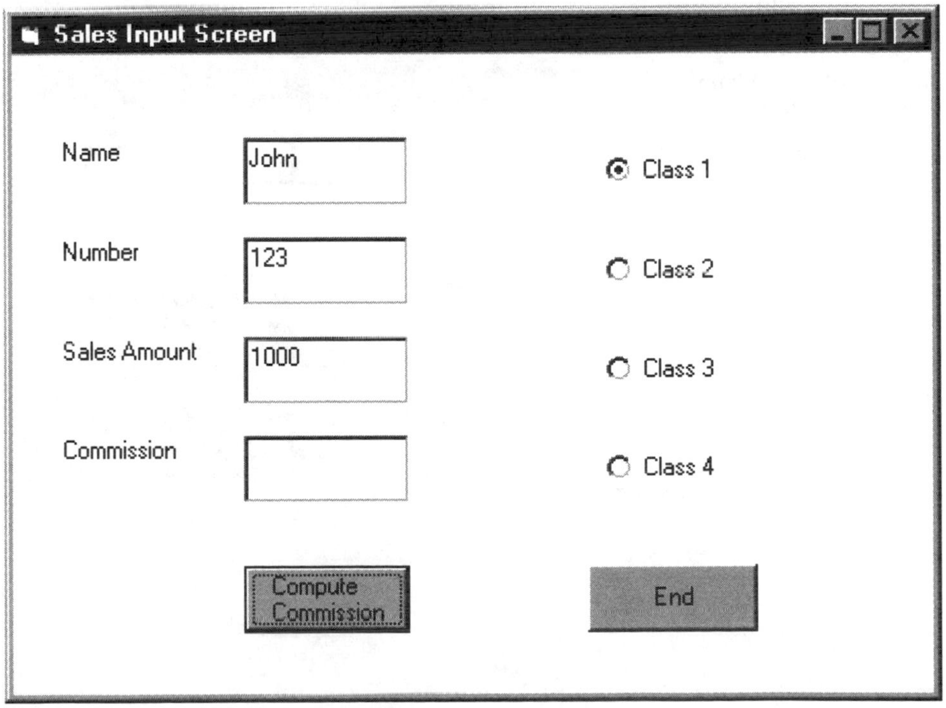

Figure 3–18
Sales Problem (Visual
Basic—Screen 3)

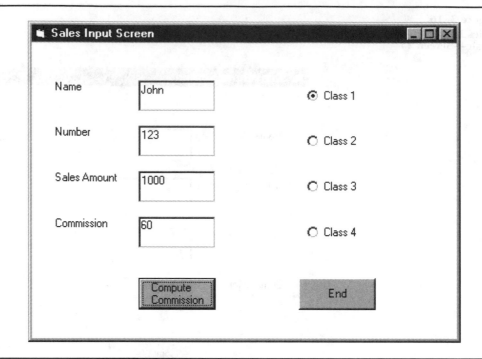

Since option buttons are used, the user cannot enter an invalid class. The user simply chooses one of the buttons. Consider, however, what would happen if the user clicked the Compute Commission button prior to selecting one of the options for class. In this case, since no class was selected, an error message needs to be output. This situation is illustrated in Figure 3–19. In Visual Basic we can use a *message box* to display information to

Figure 3–19
Sales Problem (Visual
Basic—Screen 4)

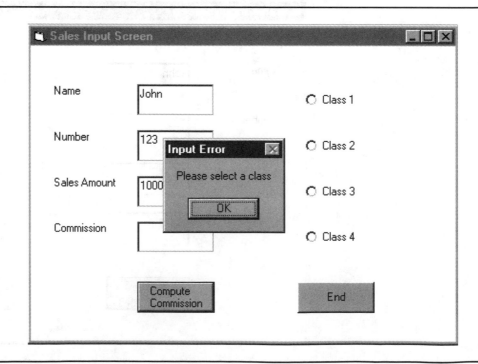

the user. After the user reads the message, the user clicks the OK button and the program execution continues.

Figure 3–20 illustrates the program that is associated with the click event of the Compute Commission button. Note that these statements very closely parallel the pseudocode in Figure 3–13. Only the IF statements that test the value of CLASS are different. Option buttons have a property called *value,* which can be either true or false. If an option button is selected, the value of the value property is true. If an option button is not selected, the value of the value property is false. Only one option button can have its value property set to true at any given time. Thus, each IF test checks the value of one of the option button's value property. Note that option button control names begin with *opt.* Note also that the "Invalid Class" error message is replaced by the MsgBox statement. This statement causes a message box to be displayed. The programmer determines both the message to be displayed and the title of the message box window. In our example, only an OK button is

Figure 3–20
Sales Problem
(Visual Basic—cmd_
COMPUTECOMMISSION_
Click)

```
Private Sub cmd_COMPUTECOMMISSION_Click()

If opt_CLASS1.Value = True Then
    If txt_SALES.Text <= 1000 Then
        RatePercent = 0.06
    Else
        If txt_SALES.Text < 2000 Then
            RatePercent = 0.07
        Else
            RatePercent = 0.1
        End If
    End If
Else
    If opt_CLASS2.Value = True Then
        If txt_SALES.Text < 1000 Then
            RatePercent = 0.04
        Else
            RatePercent = 0.06
        End If
    Else
        If opt_CLASS3.Value = True Then
            RatePercent = 0.045
        Else
            If opt_CLASS4.Value = True Then
                RatePercent = 0.05
            Else
                MsgBox "Please select a class",, "Input Error"
                RatePercent = 0
            End If
        End If
    End If
End If
lbl_COMMISSION.Caption = txt_SALES.Text * RatePercent

End Sub
```

Figure 3–21
Sales Problem (Visual
Basic— cmd_END_Click)

```
Private Sub cmd_END_Click()

End

End Sub
```

included in the message box. The programmer can display other buttons in the message box by including special numeric codes in the MsgBox statement between the two commas. Since no special code was included in the MsgBox statement in this example, only the OK button was displayed.

In this example an additional button was included with the caption "End." Figure 3–21 illustrates the program that is associated with the click event of the End button. When the user clicks the End button, the Visual Basic End statement is executed and the program execution terminates. It is usually a good idea to include an End button as part of the graphical user interface for a program.

Key Terms

decision symbol
conditional branch
pseudocode
IFTHENELSE control
   structure

connector symbol
null ELSE
sequential
   IFTHENELSE
   pattern

nested IFTHENELSE
   pattern
character-string
   constant

Exercises

1. State in your own words the purpose of a decision-making step in a solution algorithm.

2. Which of the symbols below represents the question: "Is DUE greater than or equal to CREDIT?"

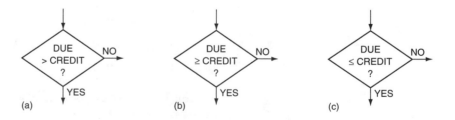

3. (a) What is pseudocode?
   (b) What are some of the advantages that the use of pseudocode offers?

4. (a) Using ANSI-approved flowcharting symbols, sketch the logic of an IFTHENELSE control structure.
   (b) State the logic of an IFTHENELSE control structure in pseudocode form.

(c) What pseudocode keywords did you use in your response to Exercise 4(b)?

(d) What indentations did you use in your response to Exercise 4(b)? Why?

5. (a) Explain what a null ELSE indicates.
   (b) Describe a problem in which a null ELSE occurs.
   (c) How is a null ELSE condition indicated on a flowchart?
   (d) How is a null ELSE condition indicated when using pseudocode?

6. How is a connector symbol used in flowcharting an IFTHENELSE control structure? Why is it used?

7. Explain how the decision-making logic represented by a sequential IFTHENELSE pattern differs from that represented by a nested IFTHEN-ELSE pattern.

8. Write a program flowchart and corresponding pseudocode to solve the following problem. Assume the input for a student is name, student number, and three grades. Output the student's name and an "S" if the average of the three grades is 65 or more. Otherwise (else), output the student's name, a "U," and the number of additional points needed for an "S."

9. Write a program flowchart and corresponding pseudocode to prepare a monthly credit card billing report. The input will contain the name of the person who has purchased on credit, the person's previous balance, total purchases, and total payments. The output lists the person's name, previous balance, total purchases, total payments, the amount subject to a finance charge, the interest, and the new balance.

    The amount subject to a finance charge is obtained by adding the total purchases to the previous balance and subtracting the total payments. If the amount subject to a finance charge is $250.00 or more, interest must be calculated by multiplying this amount by 1.5 percent. If the amount subject to a finance charge is less than $250.00, interest is calculated by multiplying this amount by 1 percent. The new balance is obtained by adding the interest to the amount subject to a finance charge.

10. Write a program flowchart and corresponding pseudocode to prepare an inventory report. The input will contain the item number, quantity, and unit price of a particular product. The inventory value will be computed by multiplying the quantity by the unit price. If the value of the inventory is more than $1000.00, then output the item number and the amount by which that item exceeds $1000.00. If the inventory value is $1000.00 or less, then output the item number and the computed inventory value. Include appropriate labels to identify the output values.

11. Write a program flowchart and corresponding pseudocode to prepare a tuition bill. The input will contain the student name, Social Security number, and total number of credits for which the student has enrolled. The bill will contain the student name, Social Security number, and

computed tuition. Total credits of 10 or more indicate that the student is full time. Fulltime students pay a flat rate of $1,000.00 for tuition. Total credits of less than 10 indicate that the student is part time. Part-time students pay $100.00 per credit for tuition.

12. Write a program flowchart and corresponding pseudocode to prepare a monthly bank statement. The input will contain the customer name, account number, old balance, total monthly deposit amount, and total monthly withdrawal amount. The statement will contain the customer name, account number, old balance, and new balance. The new balance is computed by adding the total monthly deposit amount to, and subtracting the total monthly withdrawal amount from, the old balance. If the new balance is less than $100.00, then a $5.00 service fee will be subtracted from the new balance to determine the real new balance.

13. Write a program flowchart and corresponding pseudocode to solve the following problem. Assuming that one number is input, output the number and a message indicating whether it is positive or negative. Output nothing if the number is zero.

14. Write a program flowchart and corresponding pseudocode to solve the following problem. Input a person's name, height (in inches), and weight (in pounds). If the person's height exceeds 5 feet (60 inches), and the person's weight exceeds 100 pounds, output the person's name. If the height and weight do not meet these criteria, output nothing.

15. Write a program flowchart and corresponding pseudocode to prepare a contract labor report for heavy equipment operators. The input will contain the employee name, job performed, hours worked per day, and a code. Journeyman employees have a code of J, apprentices a code of A, and casual labor a code of C. The output consists of the employee name, job performed, hours worked, and pay. Journeyman employees receive $12.00 per hour. Apprentices receive $10.00 per hour. Casual labor receives $8.00 per hour. Write two solutions, one using a nested IF pattern and another using a sequential IF pattern. (a) What output is produced by each solution? (b) Discuss which approach is more efficient and why.

16. Write a program flowchart and corresponding pseudocode for the following problem. You are given an input record that contains a student's name and three exam scores. Compute the average of the three exam scores and output a grade corresponding to the average as follows:

Average	Grade
90-100	A
80-89	B
70-79	C
60-69	D
under 60	F

Your output should be:

_____ received a grade of _____.

17. Redo Sample Problem 3.4 using a series of sequential IFTHENELSE statements to test the class. (a) Determine whether this approach works and why or why not. (b) Discuss which approach (nested IFs or sequential IFs) is more efficient and why.

18. Write a program flowchart and corresponding pseudocode to solve the following problem. Input name, age, and code for an applicant for a job in the ABC Company. A code of 1 indicates the applicant is a citizen of the United States, and a code of 2 indicates the applicant is not a U.S. citizen. The specifications for the job require that the applicant be a U.S. citizen 21 years of age or older. Your algorithm should check that these conditions are met and output an appropriate message(s) if one or both tests fail. If the applicant passes both tests, output the applicant's name only. Place only one test in each decison symbol (flowchart) or IF statement (pseudocode). Solve this problem using the nested IF approach. Solve it again using the sequential IF approach.

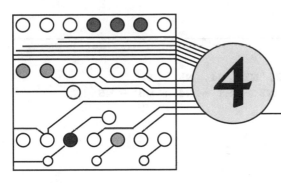

4 DOWHILE Control Structure— Counter-Controlled Loops

Objectives

Upon completion of this chapter you should be able to

- Identify, and use in program design, counters, accumulators, and program loops.
- Construct and identify the characteristics of a simple counter-controlled program loop.
- Identify, and use in program design, the DOWHILE control structure.
- Identify, and use in program design, the preparation, predefined-process, and annotation program flowcharting symbols.
- Design programs using header record logic.
- Define the terms *module, modularization, top-down design, structured programming,* and *proper program.*
- Construct a two-level structure chart.
- Design programs using top-down design, structured programming, and modularization techniques.

Introduction

The solution algorithms discussed so far have at least one characteristic in common: They show the program logic required to process only one set of input values. Generally, however, a computer program must be designed and coded to process many sets of input values. To provide for this, a **program loop** must be included in the program flowchart. A program loop is defined as a sequence of processing steps that may be repeated. The computer may reexecute the instructions. Consider, for example, the following problem: Construct an algorithm that will accept six numbers as input and will compute and output the sum of these six numbers. Figure 4–1 illustrates a solution to this problem without the use of a program loop.

First, six numbers are read into the memory locations reserved for the variables represented by the variable names N1, N2, N3, N4, N5, and N6. An assignment statement is then used to add the numbers, and the result is placed in memory under the variable named SUM. SUM is then output and the program execution stops. This solution is quite simple and straightforward. You should be familiar with all of the steps in this algorithm from previous chapters. Consider, however, the limitations of this approach. What if you were now asked to revise this algorithm to compute and output

Figure 4–1
Adding 6 Numbers
(No Loop)

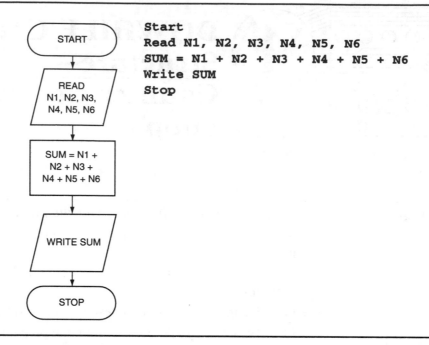

```
Start
Read N1, N2, N3, N4, N5, N6
SUM = N1 + N2 + N3 + N4 + N5 + N6
Write SUM
Stop
```

the sum of 100 numbers? You would need 100 separate variable names to represent the data being input. In addition, these 100 variable names would need to be included in the assignment statement to compute the sum. Clearly, this is not a desirable approach to take.

Let us look for a moment at how we would perform this task manually but aided by a calculator. First, we would either turn the calculator on or clear it if we had already been using it for another task. We would then enter the first number, say 5. The number 5 would appear on the display and we could then hit the + sign. The number 5 would again appear on the display. At this point we could enter a second number, say 7. A 7 would now appear on the display. When we hit the + sign this time the two numbers would be added and 12 would appear on the display. Consider the sequence of steps that occurs as we enter 4 more numbers, say 3, 4, 8, and 1, and add them together. Figure 4–2 illustrates this process.

Figure 4–2
Calculator Simulation
(No Loop)

	ACTION	SCREEN DISPLAY
1.	Clear calculator memory	
2.	Enter a number (5)	5
3.	Hit the + sign	5
4.	Enter a number (7)	7
5.	Hit the + sign	12
6.	Enter a number (3)	3
7.	Hit the + sign	15
8.	Enter a number (4)	4
9.	Hit the + sign	19
10.	Enter a number (8)	8
11.	Hit the + sign	27
12.	Enter a number (1)	1
13.	Hit the + sign	28

Figure 4–3
Calculator Simulation
(Loop)

1. Clear calculator memory
2. Enter a number   ⎫
                    ⎬ perform these steps
3. Hit the + sign   ⎭   6 times

Do you notice any repetition? Steps 2, 4, 6, 8, 10, and 12 all perform the exact same task; only the entered number is different. Similarly, Steps 3, 5, 7, 9, 11, and 13 perform the same task. The screen, meanwhile, displays sums that get increasingly closer to the final sum of 28.

Now look at Figure 4–3. It shows how this procedure can be reorganized into a simpler one using a loop.

Problem (Adding Six Numbers)

Now look at the flowchart and pseudocode (Figure 4–4) of an algorithm that illustrates this type of logic.

Figure 4–4
Adding Six Numbers

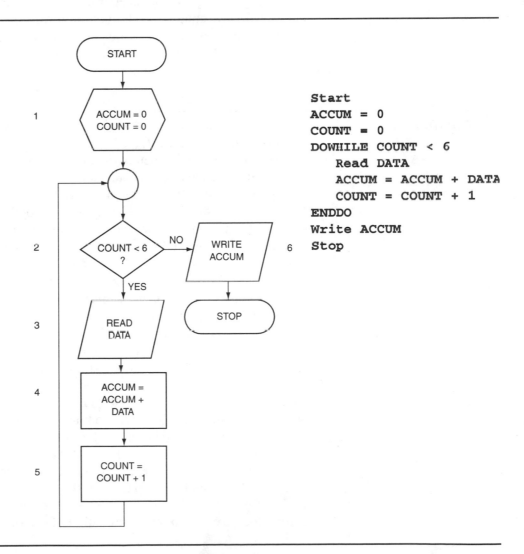

```
Start
ACCUM = 0
COUNT = 0
DOWHILE COUNT < 6
    Read DATA
    ACCUM = ACCUM + DATA
    COUNT = COUNT + 1
ENDDO
Write ACCUM
Stop
```

A new flowcharting symbol is introduced in Figure 4–4—the **preparation symbol.** It represents an operation performed on data in preparation for a major sequence of operations. Often this operation is performed before a loop is entered (as in this flowchart); in these cases, the operation is referred to as an **initialization step.** In Step 1 of this algorithm, two variables are set to 0. One is used as an accumulator (ACCUM), and the other is used as a counter (COUNT). An **accumulator** is a variable that is used to hold the sum of a group of values. This sum is computed by gradually adding (accumulating) each value to the variable each time the loop is executed. A **counter** is a special type of accumulator. A counter adds or accumulates by a constant amount, usually 1. The value of such a counter increases by 1 each time the loop is executed.

ACCUM plays the role of our calculator's memory. It is initialized to 0 just as the calculator's memory is cleared at the start of an activity. It will represent what we see on the calculator's screen when we hit the + sign. Simply put, ACCUM is used to hold the sum of the numbers so far, often called a **partial sum.** COUNT, on the other hand, is used to keep track of how many numbers have been added so far. When we add a series of numbers using a calculator, we keep track of how many we have already added and how many remain to add. In our algorithm, we must name a variable that the computer can use for this task. The computer increases the value of COUNT (and then checks its value) to know when to stop adding numbers.

Simulation (Adding Six Numbers)

Now look at what happens during one cycle of the loop in Figure 4–4. First, a test is made (Step 2): Is COUNT less than 6? If so, a number is read (let's say 5) and stored in the memory location represented by the variable called DATA (Step 3). This step is equivalent to the calculator step "Enter a number." Now look at Step 4. Do you recognize an assignment statement? Notice that the variable ACCUM appears on both sides of the assignment statement. The computer will add the value of DATA (5, for example) to the current value of ACCUM (0 at the moment) and place that result back into the storage location used for the variable ACCUM. ACCUM now contains the value 5. We have lost the previous value of ACCUM, because this statement assigned a new value to it (overlaying the previous value in the storage location). Step 4 is thus equivalent to the calculator step "Hit the + sign." The same kind of process affects the variable COUNT in Step 5. The computer adds 1 (a constant) to the current value of COUNT (0 at the moment), and places the result back into the storage location represented by the variable COUNT. COUNT now holds the value 1. Look again at ACCUM and COUNT. Can you see that ACCUM does in fact hold the sum of the numbers so far? Does COUNT indicate how many numbers have been added so far? The flowline then takes us back to the test that determines if COUNT is less than 6. Since this is still true, the "yes" path is again taken and the READ statement is executed. Continue this process with five more numbers—7, 3, 4, 8, and 1. Keep track of the values for DATA, ACCUM, and COUNT each time through the loop. Check your results with Figure 4–5 before you go on. It shows a simulation of the steps in this algorithm.

Figure 4–5
Adding Six Numbers—
Simulation

INPUT: 5
7
3
4 ☐ VALUE CHANGES
8 IN THIS STEP
1

STEP	ACCUM	COUNT	DATA
1	☐0	☐0	UNDEFINED
3	0	0	☐5
4	☐5	0	5
5	5	☐1	5
3	5	1	☐7
4	☐12	1	7
5	12	☐2	7
3	12	2	☐3
4	☐15	2	3
5	15	☐3	3
3	15	3	☐4
4	☐19	3	4
5	19	☐4	4
3	19	4	☐8
4	☐27	4	8
5	27	☐5	8
3	27	5	☐1
4	☐28	5	1
5	28	☐6	1

When COUNT finally reaches 6, the answer to the question asked at the beginning of the loop will be NO and the WRITE statement will be executed to output the sum of the six numbers. In this example, the sum should be 28, which is the most recent value of ACCUM. The program execution will then stop. Notice that the value of ACCUM is not output until the loop is exited; that is, until all six numbers have been added. This sequence of operations makes sense, since the computer can't output the sum until it finishes computing the sum, and the computer can't finish computing the sum until all numbers have been read and processed.

The DOWHILE Loop

The previous example was a simple but informative one. You can see that the "yes" flowline extending from the decision symbol in Figure 4–4 causes three steps to be executed and then flows back toward the beginning of the flow-chart to the small circular symbol. Recall from Chapter 3 that this symbol is a connector symbol. It serves as a collector at the beginning of the loop. As before, it has two flowlines entering and only one exiting. It performs no action of its own. Its presence on the flowchart only serves to emphasize that there is only one entrance point to the loop (at the connector symbol) and only one exit from it (at the decision symbol). If (and only if) the tested condition is true (COUNT < 6), the processing steps along the true ("yes") path are executed. If the tested condition is not true, the false ("no") path is followed. If the false path is taken, we say that the program loop is exited.

This loop pattern, called the **DOWHILE loop,** is the third basic pattern of structured program logic. Note that the DOWHILE pattern is a **leading-decision program loop.** The test to determine whether the loop should be executed or exited is encountered immediately upon entering the loop. In other words, the test immediately follows the connector symbol. Whether the additional steps inside the loop are executed depends on the outcome of the test. Notice the significance of the fact that, if the tested condition is not true, the loop is exited immediately thereafter. Thus, if the tested condition is not true the first time it is tested, the remaining steps in the loop are not executed at all.

As outlined above, the DOWHILE loop has three basic structural characteristics that must be adhered to. To create a properly formed DOWHILE loop you must:

1. Place the loop test before any other step within the loop (leading decision).

2. Place the loop steps in the "yes" path of the loop test.

3. Indicate that the loop will exit in the "no" path of the loop test.

Make sure that you can identify these characteristics in the DOWHILE loop in the previous example and in any algorithm you write using the DOWHILE loop.

The general form of the DOWHILE pattern is shown in Figure 4–6. To help you become familiar with this pattern, it is flowcharted in two ways.

Figure 4–6
DOWHILE Loop—Generic

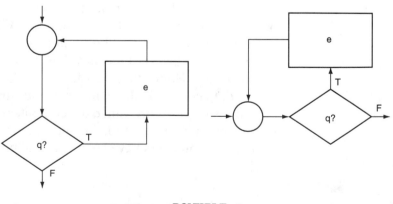

```
DOWHILE q
    e
ENDDO
```

The same control structure appears in each representation; you should learn to recognize and use either one. First, condition q is tested. If q is true, statement e is executed and control returns to the test of q. If q is false, control passes to the next processing step. The DOWHILE pattern is always set up this way—the steps in the loop are executed while the outcome of the test is true, and the loop is exited when the outcome is false.

DOWHILE Pseudocode

Now look at the pseudocode representation in Figure 4–4. Note the keywords DOWHILE and ENDDO. They are aligned at the left and mark the beginning and ending of the program loop, respectively. The initialization steps are placed before the loop, that is, on the line above the DOWHILE statement. The actual loop steps that occur in the "yes" path on the program flowchart are placed on the lines below the DOWHILE statement and directly above the ENDDO statement. The WRITE instruction that occurs in the "no" path outside of the loop on the program flowchart is placed directly after ENDDO. In pseudocode, the steps within the loop ("yes" path in the flowchart) are always placed between DOWHILE and ENDDO. Similarly, the steps after the loop ("no" path in the flowchart) are always placed on the line after ENDDO. All processing steps within the loop (the "yes" path on the flowchart) are indented a few positions for clarity.

Counter-Controlled Loops

It is also very important to look at the technique used to control the loop. In this example a counter (COUNT) is used to determine whether or not the loop steps will be repeated yet another time. This is an example of a **counter-controlled loop.** The algorithm clearly shows the number of times the loop steps will be done (6 times in this case). A counter-controlled loop has two basic characteristics:

1. The loop is controlled by a counter.
2. The number of times that the loop will be executed is known or preset.

These characteristics are shown pictorially in Figure 4–7. Each loop is executed a predetermined number of times. In the flowchart to the left, the COUNT is initialized to 0 before the loop is entered, and then tested in the first step of the loop. The number used in this test always corresponds to the number of times the loop is to be executed. After the processing steps within the loop are completed, the count is incremented by one and the test is made again. COUNT is often referred to as the **loop control variable.** In the flowchart to the right in Figure 4–7, a slightly different approach is used. The count is initialized to a number representing how many times the loop is to be done. Then the loop test determines if the count is still greater than 0. If so, the count will be decremented by one (rather than incremented) after the processing steps in the loop are executed. Do you see why? Both flowcharts accomplish exactly the same thing; they just approach it in two different ways. Both ways are satisfactory, and you will see examples of each throughout the book. Make sure you can identify

Figure 4–7
Simple Counter-Controlled
Loop—Generic

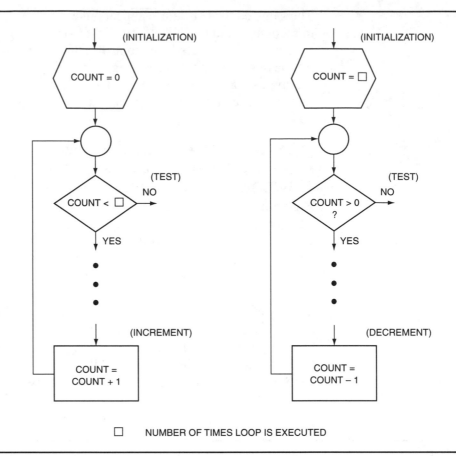

☐   NUMBER OF TIMES LOOP IS EXECUTED

each of these steps in the previous example as well as in any algorithm you write that uses a counter-controlled loop.

Sample Problem 4.1 (Payroll with Counter Loop)

Problem:

Redo the payroll problem from Chapter 3 to process the payroll data for exactly ten employees.

Solution:

Since we want to repeat the same processing steps for each employee, we can code the steps just once and use a counter-controlled DOWHILE loop structure to repeat the processing steps ten times. A solution is shown in program flowchart form in Figure 4–8 and in pseudocode form in Figure 4–9.

A counter (COUNT) is used to control the loop. It is initialized to 0 at the beginning of the program. The DOWHILE loop is structured with the test first, as required: COUNT is checked for a value less than 10. If the "yes" path is taken, then the processing steps in the loop will be executed for one employee.

Look at these steps closely. The sequence of operations is the same as the sequence of operations we used in Figure 3–6 (Chapter 3). Remember, however, that that solution processed data for only one employee. In this example, after the WRITE statement is executed, the processing for one employee is

**Figure 4–8
Payroll Problem—Ten
Employees (Flowchart)**

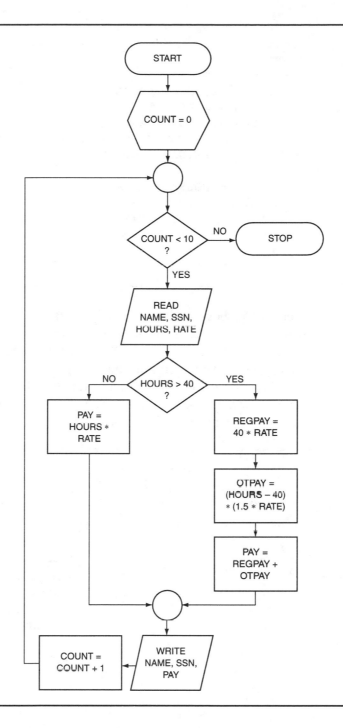

complete, the COUNT is incremented by 1, and control is returned to the beginning of the loop. This series of actions is repeated ten times (until the data for all ten employees has been processed). At that point the value of COUNT is 10, the "no" path is taken, and program execution stops.

Modularization

You may have noticed that our flowcharts and our pseudocode are becoming more complicated. The flowchart can barely fit on one page, and the

Figure 4–9
Payroll Problem—Ten
Employees (Pseudocode)

```
Start
COUNT = 0
DOWHILE COUNT < 10
   Read NAME, SSN, HOURS, RATE
   IF HOURS > 40 THEN
      REGPAY = 40 * RATE
      OTPAY = (HOURS - 40) * (1.5 * RATE)
      PAY = REGPAY + OTPAY
   ELSE
      PAY = HOURS * RATE
   ENDIF
   Write NAME, SSN, PAY
   COUNT = COUNT + 1
ENDDO
Stop
```

pseudocode shows several levels of indentation. This happens when several structures are used together in the same algorithm. In this example, an IF-THENELSE is nested inside a DOWHILE loop. Imagine the complexity when three, four, or even more structures are needed in the same problem solution.

This apparent complexity can be lessened by the use of a technique called **modularization.** Consider an alternative solution to this problem shown in Figures 4–10, 4–11, and 4–12.

Figure 4–10
Payroll Problem—Ten
Employees (Overall Control)

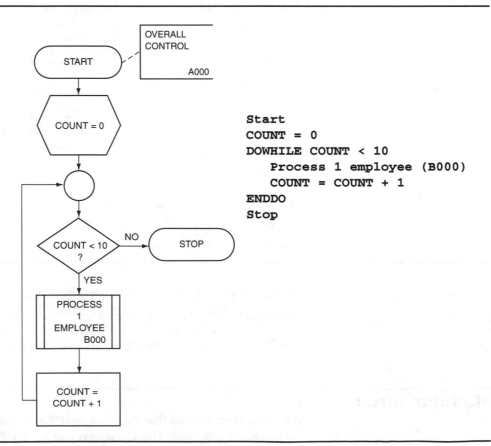

```
Start
COUNT = 0
DOWHILE COUNT < 10
   Process 1 employee (B000)
   COUNT = COUNT + 1
ENDDO
Stop
```

Figure 4–11
Payroll Problem—Process
Employee Record
(Flowchart)

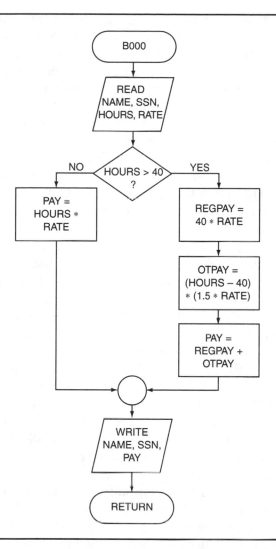

Figure 4–12
Payroll Problem—Process
Employee Record
(Pseudocode)

```
B000
Enter
Read NAME, SSN, HOURS, RATE
IF HOURS > 40 THEN
    REGPAY = 40 * RATE
    OTPAY = (HOURS - 40) * (1.5 * RATE)
    PAY = REGPAY + OTPAY
ELSE
    PAY = HOURS * RATE
ENDIF
Write NAME, SSN, PAY
Return
```

The flowchart in Figure 4–10 is much simpler and easier to follow than the one in Figure 4–8. The counter is still there, initialized, tested, and incremented as before, but the steps to compute the pay for one employee are replaced by a single box identified in two ways. It is given a descriptive name (process 1 employee) and a label (B000). The box itself is called a predefined-process symbol. The **predefined-process symbol** is used to identify a series of steps shown on another flowchart. These steps are given a label for reference purposes and together make up a **module.** This modularization technique allows us to concentrate on the overall processing the program needs to do, instead of being overwhelmed by the details early on.

Since each module is identified in our program by a label, we should also give a label to the main processing module, that is, the one we start with. We will call this module the overall control module (also known as the driver module), and give it an identifying label of A000. We indicate this next to the START symbol in another flowcharting symbol called the annotation symbol. The **annotation symbol** can be used to further explain any step in the flowchart. It is a documentation symbol, not an additional processing step. The choice of module descriptive names and labels is either left up to the programmer or dictated by company standards. As with variable names, module names should be chosen to indicate what the modules actually do.

A module that is referenced in a predefined-process symbol needs to be described in another flowchart or in pseudocode representation. Module B000 is shown in Figures 4–11 and 4–12. Notice that the flowchart does not begin with START because this module is not used at the start of program execution. Instead, we identify the module by placing its label in the first symbol. Thus, the label indicates a linkage between the two flowcharts. Similarly, when the steps within the module are complete, a STOP is not appropriate, since we have not yet completed the algorithm. We need to return control (go back) to module A000, which will continue processing.

To summarize, when a program is divided into several parts, or modules, several flowcharts or pseudocode representations will be needed. The overall control module can be designed first, leaving details until later. This approach is often called **top-down design.** Only the overall control module contains a START and a STOP. We refer to the overall control module as the **calling module** (or **callee**) because it references other modules. We refer to the other modules as **called modules** because they are referenced (called) by the main module. The called modules are identified by labels (reference numbers) at the beginning of their flowcharts, and each one will return control (RETURN) back to the calling module (the main module) as its last step. This logic can also be indicated in the pseudocode by the appropriate statements. It is important to understand that, when module B000 returns control to module A000, the step in A000 following the predefined-process symbol will be executed next. A000 does not restart from the beginning. It is also possible for a module to be both a calling module and a called module. We will see examples of this later in the book.

Structure Charts

It might be valuable at this point to step back and look at the big picture. We already know that an information-processing system may be composed of a single program or of several programs. This general information is shown in a system flowchart. A system flowchart typically shows the flow of work within a system; that is, it shows what inputs are needed for what processes, and what processes produce what outputs. Figure 4–13 shows the system flowchart for our payroll problem.

We have also seen in this chapter that a program can be composed of one or more modules. Each module is a segment of logically related code, a part of a complete program that gets executed to solve a problem. As much as possible, each module should be independent of all other modules. It should constitute a logical unit of work, performing one or a small number of functions of the overall problem-solving task.

Figure 4–14 shows a new graphic representation, namely a **structure chart,** or **hierarchy chart,** which shows the potential flow of control within one program. In other words, a structure chart shows the relationships of all modules within a program. It is similar to an organizational chart in a company. The top box shows the main controlling module or driver module. All lower-level boxes represent modules that may be given control during program execution.

The example in Figure 4–14 is very simple, since the program we have just looked at has only two modules. Now let's look at a more complex generic structure chart shown in Figure 4–15.

In this example there are six modules, each indicated by one box on the structure chart. For simplicity, only module numbers are used. Module A000, the overall control module, may call on three lower-level modules (B000, B010, and B020) at various points in its processing. This structure is likewise shown in the program flowchart in Figure 4–16.

Figure 4–13
Payroll Problem (System Flowchart)

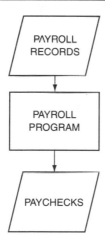

Figure 4–14
Payroll Problem (Structure Chart)

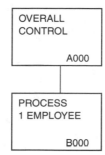

Figure 4–15
Generic Structure Chart

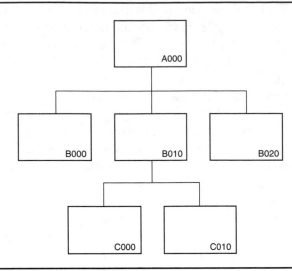

Figure 4–16
Generic Program Flowchart
(Overall Control)

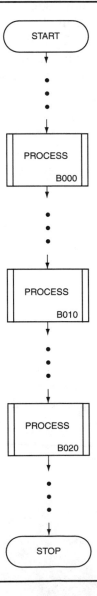

The structure chart in Figure 4–15 does not show any module references below B000 and B020. We can conclude that these two modules do not call any lower-level modules during execution. (See Figure 4–17.) However, module B010 may refer to two lower-level modules (level 3 since B010 is itself level 2) during execution. (See Figure 4–18.) Neither of the level 3 modules (C000 and C010) calls any lower-level modules. (See Figure 4–19.) It is important to understand that each called module returns control to its calling module at the completion of its execution. For example, C000

Figure 4–17
Generic Program Flowchart (Modules B000 and B020)

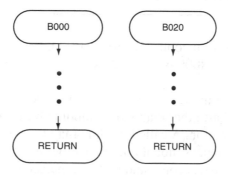

Figure 4–18
Generic Program Flowchart (Module B010)

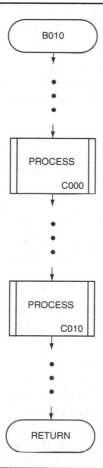

Figure 4–19
Generic Program Flowchart
(Modules C000 and C010)

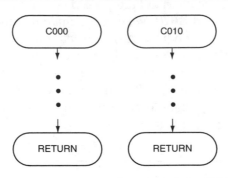

and C010 return control to B010; B000, B010, and B020 return control to A000. When A000 is finished executing, processing for that program is complete.

It is also important to note that no execution order is ever implied on a structure chart other than which module may call which other module(s) during execution. A called module may be invoked any number of times or, in some instances, not at all. On a structure chart, left-to-right order does not imply first, second, and so forth in execution sequence.

Header Record Logic

Let us now turn our attention back to the mechanisms by which a loop can be controlled. This chapter has introduced DOWHILE loops and the counter approach for controlling them. Recall that a simple counter-controlled loop is always executed a preset number of times. In our two previous examples, the limits were 6 (adding problem) and 10 (payroll problem). We now look at a more general and somewhat more flexible approach to loop control that builds on simple counter-controlled loops. This approach is called **header record logic.** In the header record logic approach, a counter is still used to control the loop as before. However, the number of loop iterations can vary with each program execution. This flexibility is provided by inputting a special record before any of the regular input records. This special record is called a **header record,** and it specifies how many additional input records will follow. The additional input records contain the regular data that will be processed by the program. It is important to understand that the header record is a separate record and not part of the first regular input record.

For example, we could have included a header record containing a 10, followed by 10 employee records in our payroll problem. If we set the logic up properly, the same algorithm should work at a later time if the header record is changed to 50, followed by 50 employee records. The general logic required to accomplish this processing is shown in Figure 4–20.

These flowcharts expand the notion of simple counter-controlled loops, as shown in Figure 4–7. Both flowcharts include the addition of an initial input step to read the header record information. In this example, we have used the variable named TOTNUM to represent the total number of records to be processed. The flowchart on the left (incrementing the count) refers to TOTNUM in the loop test instead of a specific value such as 6 or 10.

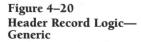

Figure 4–20
Header Record Logic—
Generic

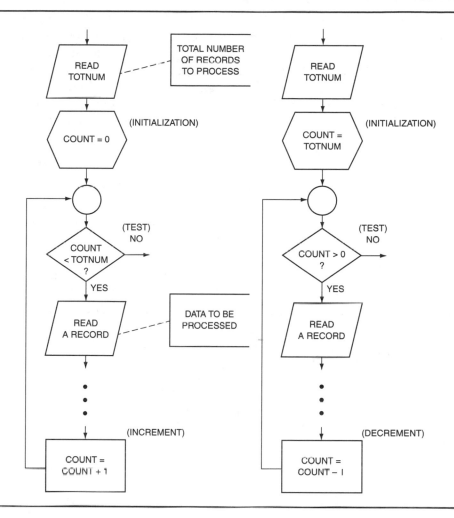

The flowchart on the right (decrementing the count) indicates that COUNT will initially be set to the value of TOTNUM instead of a specific value such as 6 or 10. In this way the algorithm becomes more flexible. No mention is made of any specific number on the program flowchart. Also note the second READ statement in each of these flowcharts. This READ step is positioned as the first step within the DOWHILE loop; it inputs the regular data to be processed, one record at a time. This is the step that would actually input the employee records or the individual numbers to compute a sum. Make sure you understand the purpose of the two READ steps. The first READ is done only once—it inputs the header record. The second READ is done every time the loop steps are executed—each time reading one of the regular records containing data to be processed.

Sample Problem 4.2 (Averaging Problem Without Modules)

Problem:

An instructor at Cloverdale School desires a computer program to compute and print a student's term average. The individual scores earned by the student will be input, one at a time, and will need to be accumulated. To determine the student's average, the scores' sum will be divided by the number of scores. Because the number of individual scores that must be added will depend on the number of assignments completed, a special input record containing the student's name and number of scores to be added will be provided as the first input to the program whenever it is used. The individual scores will then follow that record. The output is to contain the student's name, number of assignments completed, and term average computed during processing.

Solution:

A solution to this problem is shown in Figure 4–21 (flowchart) and Figure 4–22 (pseudocode).

This algorithm accumulates the value of the scores so that the average can be computed. The processing can be done using the same technique for adding as was used in Figure 4–4. What sets this problem apart from the previous one is that we cannot just add six numbers—that is, we cannot

Figure 4–21
Averaging Problem—No Modules (Flowchart)

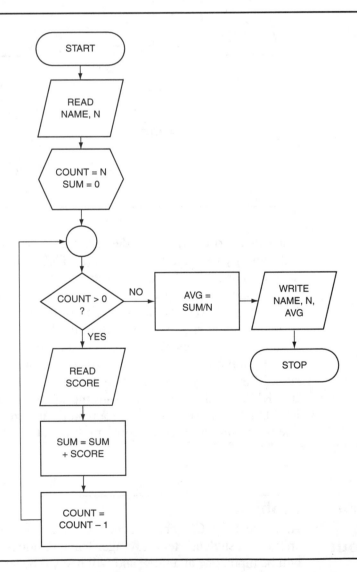

Figure 4–22
Averaging Problem—No
Modules (Pseudocode)

```
Start
Read NAME, N
COUNT = N
SUM = 0
DOWHILE COUNT > 0
   Read SCORE
   SUM = SUM + SCORE
   COUNT = COUNT - 1
ENDDO
AVG = SUM/N
Write NAME, N, AVG
Stop
```

place a 6 or any other known number in our loop test. How, then, can we know how many times to execute the loop steps? Remember that the first input record will contain the name of the student and the number of assignments completed. This number will be used in the loop test. Since this data needs to be input, the first step in Figures 4–21 and 4–22 shows a READ statement with the variable N representing the number of assignments completed. This record is the header record—it contains not only the number of assignments completed but also the name of the student. The regular records contain the individual scores.

Notice that the loop is still controlled by a counter. However, the initial value of the counter (COUNT) is set to N (just input), not to a fixed number (i.e., a constant such as 10). Notice also that we are decrementing the count in this example. Consider what changes you would have to make to increment the count instead. Both approaches are satisfactory.

When COUNT finally reaches 0, we exit the loop and compute the student's average. This is accomplished by dividing the accumulated sum by the total number of scores. Notice that the value of N never changes throughout program execution. N is still equal to its initial input value. One common mistake of the beginner is to include the computation of the average (AVG = SUM/N) inside the loop. This is very inefficient because the average depends on the final value (last partial sum) of SUM. Remember, the variable SUM is being used as an accumulator of the partial sum of the student scores. The complete sum isn't known until all the scores have been accumulated. It is thus appropriate to compute the average only upon exiting the loop.

Sample Problem 4.3 (Averaging Problem Using Modules)

Problem:

Redo Sample Problem 4.2 using a modular approach as outlined in the structure chart in Figure 4–23.

Solution:

The overall control module is shown in Figure 4–24 (flowchart) and Figure 4–25 (pseudocode). This module (A000) reads the header record,

Figure 4–23
Averaging Problem—
Structure Chart)

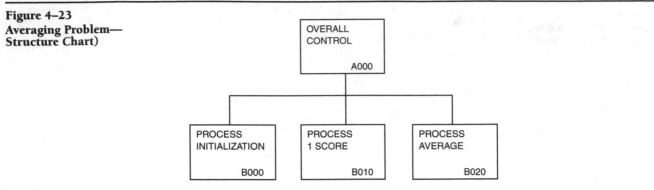

Figure 4–24
Averaging Problem—Overall
Control (Flowchart)

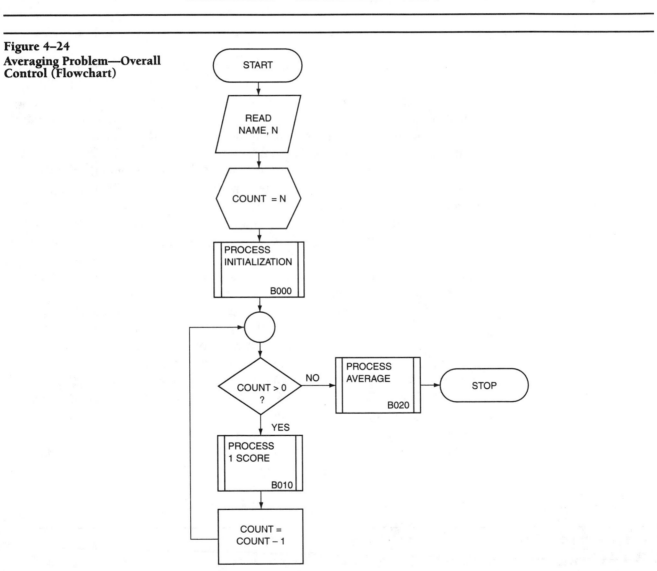

controls the DOWHILE loop, and calls three lower-level modules during the course of its processing. Module B000 is called prior to entering the loop to initialize the variable named SUM to 0. This module, which is fairly trivial, is shown in Figure 4–26. We could have initialized COUNT in this module as well, but the general approach in this book is to show all the steps related

Figure 4–25
Averaging Problem—Overall
Control (Pseudocode)

```
Start
Read NAME, N
COUNT = N
Process initialization (B000)
DOWHILE COUNT > 0
   Process 1 score (B010)
   COUNT = COUNT - 1
ENDDO
Process average (B020)
Stop
```

to loop control in the overall control module. Another module (B010) is referenced inside the loop. As the name of the module implies, it performs the processing associated with one score. Figure 4–27 shows the details of B010. As you can see, this module is also fairly trivial. An individual score is first input (SCORE), and then it is accumulated using the variable SUM. At this point B010 returns control to A000, where the counter is decremented and the test is again made to see if any scores remain. Again, we could have decremented COUNT in module B010, but we left this step in overall control, as it is part of the loop control process. When the count reaches 0, the loop is exited and a third module (B020) is called to compute and output the average. This module is shown in Figure 4–28.

This problem solution could have been broken into modules in any of several ways. In this example, we have, as before, one main controlling module; but this time the problem solution is broken down into three lower-level modules. Let us look at each module and how it interacts within the program as a whole. The overall control module (A000) has control when processing begins. During processing, A000 may give control (once or more than once) to any of the other three modules. When any of these modules completes its processing, it returns control to A000. Since all three modules are at the same level, they cannot communicate directly with each other. Each can only be given control from A000, and each can only return control to A000. B000, B010, and B020 are all relatively trivial modules—you might wonder why we even bother to design them as separate modules. Typically, a complete problem solution involves steps like printing headings (we'll look at this in Chapter 5), writing totals, and doing

Figure 4–26
Averaging Problem—Process
Initialization

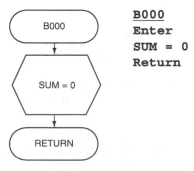

```
B000
Enter
SUM = 0
Return
```

Figure 4–27
Averaging Problem—
Process One Score

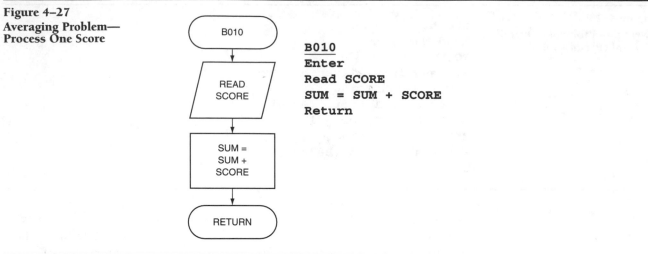

```
B010
Enter
Read SCORE
SUM = SUM + SCORE
Return
```

Figure 4–28
Averaging Problem—
Process Average

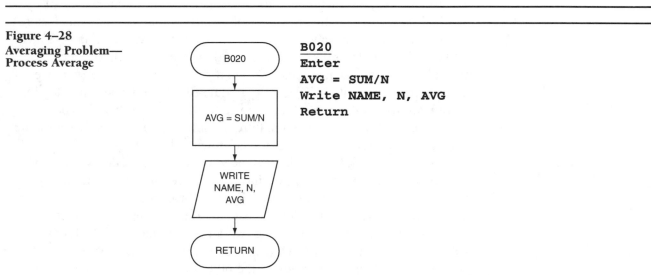

```
B020
Enter
AVG = SUM/N
Write NAME, N, AVG
Return
```

initialization. Each of these tasks can become complex, and, more importantly, each can be performed in a relatively generic fashion, independent of other processing in the algorithm. At some later point, we may even need to break the processing of an individual input record into several parts, thus creating a third level on the structure chart. As you study each of these modules, you will see that the steps within the modules are precisely those shown in Figures 4–21 and 4–22.

The No-Data Condition

Before we leave this problem, an important question needs to be addressed: What if the value read in for N is less than or equal to 0? In this case, COUNT will be set to either 0 or a negative value after the name record is input. When the test is then made the first time to check if COUNT is greater than 0, the "no" path will be taken immediately, since the condition is not true even the first time. The step immediately following the loop is the computation of the average, which involves a division by N. If N is negative, the average computed will be 0. (Do you see why?) If N is 0, a division by 0 will be attempted, and an error will result. We can handle these two cases by adding an IFTHENELSE statement right after N is input, as shown in Figures 4–29 and 4–30. Under this test the computer will check the current value of N and output a special message if the current value of N is 0 or negative. The program execution will then stop. If the "no" path is taken as a result of that first test, we know that N must be positive, and we can proceed to compute the average as was shown in the previous example.

Notice the structures that are now part of our program. There is a DOWHILE loop completely nested in the "no" path of the IFTHENELSE statement. Do you see it? Do you also see the role that each connector plays?

Figure 4–29
Averaging Problem with
No-Data Test (Flowchart)

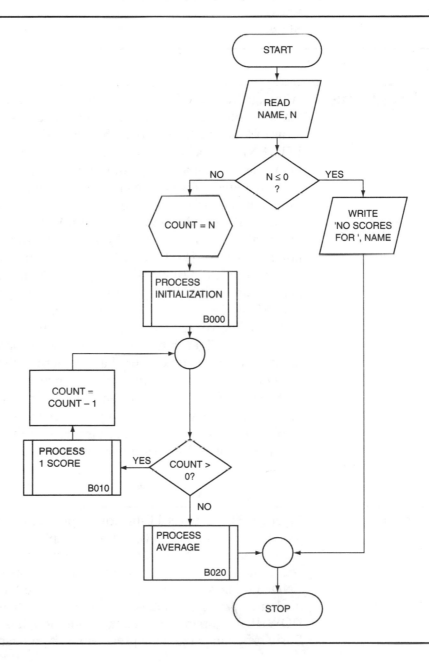

Figure 4–30
Averaging Problem with
No-Data Test (Pseudocode)

```
Start
Read NAME, N
IF N ≤ 0 THEN
   Write 'No scores for ', NAME
ELSE
   COUNT = N
   Process initialization (B000)
   DOWHILE COUNT > 0
      Process 1 score (B010)
      COUNT = COUNT - 1
   ENDDO
   Process average (B020)
ENDIF
Stop
```

Proper Programs

Although you may find it hard to realize at this time, it is important to note that any solution algorithm can be expressed using only the three basic patterns of logic we have learned thus far: SIMPLE SEQUENCE, IFTHENELSE, and DOWHILE. As mentioned earlier, this approach is known as **structured programming.** When we construct an algorithm using only the three basic patterns of structured programming, we are at the same time taking advantage of another idea set forth by Bohm and Jacopini: the **building-block concept.** We have noted already that each basic pattern is characterized by a single point of entrance and a single point of exit. A SIMPLE SEQUENCE may be only a single statement, or it may be a series of single statements. It may also include IFTHENELSE patterns and DOWHILE patterns, and these may in turn include other SIMPLE SEQUENCEs comprising single statements, IFTHENELSEs, and DOWHILEs. We say that the contained patterns are nested.

A solution algorithm should have only one entry point and one exit point. At the same time, every basic pattern in the algorithm should also have one entry and one exit point. A computer program representation of such an algorithm can be viewed conceptually as a single statement. A program that can be viewed as a single statement is called a **proper program.** Look again at some of the algorithms presented thus far in this book—they are all examples of proper programs.

Enrichment (Basic)

Figure 4–31 illustrates a listing of the program that solves the DOWHILE loop problem (Figure 4–4). In this example we implement the DOWHILE loop with a construct in Basic that is very similar to DOWHILE pseudocode. The keyword LOOP is used in Basic instead of the keyword ENDDO. The same type of indentation is used in the Basic program, and the logic of the Basic DOWHILE loop is identical to the logic of the DOWHILE loop in pseudocode. In addition, most of the statements in the Basic program parallel the pseudocode. Again, an Input statement is used

Figure 4–31
DOWHILE Loop Problem
(Basic List)

```
CLS
COUNT = 0
ACCUM = 0
DO WHILE COUNT < 6
    PRINT "Input a number";
    INPUT NUMBER
    ACCUM = ACCUM + NUMBER
    COUNT = COUNT + 1
LOOP
PRINT "The sum of the numbers is "; ACCUM
END
```

Figure 4–32
DOWHILE Loop Problem
(Basic Run)

```
Input a number? 1
Input a number? 2
Input a number? 3
Input a number? 4
Input a number? 5
Input a number? 6
The sum of the numbers is   21
```

to request a number from the user. Since the Input statement is included within the loop, it will be executed six times and the user will be prompted for six numbers. The Print statement is used again to output directions to the user. Note that these directions will be printed six times, since the Print statement is also included within the loop. Identifying text was added in the last Print statement to make the output more readable.

Figure 4–32 illustrates the output that will be produced when the program is executed. After the user enters the first number (1 in this case), the user is prompted to enter another number. As the user enters each number, the number is accumulated and stored in the variable ACCUM. After six numbers have been entered by the user, the sum (21 in this case) is output with an identifying label.

Enrichment (Visual Basic)

Figure 4–33 illustrates the graphical user interface for the DOWHILE loop problem (Figure 4–4).

In this example, only one control is created—a command button. When the user clicks this command button, a special window called an *input box* is presented to the user, as illustrated in Figure 4–34. The input box is another way (in addition to the text box control) to accept input from the user. At this point the user should enter a number and click the OK button. This same input box will be presented five more times as the user enters five additional numbers. After the last number is input and the user clicks the OK button, a message box is presented displaying the sum of the six numbers, as shown in Figure 4–35.

Figure 4–33
DOWHILE Loop Problem
(Visual Basic—Screen 1)

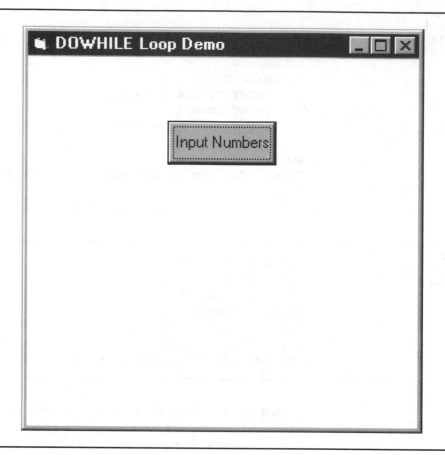

Figure 4–34
DOWHILE Loop Problem
(Visual Basic—Screen 2)

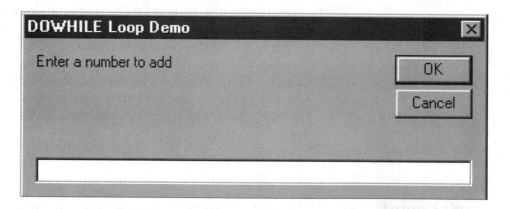

Figure 4–36 illustrates the program that is associated with the click event of the Input Numbers button. In this example we implement the DOWHILE loop with a construct in Visual Basic that is very similar to DOWHILE pseudocode. The keyword LOOP is used in Visual Basic instead of the keyword ENDDO. The same type of indentation is used in the Visual Basic program, and the logic of the Visual Basic DOWHILE loop is identical to the logic of the DOWHILE loop in pseudocode. In addition, most of the statements in the Visual Basic program parallel the pseudocode. An InputBox$ statement is used to request a number from the user. This

Figure 4–35
DOWHILE Loop Problem
(Visual Basic—Screen 3)

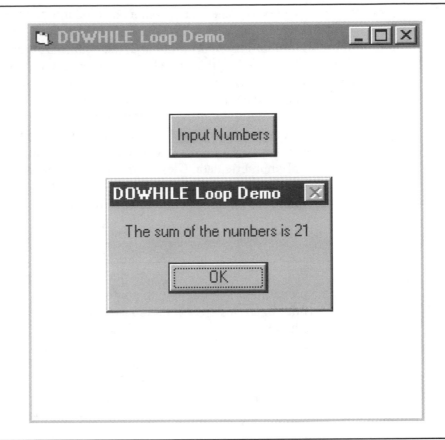

Figure 4–36
DOWHILE Loop
Problem (Visual Basic—
cmd_INPUT_Click)

```
Private Sub cmd_INPUT_Click()

Cnt = 0
Accum = 0
Do While Cnt < 6
    Number = InputBox$("Enter a number to add", "DOWHILE Loop Demo")
    Accum = Accum + Number
    Cnt = Cnt + 1
Loop
MsgBox "The sum of the numbers is " & Accum,,"DOWHILE Loop Demo"

End Sub
```

statement causes the input box window to be displayed. Since the InputBox$ statement is included within the loop, it will be executed six times and the user will be prompted for six numbers. The programmer determines both the message to be displayed and the title of the input box window. The programmer has no control over the buttons that will be displayed in the input box. An OK button and a Cancel button are always displayed. When a user enters a value into the input box and clicks the OK button, that value is assigned to the variable named Number. The value of Number is then accumulated, the counter is incremented, and the loop test is executed. If the user clicks the Cancel button instead of the OK button, no value will be assigned to Number. This situation could cause an error to occur since the value of the variable Number may not always be defined when the assignment statement following the InputBox$ statement is executed. In addition, if the user enters a non-numeric value in the input box, another type of error may occur since the variable Number is meant to hold only numeric data. Clearly, this program is not complete. Potential errors are likely. We will discuss some of these issues in later chapters. At this point, we simply need to realize this program's limitations.

Key Terms

program loop	counter-controlled loop	called module
preparation symbol	loop control variable	structure (hierarchy)
initialization step	modularization	chart
accumulator	predefined-process	header record logic
counter	symbol	header record
partial sum	module	structured
DOWHILE loop	annotation symbol	programming
leading-decision	top-down design	building-block concept
program loop	calling module (callee)	proper program

Exercises

1. State in your own words the purpose of a program loop.

2. What does it mean to say that a loop is "exited"?

3. (a) Using ANSI-approved flowcharting symbols, sketch the logic of a DOWHILE control structure.
   (b) State the logic of a DOWHILE control structure in pseudocode form.
   (c) What pseudocode keywords did you use in your response to Exercise 3(b)?
   (d) What indentations did you use in your response to Exercise 3(b)? Why?

4. (a) Why do we call the DOWHILE pattern a leading-decision loop?
   (b) What is particularly significant about the potential effects of this execution sequence?

5. Explain how the building-block concept can be used in developing a solution algorithm.

6. What is a proper program?

7. Name the three basic patterns of structured programming.

8. (a) What is a counter-controlled program loop?
   (b) Draw a generic program flowchart to explain header record logic.
   (c) How are the loop constructions in Exercises 8(a) and (b) similar?
   (d) How do they differ?

9. Use Figure 4–4 to answer the following questions.
   (a) What would happen if the step COUNT = 0 were placed inside the loop?
   (b) What would happen if the step ACCUM = 0 were placed inside the loop?
   (c) What would happen if the step Write ACCUM were placed inside the loop?
   (d) What would happen if only three numbers were input?
   (e) What would happen if ten numbers were input?
   (f) How could you change the algorithm to work for ten numbers?

10. (a) Using ANSI-approved flowcharting symbols, sketch the logic showing the processing steps required to output the first ten numbers (the numbers 1 to 10). Use a counter-controlled program loop.
    (b) State the logic of Exercise 10(a) in pseudocode form.

11. (a) Using ANSI-approved flowcharting symbols, sketch the logic showing the processing steps required to compute and output the square (number times number) and cube (number times number times number) for each of the numbers 1 through 100. Use a counter-controlled program loop.
    (b) State the logic of Exercise 11(a) in pseudocode form.

12. Construct a program flowchart and corresponding pseudocode describing the processing steps needed to solve the following problem: Initial values of 5.00 and 3.00 are to be assigned to A and B, respectively. The value for C, which is 95 percent of A, is to be computed. A, B, and C are to be printed. A is to be increased by twice the value of B. B is to be increased by 10 percent. The steps beginning with the computation of a value for C are to be repeated five times, and then program execution should terminate. Be sure to plan a well-structured program.

13. Assume the problem statement in Exercise 12 is modified as follows: A new value is to be computed for C on the first, third, and fifth passes through the loop only; otherwise, C is not to be changed. Construct a program flowchart and corresponding pseudocode for this revised algorithm.

14. Do a procedure execution of your solutions to Exercises 12 and 13. Be sure to list all the variables you used in the design, and to show how their values change with each iteration of the loop. Do not make any assumptions.

15. Construct a program flowchart and corresponding pseudocode to develop a solution algorithm for a program that will compute and print the sum of the numbers 1, 3, 5, 7, . . . , 99. Be sure to plan a well-structured program.

16. The Fibonacci series is defined to be the following numbers:

$$0, 1, 1, 2, 3, 5, 8, \ldots$$

where each number is the sum of the previous two numbers. Construct a program flowchart and corresponding pseudocode that will compute and output the first number greater than 100 in the above series. No input is required.

17. Construct a program flowchart and corresponding pseudocode to compute and print a sum as shown below:

$$1^1 + 2^2 + 3^3 + 4^4 + \cdots + N^N$$

N will be input.

18. N factorial (N!) is defined as the following series of numbers:

$$N! = N \times (N - 1) \times (N - 2) \times (N - 3) \times \cdots \times 1$$

Construct a program flowchart and corresponding pseudocode to compute N!, and output both N and N!. N will be input, and N! should only be computed if N is greater than 0. If it is not, output an appropriate message.

19. The ABC Company needs a weekly payroll report for its salespeople. Input to the program is a salesperson's name, number, and weekly sales. Output is the salesperson's name, number, and pay. Each salesperson receives a base pay of $300.00 as well as a 10 percent commission on his or her total sales up to and including $500.00. Any sales over $500.00 merit a 15 percent commission for the employee. (For example, if sales = $600.00, then pay = $300.00 + $50.00 [or 10 percent * 500] + $15.00 [or 15 percent * 100] = $365.00.) Use a DOWHILE loop and a counter to compute the weekly payroll for exactly 20 employees. Be sure to plan a well-structured solution. Design this algorithm using both a modular approach and a nonmodular approach, using both flowcharts and pseudocode. Include a structure chart with your modular solution.

20. Redo the solution to Exercise 19 to process sales data for any number of employees. Assume that the total number of employees for whom data is to be processed will be indicated on the first input record. This record will be followed by all the employee records. Be sure to check that the header record contains a positive number. Design this algorithm using both a modular approach and a nonmodular approach, using both flowcharts and pseudocode. Include a structure chart with your modular solution.

21. Redo the solution to Sample Problem 3.1 to process payroll data for any number of employees. Assume that the total number of employees for whom data is to be processed will be indicated on the first input record. This record will be followed by all the employee records. Be sure to check that the header record contains a positive number. Design this algorithm using both a modular approach and a nonmodular approach, using both flowcharts and pseudocode. Include a structure chart with your modular solution.

22. You are in a pumpkin patch looking for the great pumpkin. The first input record indicates how many pumpkin weight records follow. Several input records, each containing the weight of a pumpkin, follow the first input record. Assume that all the pumpkin weights are greater than zero. You are to find the largest weight and the average weight of all the pumpkins. You are to output each weight, as well as the largest weight and the average weight. Include an initial IF in your design that will output a descriptive message if the header record indicates that there are no input records to process. Design this algorithm using both a modular approach and a nonmodular approach, using both flowcharts and pseudocode. Include a structure chart with your modular solution.

23. Redo the solution to Sample Problem 4.3 to process data for any number of students. Assume that the total number of students will be the first input, followed by the name record for the first student. This record will then be followed by the individual scores for that student. After the scores for one student have been read, a name record for the next student will follow, and so on. Be sure to check that both the total number of students and the number of assignments completed for each student are positive numbers. Use the following structure chart to guide you in the modular design of this algorithm. Construct a program flowchart and corresponding pseudocode for each module in your solution.

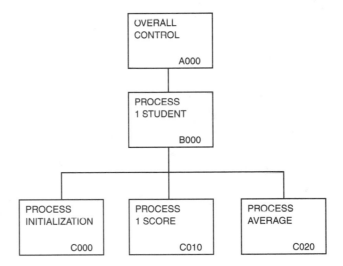

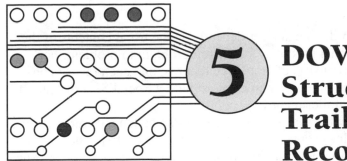

5 DOWHILE Control Structure— Trailer Record Logic

Objectives

Upon completion of this chapter you should be able to

- Distinguish between header record logic and trailer record logic.
- Design programs using trailer record logic.
- Distinguish between heading, detail, and total lines.
- Design programs that require heading, detail, and total lines.
- Design the logic needed to handle invalid input data.
- Define and distinguish between the priming read and the loop read.
- Design the logic required for automatic end-of-file processing.
- Design a program that outputs headings on every page of a report.

Introduction

In the previous chapter, the concept of a loop was introduced. Specifically, the DOWHILE loop was used in the solutions for all of the problems. In this chapter, we will continue to use the DOWHILE loop. Remember what characterizes this type of loop. The test to determine whether or not the processing steps within the loop should, in fact, be executed always comes first within the loop structure. Also, the test is worded so that the loop steps are always executed in the "yes" (true) path, and exited in the "no" (false) path. We also looked at the very important issue of loop control; that is, which factor determines when the loop should be exited. In Chapter 4 we began with the concept of the simple counter-controlled program loop, and then expanded that idea to a specific technique called header record logic. Both approaches use a counter to control the loop. In header record logic, the first input record (the header record) contains a number that specifies how many times to execute the loop. In this chapter we will explore a different procedure for loop control called **trailer record logic.**

As the name **trailer record logic** implies, this approach involves the use of a **trailer record** (last input record) to control the loop. This last record serves as a signal to the computer that no more records are to be processed. Because this record serves as an indicator that no more records are to follow, it must contain some special information that differentiates it from the rest of the input, and that can be used in the loop test to determine when all input has been processed. The question is: What type of signal should we place in a trailer record? The answer depends on the usual contents of the input records. The signal used may vary from problem to problem. For example, if the input consists of employee records, and each record contains a Social Security number, then a record with a Social Security number of 0 could serve as a trailer record.

The key requirement is that a trailer record (also called a **dummy data value** or **sentinel value**) contain a value in the particular field chosen for the loop test that is different from any possible value for the field. (No one, for example, has a Social Security number of 0.) That is, we must be sure that our choice of the trailer value will not occur as a valid value for the field in other input records. If this were to happen, none of the records following the record containing the trailer value as a valid value would be input or processed. In addition, a trailer record may need to contain values for all fields even though only one of these values will be tested. It is also important to understand that a DOWHILE loop controlled by a trailer record does not require a counter for loop control. Let us explore this concept with a specific example.

Sample Problem 5.1 (Defective Parts Without Modules)

Problem:

The Car/Go Manufacturing Company produces a large number of automotive parts each year in its two plants. Some of these parts are returned to the main sales office because of defects in manufacture. An input record is prepared for each defective part, containing a code, part number, type of part, and date returned. The code is either 1 or 2, indicating whether plant 1 or plant 2 made the defective part.

Car/Go needs a read-and-print program to process these records and produce a listing of their contents. In addition, the number of defective parts manufactured by each plant is to be totaled for future reference. A trailer record containing a plant code of 9 is to signal the end of the input (see Figure 5–1). The output is to consist of a printed listing of the contents of the input records, followed by the total computed for each plant.

Solution:

A solution to this problem is shown in both flowchart and pseudocode forms in Figures 5–2 and 5–3.

Figure 5–1
Defective Parts Problem—
Input Format

Plant Code	Part #	Part Type	Date Returned
2	L45603	TAILLIGHT	04/16/98
1	W07722	WIPER BLADE	04/17/98
1	C19654	CLOCK	04/16/98
2	D33045	DOMELIGHT	04/20/98
:	:	:	:
9	999999	END OF FILE	00/00/00

Figure 5–2
Defective Parts Problem
(Flowchart)

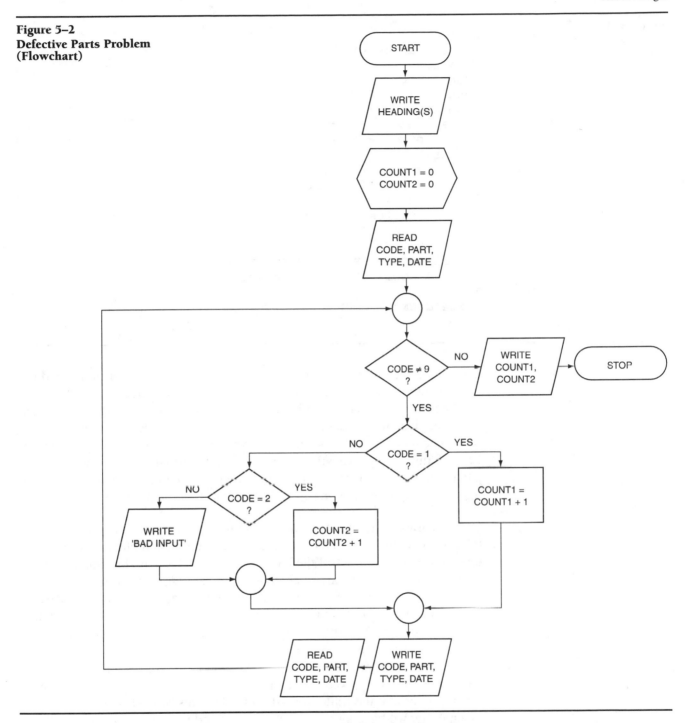

Heading Lines The algorithm begins with an output statement that produces one or more headings. A **heading line** serves as a title to a report that is output. Headings are almost always used on business reports to identify them to readers. A report might include a report heading such as "PAYROLL REPORT" or "DEFECTIVE PARTS REPORT." It might also include one or more column headings such as "NAME," "HOURS," "RATE," and so on. It is not usually necessary to define the headings in the early stages of algorithm development. The detailed text of the

Figure 5–3
Defective Parts Problem
(Pseudocode)

```
Start
Write heading(s)
COUNT1 = 0
COUNT2 = 0
Read CODE, PART, TYPE, DATE
DOWHILE CODE ≠ 9
   IF CODE = 1 THEN
      COUNT1 = COUNT1 + 1
   ELSE
      IF CODE = 2 THEN
         COUNT2 = COUNT2 + 1
      ELSE
         Write 'Bad Input'
      ENDIF
   ENDIF
   Write CODE, PART, TYPE, DATE
   Read CODE, PART, TYPE, DATE
ENDDO
Write COUNT1, COUNT2
Stop
```

headings can be worked out later, but an indication that one or more headings will be output should be included in the design at this point. Notice that headings are output at the beginning of processing; therefore, this output step is not included in the loop. This makes sense, since a title is usually shown only once—at the start of a report, not preceding every line within the report. Later in this chapter we will look at the logic to output headings on every page of the report. At this point, however, our design indicates that the headings will be output only once—at the beginning of the report.

Detail Lines In the next step, two counters are initialized to 0 to keep a tally of the number of defective parts produced by each plant. These counters are not used to control the loop, as was the case with header record logic. At this point, we are ready to process each input record, so the first record is input. Notice that the READ statement refers to four variables, each representing one of the input fields. Notice also that the READ statement in Figure 5–2 is followed by a connector indicating the beginning of the DOWHILE loop.

Now notice the test at the beginning of the loop. We need to know if the loop steps should be executed; that is, is the record we've just read a normal input, or is it the trailer record? If CODE (just input) is not 9, we assume that we have a normal input record and proceed with the "true" path—the actual processing steps within the DOWHILE loop. A nested IFTHENELSE structure checks to see if the code is 1 or 2. The appropriate counter is then increased, because we need to keep track of the number of defective parts from each plant. If both tests fail, the code must be invalid, because the company has only two plants, 1 and 2. In this case we output an error message indicating that the input is invalid.

Both IFTHENELSE structures are then closed with their respective connectors on the flowchart and ENDIFs in the pseudocode. The contents of the input record are output. Note that if the code is in fact invalid, two lines of output are generated: an error message ("Bad Input") and the contents of the input record itself. We can then see the contents of all the invalid records, with an error message preceding each one.

Note that the last WRITE statement within the loop is executed each time the loop steps are processed. It causes one line of output to be printed for each input record. This output is an example of a **detail line;** that is, a line of output associated with one input record. Detail lines are always output in a step within the main processing loop. Remember, though, that heading lines are output before the loop is entered.

The last step in the DOWHILE loop is a READ statement that is identical to the first READ statement. This statement causes the next available record to be input; then the loop processing is started again, and the initial test is made to determine whether the code just input is 9. If this second record is not the trailer record (CODE is not 9), the loop steps are repeated for the record and a third record is read. This processing continues until all the input records have been tested and output. When the trailer record is finally input, the loop test is not true (since the code is 9). Notice the double negative; that is, a code of 9 means that the test for a code not equal to 9 is false. Why this confusing verbiage? Remember, the test must be worded in such a way as to cause the loop steps to be done in the true path and the loop exit to be the false path.

Total Lines When the loop is finally exited, the values for the two counters are output. This is an example of a **total line;** that is, a line that represents cumulative information from one or more input records. Total lines are typically output after the loop is exited. It is important to remember the differences between a heading line, a detail line, and a total line; similarly, you must remember where the statement for each type of line should be written relative to the loop.

Priming Read and Loop Read In trailer record logic there are always two READ statements in the algorithm that look exactly the same. The first READ statement, placed before the loop, causes the first record to be input. This READ statement is called the **priming read,** because it gets the computer ready (primes the computer) to make the loop test. The second READ statement, called the **loop read,** is within the loop—usually the loop's last statement. It causes the next available input record to be read each time the loop steps are executed.

Both of these READ statements are essential for successful program operation. If we omitted the priming read in this example, the value of CODE would be undefined when the loop test was first attempted. If we omitted the loop read, no more records would be input, and the initial value of CODE would be tested over and over again. Because the trailer record would never be input, the loop steps would be repeated indefinitely. An infinite loop would result, eventually causing an error condition to be recognized by the system and signaled to the user or application program.

Look over this algorithm once again and concentrate on finding each control structure. We have a series of SIMPLE SEQUENCE statements and a DOWHILE loop, containing a nested IFTHENELSE structure, containing additional SIMPLE SEQUENCE statements. Convince yourself that this is, in fact, a proper program. You might have noticed that this solution contains no modular breakdown. In our next example, we will take this same algorithm, redesign it using several modules, and include a test to handle the situation where the first input is the trailer record.

Sample Problem 5.2 (Defective Parts Using Modules)

Problem:

Redo Sample Problem 5.1 to construct a modular design, and include a test to determine if there is any input data.

Solution:

This problem solution can be broken into modules in any of several ways. The structure chart in Figure 5–4 illustrates one possible construction.

In this example we have, as before, one main controlling module; but this time the problem solution is broken down into four lower-level modules. The modular breakdown is very similar to Sample Problem 4.3 in Chapter 4; however, in the present case we have included an additional module to process the headings. This module is numbered B000, and the other three level-2 modules are renumbered accordingly. You might notice that modules B020 and B030 have been given general names, whereas in Chapter 4 the names were more specific. The process 1 score module in Sample Problem 4.3 took care of detail processing; the process average module in Sample Problem 4.3 took care of total processing.

Now let's look at the flowchart (Figure 5–5) and the pseudocode (Figure 5–6) for module A000.

As you can see, there are four predefined-process symbols in the flowchart, each referring to one of the modules. The headings module (B000) is called first. Its execution and return of control to A000 is followed immediately by a call to the initialization module (B010). After the first record is read, an IFTHENELSE statement directs the computer to check whether the CODE just input is 9. If so, the trailer record has been read first, either by accident or because there are no data records to process. A special message is output and program execution stops. This part of the logic is analogous to the test made to determine if the header record read as input contains a positive number (see Figures 4–29 and 4–30). In the present example, if the first code is not 9, then we can assume the record is a normal data record and needs to be processed. The DOWHILE loop is shown as before, but this time the details are left to module B020. Any current input record that is not the trailer record will be processed. Then the next record will be input. In this type of logic, each time the loop is executed, the record already input is processed and then the next record is read. Can you find the priming and loop reads in A000? After all records have been processed, the loop will be exited and the total lines will be output. Notice that another module (B030) is referred to when the loop is exited. We will now look at the details of each of the four modules called by A000.

B000 (Figure 5–7), B010 (Figure 5–8), and B030 (Figure 5–9) are all relatively trivial; however, since each of these tasks can become more

Figure 5–4
Defective Parts Problem
(Structure Chart)

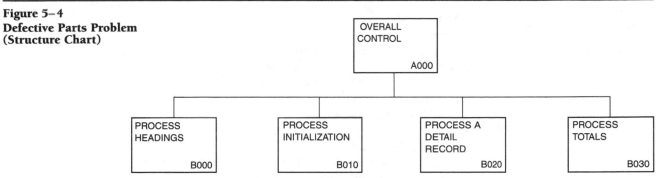

Figure 5–5
Defective Parts Problem—
Overall Control (Flowchart)

Figure 5–6
Defective Parts Problem—
Overall Control
(Pseudocode)

```
A000
Start
Process headings (B000)
Process initialization (B010)
Read CODE, PART, TYPE, DATE
IF CODE = 9 THEN
   Write 'No data'
ELSE
   DOWHILE CODE ≠ 9
      Process a detail record (B020)
      Read CODE, PART, TYPE, DATE
   ENDDO
   Process totals (B030)
ENDIF
Stop
```

Figure 5–7
Defective Parts Problem—
Process Headings

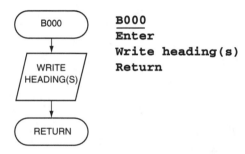

```
B000
Enter
Write heading(s)
Return
```

Figure 5–8
Defective Parts Problem—
Process Initialization

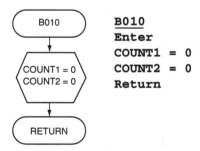

```
B010
Enter
COUNT1 = 0
COUNT2 = 0
Return
```

Figure 5–9
Defective Parts Problem—
Process Totals

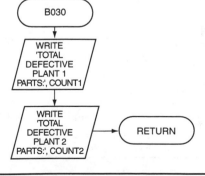

```
B030
Enter
Write 'Total defective
   plant 1 parts:', COUNT1
Write 'Total defective
   plant 2 parts:', COUNT2
Return
```

complex, we have defined each as a separate module. B020 (Figures 5–10 and 5–11) is more significant and probably a more obvious module. At some later point, we may even need to break the processing of a detail record into several parts, thus creating a third level on the structure chart. As you study each of these modules, you will see that the steps within the modules are like those shown in Figures 5–2 and 5–3. The only slight variation is in module B030. In Figure 5–9 we have written two lines, not one, and we have added an identifying label to each counter value that is output. This information increases the readability of the report.

Figure 5–10
Defective Parts Problem—
Process Detail Record
(Flowchart)

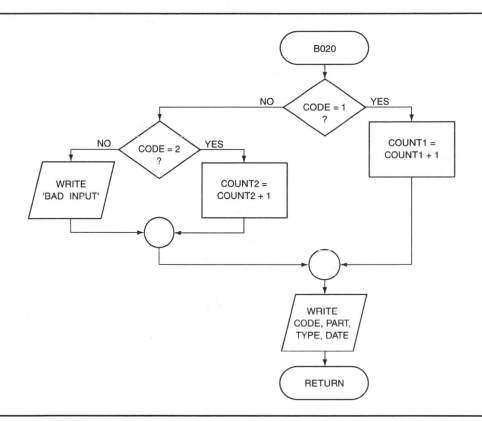

Figure 5–11
Defective Parts Problem—
Process Detail Record
(Pseudocode)

```
B020
Enter
IF CODE = 1 THEN
    COUNT1 = COUNT1 + 1
ELSE
    IF CODE = 2 THEN
        COUNT2 = COUNT2 + 1
    ELSE
        Write 'Bad Input'
    ENDIF
ENDIF
Write CODE, PART, TYPE, DATE
Return
```

Automatic End-of-File Processing

It is not always necessary to physically place a trailer record at the end of the input. Most language-processor programs (interpreters or compilers) support a built-in function for recognizing when the end of file has been reached, even if a trailer record is not provided as input. The main design of the algorithm is not affected in such a case. The only change that needs to be made is the wording of the test to determine if there is any more input. Instead of checking for a specific trailer value, we can simply test for the generic name of the function, for example, "End of File" or, even more simply, EOF. Each programming language provides a specific way to do this test; but at design time simply noting that a check for an EOF condition is needed is sufficient. If we design our algorithm in this way, we are utilizing what is called an **automatic end-of-file facility.**

Figures 5–12 and 5–13 illustrate the flowchart and pseudocode for one approach to this problem. As you can see, the steps in the algorithm are like

Figure 5–12
Automatic End of File
(Flowchart)

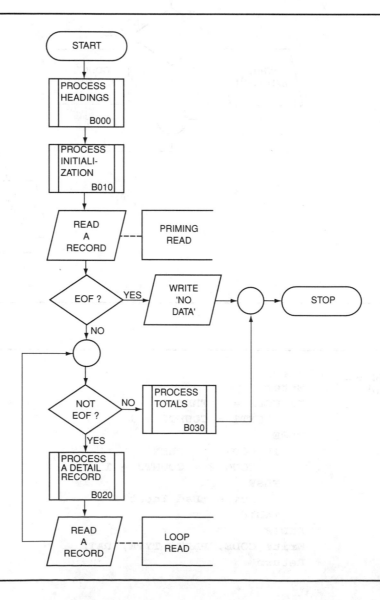

Figure 5–13
Automatic End of File
(Pseudocode)

```
A000
Start
Process headings (B000)
Process initialization (B010)
Read a record
IF end of file (EOF) THEN
   Write 'No data'
ELSE
   DOWHILE not end of file (not EOF)
      Process a detail record (B020)
      Read a record
   ENDDO
   Process totals (B030)
ENDIF
Stop
```

those shown in our trailer record logic example. Both the priming read and the loop read are still present. The wording of each test, however, is different: Instead of checking for a specific value, the first IFTHENELSE tests whether end of file (EOF) has been reached. The test result will be true only if there is no input data. We sometimes call this the **empty file condition.** It may seem unnecessary to check for this condition, but the condition happens more often than you may expect. The second test—a check for a "not EOF" condition—occurs at the beginning of a DOWHILE structure. If "not EOF" is true, the loop steps in the true path of the structure are executed. Remember, having the true path within the loop is a DOWHILE loop requirement.

Sample Problem 5.3 (Defective Parts with Multiple Headings)

Problem:

Redo the solution to Sample Problem 5.2 to output headings on every page of the report, not just on the first page. In addition, number each page. Use automatic end-of-file processing in the solution.

Solution:

To output headings at the top of every page, we will need to know when the bottom of every page (and hence the top of the next page) is reached. We will use a counter (LINECNT) to keep track of the number of detail lines that have been output on a page at any given time. LINECNT will be initialized to 0. Each time a detail line is output, we will increase the value of LINECNT by 1. When the value of LINECNT reaches a predetermined maximum (55 in this example), a new page will be started, and the heading lines will be the next lines written as output. The maximum value of LINECNT will determine the maximum number of detail lines printed on one page. We will use another counter (PAGECNT) to keep track of which page is currently being written as output. PAGECNT will be initialized to 1. Its value will be increased by 1 each time the heading lines are output. Its current value will be output whenever the heading lines are output. The structure chart for this problem is shown in Figure 5–14.

The headings module (C000) is not controlled directly from A000 as it was in our earlier solution (Figure 5–4). When the detail-processing module is given control, it determines whether heading lines need to be printed. If not, it can simply process and print a detail line. In this way, the headings are directly tied to the detail lines. We might think of the logic as follows: Before a detail line can be output, we must check to see if any room exists on the current page. If so, we simply write out the detail line. If not, we start a new page, write the heading information, and then output the detail line. The total lines will be output on the same page as the last detail line—even if the maximum number of lines (55 in this case) has been output. (Users of a report prefer to see totals in relation to the rest of the report, not alone on a separate page.) Figures 5–15 and 5–16 illustrate the overall control module for this algorithm. It is similar to the previous overall control module, except that no call to the headings module is included. Remember, only the detail-processing module can give control to the headings module.

The initialization module (B000) is shown in Figure 5–17. The two counters PAGECNT and LINECNT have been added to this module. PAGECNT is initialized to 1, since we want the first page of our report to be numbered 1. LINECNT is initialized to 55—not to 0 as you may have expected. If we had set LINECNT to 0, no headings would have been printed on the first page. We need to "fool the computer" into thinking that we are already at the bottom of a page before we even start. In this way, the first time the value of LINECNT is checked, it will cause a new page to be started and the desired headings to be output.

The total processing module (B020) is shown in Figure 5–18. Except for its reference number, it is like the total processing module of our earlier solution.

The detail-processing module (B010) is shown in Figures 5–19 and 5–20. Before CODE is checked, LINECNT is checked to see if its value is equal to or exceeds 55. If so (as it will be the first time), the headings

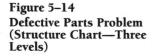

Figure 5–14
Defective Parts Problem (Structure Chart—Three Levels)

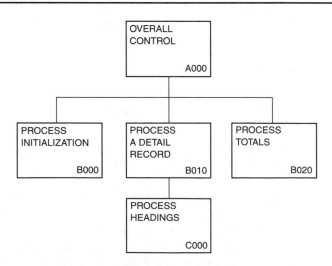

Figure 5–15
Defective Parts Problem—
Multiple Headings—Overall
Control (Flowchart)

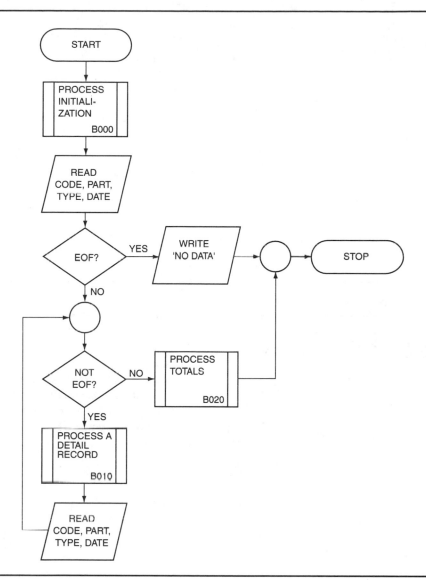

Figure 5–16
Defective Parts Problem—
Multiple Headings—Overall
Control (Pseudocode)

```
A000
Start
Process initialization (B000)
Read CODE, PART, TYPE, DATE
IF EOF THEN
   Write 'No data'
ELSE
   DOWHILE not EOF
      Process a detail record (B010)
      Read CODE, PART, TYPE, DATE
   ENDDO
   Process totals (B020)
ENDIF
Stop
```

Figure 5–17
Defective Parts Problem—
Multiple Headings—Process
Initialization

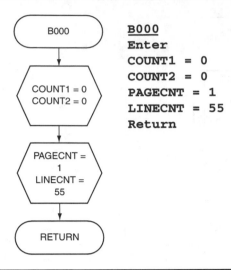

```
B000
Enter
COUNT1 = 0
COUNT2 = 0
PAGECNT = 1
LINECNT = 55
Return
```

Figure 5–18
Defective Parts Problem—
Multiple Headings—Process
Totals

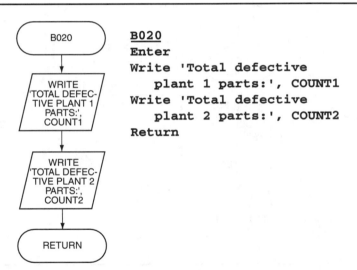

```
B020
Enter
Write 'Total defective
    plant 1 parts:', COUNT1
Write 'Total defective
    plant 2 parts:', COUNT2
Return
```

module is called to output the appropriate headings. The normal detail processing occurs and a detail line is output. If the plant code within the next input record is invalid, the "Bad Input" line is output, and LINECNT is again increased by 1. It is important to see that the detail processing must be done, whether or not the headings are output. This logic is provided for in the design by the use of the null ELSE clause located in the first IFTHEN-ELSE statement in the detail-processing module. Note also that there are three IFTHENELSE statements in this module. Can you see that the first two IFs are sequential and that the third IF is nested within the second IF?

Finally, the headings module (C000) is shown in Figure 5–21. In this example, we assume that both report and column headings are to be output. PAGECNT is written on the same line as the report heading. LINECNT is set back to 0, since we are starting a new page and no detail lines have yet been output on the page. PAGECNT is then increased by 1 so that the next page will be numbered correctly.

Figure 5–19
Defective Parts Problem—
Multiple Headings—Process
Detail Record (Flowchart)

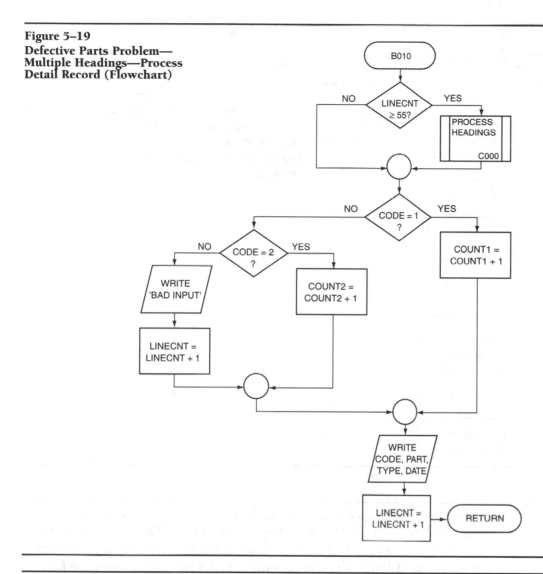

Figure 5–20
Defective Parts Problem—
Multiple Headings—Process
Detail Record (Pseudocode)

```
B010
Enter
IF LINECNT ≥ 55 THEN
    Process headings (C000)
(ELSE)
ENDIF
IF CODE = 1 THEN
    COUNT1 = COUNT1 + 1
ELSE
    IF CODE = 2 THEN
        COUNT2 = COUNT2 + 1
    ELSE
        Write 'Bad Input'
        LINECNT = LINECNT + 1
    ENDIF
ENDIF
Write CODE, PART, TYPE, DATE
LINECNT = LINECNT + 1
Return
```

Figure 5–21
Defective Parts Problem—
Multiple Headings—Process
Headings

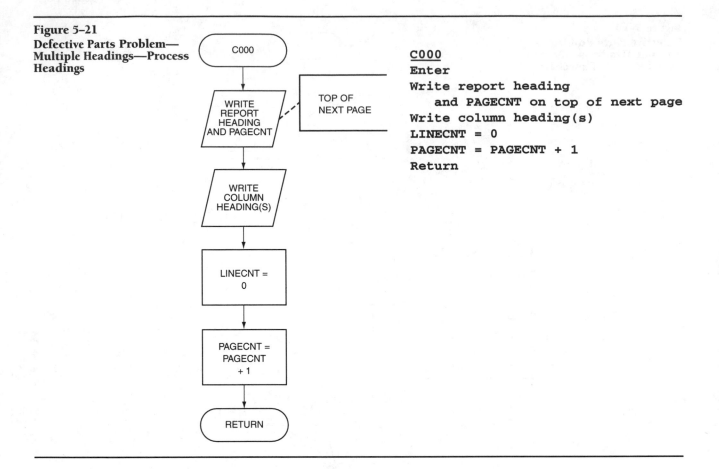

```
C000
Enter
Write report heading
    and PAGECNT on top of next page
Write column heading(s)
LINECNT = 0
PAGECNT = PAGECNT + 1
Return
```

Multiple Headings— Summary

Before we look at another algorithm, let us summarize what we have learned about multiple headings. We saw that two additional counters are needed when keeping track of how many lines on a given page have been output so far (LINECNT) and how many pages have been output so far (PAGECNT). These counters are initialized, incremented, and tested in much the same way in any problem that outputs multiple headings and page numbers. These functions are often used in application packages. For example, word processors use this type of logic to output page numbers, headers, and footers. Likewise, a database management program uses similar logic to generate a page overflow.

Figure 5–22 shows the general processing requirements for multiple heading logic. Partial flowcharts for the three modules, B000 (process initialization), B010 (process a detail record), and C000 (process headings), illustrate the specific steps.

Sample Problem 5.4 (Credits Problem)

Problem:

Design an algorithm to read individual records containing student names, addresses, and total numbers of accumulated credits as input. The names and addresses of all students who have earned 60 or more

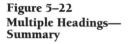

**Figure 5–22
Multiple Headings—
Summary**

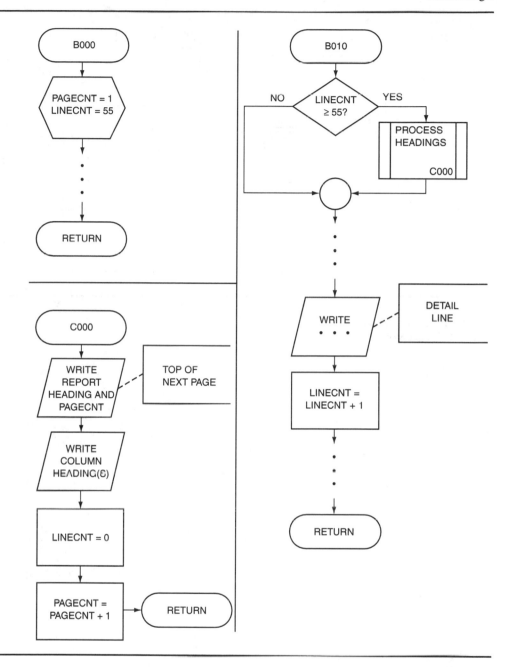

credits should be printed as output. For other student records, no action is required. Program execution should terminate when a trailer record containing a negative credits amount is input. Headings are to be written on every page, and the pages are to be numbered.

Solution:

The structure chart for a solution to this problem is shown in Figure 5–23.

The four modules have exactly the same names as four of the modules used in our previous design (Figure 5–14)—only the totals module is missing. Figures 5–24 and 5–25 illustrate the flowchart and pseudocode

110

Chapter 5

Figure 5–23
Credits Problem (Structure Chart)

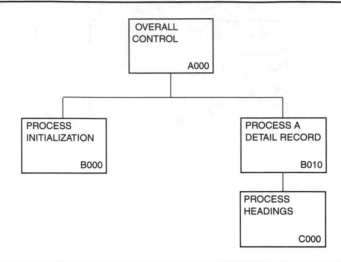

Figure 5–24
Credits Problem—Overall Control (Flowchart)

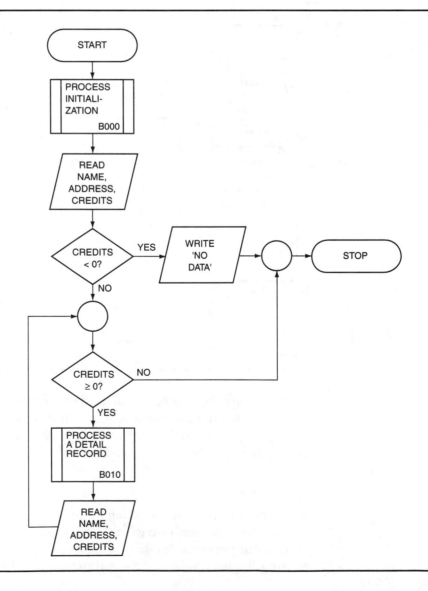

Figure 5–25
Credits Problem—Overall
Control (Pseudocode)

```
A000
Start
Process initialization (B000)
Read NAME, ADDRESS, CREDITS
IF CREDITS < 0 THEN
   Write 'No data'
ELSE
   DOWHILE CREDITS ≥ 0
      Process a detail record (B010)
      Read NAME, ADDRESS, CREDITS
   ENDDO
ENDIF
Stop
```

for the overall control module (A000). The overall structure of this module is the same as that of A000 in our previous solution; however, there are a few minor differences in details. First, the two READ statements contain different variable names. The three variables—NAME, ADDRESS, and CREDITS—are the values that need to be input for each student.

A second difference is in the actual test that is made in both the first IFTHENELSE statement and the DOWHILE loop. This test corresponds to the requirement that a trailer record containing a negative number for the credits field be used.

The only other difference in this solution is the omission of a totals module, which is usually invoked after loop processing is complete. In this problem, however, we are not asked to compute or output any total information. For example, we do not need to count the number of student records or accumulate the total number of credits for all the students. (Doing so is left as an exercise.)

The detail-processing module (B010) is shown in Figures 5–26 (flowchart) and 5–27 (pseudocode). To begin with, we check to see if the value of LINECNT equals or exceeds 55. If so, the headings module is called to output the headings on a new page. This IFTHENELSE construct is then immediately followed by another IFTHENELSE construct. The second IFTHENELSE checks to see if the current student's credits equal or exceed 60. Remember, the data for the current student was read as input by A000. If the value of CREDITS is greater than or equal to 60, the student name and address are output and the value of LINECNT is incremented by 1. You might wonder why the value of student credits (CREDITS) was not also output. If you reexamine the problem statement, you will notice that it specifies only that the name and address of each student be output. If the value of CREDITS is less than 60, nothing is to be output. The null ELSE clause in the design reflects this logic. It is interesting that this module contains two sequential (not nested) IFTHENELSE statements, and each contains a null ELSE clause.

Finally, the initialization module (B000) and the headings module (C000) are shown in Figures 5–28 and 5–29. Notice that, in B000, no counters are set to 0, as was done in the previous example. Remember, we are not being asked to count or accumulate anything other than the required computations for line count and page count. Typically, if a total of some type is required, a counter and/or accumulator must be set to some initial value, like 0, in the initialization module. That same counter and/or

Figure 5–26
Credits Problem—Process
Detail Record (Flowchart)

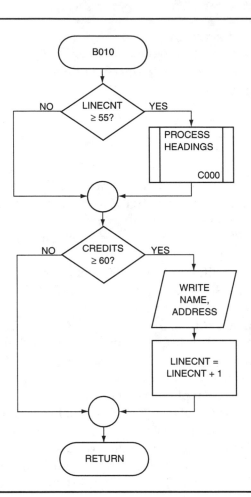

Figure 5–27
Credits Problem—Process
Detail Record (Pseudocode)

```
B010
Enter
IF LINECNT ≥ 55 THEN
    Process headings (C000)
(ELSE)
ENDIF
IF CREDITS ≥ 60 THEN
    Write NAME, ADDRESS
    LINECNT = LINECNT + 1
(ELSE)
ENDIF
Return
```

Figure 5–28
Credits Problem—Process
Initialization

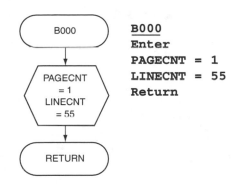

```
B000
Enter
PAGECNT = 1
LINECNT = 55
Return
```

Figure 5–29
Credits Problem—Process
Headings

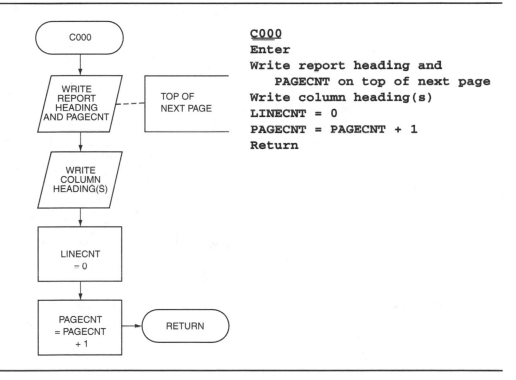

```
C000
Enter
Write report heading and
     PAGECNT on top of next page
Write column heading(s)
LINECNT = 0
PAGECNT = PAGECNT + 1
Return
```

accumulator is incremented in the detail-processing module, and a total module is designed to output the final value of the counter and/or accumulator.

DOWHILE Loop Control— Summary

In Chapters 4 and 5 we introduced the DOWHILE control structure and four approaches to loop control. Chapter 4 focused on counter loops (simple and header record) and Chapter 5 focused on end-of-file control (trailer record and automatic). Figure 5–30 (flowcharts) and Figure 5–31 (pseudocode) illustrate the basic steps required to read and write several records. Each of the four approaches to loop control is shown; however, the initial test for an empty file is omitted for simplicity. Make sure you understand the differences among these four approaches.

Figure 5–30
Types of DOWHILE Loop
Control (Flowcharts)

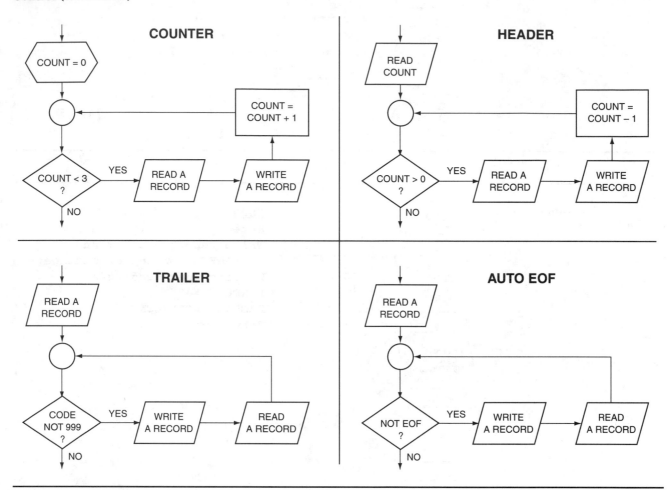

Figure 5–31
Types of DOWHILE Loop
Control (Pseudocode)

```
   COUNTER                      HEADER

COUNT = 0                 Read COUNT
DOWHILE COUNT < 3         DOWHILE COUNT > 0
   Read a record             Read a record
   Write a record            Write a record
   COUNT = COUNT + 1         COUNT = COUNT + 1
ENDDO                     ENDDO


   TRAILER                     AUTO EOF

Read a record             Read a record
DOWHILE CODE not 999      DOWHILE not EOF
   Write a record            Write a record
   Read a record             Read a record
ENDDO                     ENDDO
```

**Enrichment
(Basic)**

Figure 5–32 illustrates a listing of the program that solves the Credits Problem (Figures 5–24 through 5–29). In Basic each module (except the overall control module) is considered a Subprogram and is identified by a *Sub* statement followed by the name of the module. The *End Sub* statement denotes the end of each module or subprogram. In addition, a *Rem* statement identifying the module number is listed at the beginning of each module. A Rem statement is simply a remark or comment and is ignored by the computer. We use Rem statements to clarify program statements, making them easier to follow.

In Basic, all subprograms that are accessed in a program must be stated or "declared" at the beginning of the program. Thus, our first three statements are *Declare Sub* statements for the called modules. Note that in Basic we use the keyword *Call*, followed by the module name, to invoke a module. The overall control module is very similar to the pseudocode in Figure 5–25. In this example, however, we use a *Read* statement instead of an Input statement. The Read statement does not accept user input. Rather, *Data* statements containing the actual data to be input are listed at the end of the overall control module. Each time the Read statement is executed, three data items are input from one of the Data statements. These three pieces of data are then stored in the appropriate variables listed in the Read statement. For example, the first time the Read statement is executed, "John" is stored in the variable NAME$, "111 Main St." is stored in the variable ADDRESS$, and 60 is stored in the variable CREDITS. The second time the Read statement is executed, "Mary" is stored in the variable NAME$, "222 Oak St." is stored in the variable ADDRESS$, and 70 is stored in the variable CREDITS. Note that the trailer record (the last Data statement) contains three values. Every time the Read statement is executed, three values must be input since the Read statement contains three variables. However, only the variable CREDITS is tested to determine when to exit the loop. The value of –1 is used to signal the end of the input. In this example, the Read and Data statements are used to receive input. We could have also used the Input statement to receive the data interactively from the user as we did in previous chapters.

The statements for each module or subprogram are listed after the overall control module. In our design examples we assumed that all variables were global in scope. If a variable is global, all modules have access to its value. In contrast, local variables can only be accessed within one module. In Basic we must use a *Shared* statement for each global variable, that is, each variable whose value is shared with another module. For example, the value of LINECNT is shared among modules B000, B010, and C000. Note that the Shared statement is only used within subprograms and, thus, is not necessary in A000.

The statements in B000, B010, and C000 are very similar to the pseudocode in Figures 5–27, 5–28, and 5–29. Only minor differences in syntax exist. For example, in Basic the tests for "greater than or equal to" in module B010 specify the logical operators > and = side by side as >=. Also, a null else clause in Basic is indicated by the absence of the keyword ELSE.

Figure 5–32
Credits Problem (Basic List)

```
DECLARE SUB ProcessInitialization()
DECLARE SUB ProcessDetailRecord()
DECLARE SUB ProcessHeadings()

REM A000 - Overall Control Module
CALL ProcessInitialization
READ NAME$, ADDRESS$, CREDITS
IF CREDITS < 0 THEN
        PRINT "No data to process"
ELSE
        DO WHILE CREDITS >= 0
                CALL ProcessDetailRecord
                READ NAME$, ADDRESS$, CREDITS
        LOOP
END IF
DATA "John", "111 Main St.", 60
DATA "Mary", "222 Oak St.", 70
DATA "Jane", "333 First Ave.", 50
DATA "Bill". "444 Cedar St.", 100
DATA "Terry", "555 Main St.", 65
DATA "Sue", "666 Oak Dr.", 59
DATA "Andy", "777 Star Ct.", 61
DATA "End","No St.", -1
END


REM B000
SUB ProcessInitialization
SHARED LINECNT
SHARED PAGECNT
PAGECNT = 1
LINECNT = 55
END SUB


REM B010
SUB ProcessDetailRecord
SHARED LINECNT
SHARED CREDITS
SHARED NAME$
SHARED ADDRESS$
IF LINECNT >= 55 THEN
        CALL ProcessHeadings
END IF
IF CREDITS >= 60 THEN
        PRINT NAME$, ADDRESS$
        LINECNT = LINECNT + 1
END IF
END SUB


REM C000
SUB ProcessHeadings
SHARED LINECNT
SHARED PAGECNT
PRINT "CREDITS REPORT", "Page"; PAGECNT
PRINT
PRINT "NAME", "ADDRESS"
PRINT
LINECNT = 0
PAGECNT = PAGECNT + 1
END SUB
```

Figure 5–33
Credits Problem (Basic Run)

```
CREDITS REPORT      Page 1

NAME       ADDRESS

John       111 Main St.
Mary       222 Oak St.
Bill       444 Cedar St.
Terry      555 Main St.
Andy       777 Star Ct.
```

Figure 5–33 illustrates the output that will be produced when the program is executed. Note that detail lines are output only for those records where the value of CREDITS is greater than or equal to 60. Note also that the trailer record is not output.

Enrichment (Visual Basic)

Figure 5–34 illustrates the graphical interface for the Credits Problem (Figures 5–24 through 5–29). Although this example is based on the Credits Problem, some modifications to the original problem have been made. In this example, only the student name and number of credits are input. The address was left out to simplify the problem. A text box is used to input the student name and a new control, a *horizontal scroll bar*, is used to input the number of credits. The scroll bar is given a minimum value of 1 and a maximum value of 100; that is, only credit values between 1 and 100 can be input. In this way, no data validation is necessary. When the

Figure 5–34
Credits Problem (Visual Basic—Screen 1)

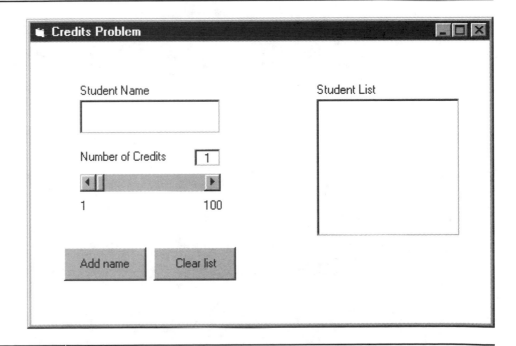

user clicks one of the small arrows to the left or right of the scroll bar, the value of credits is increased or decreased by one. This value is also displayed in a small label control above the scroll bar. Another new control, called a *list box,* is shown on the right of the screen. This control will be used to display the name of each student whose credits are greater than or equal to 60. Two command buttons are created, one to add a student name to the list and one to clear all student names from the list.

Figure 5–35 illustrates the screen after the user has entered the name and credits and has clicked the Add name button. Note that the student name John appears in the list box since the value of credits is equal to 60.

Figure 5–36 illustrates the screen after the user has entered another name and credits and has again clicked the Add name button. Note that the student name Mary appears in the list box since the value of credits is greater than 60. Note also that this second name is added to the list box; that is, Mary is listed in addition to John, not in place of John.

Figure 5–37 illustrates the screen after the user has entered another name and credits and has again clicked the Add name button. This time, the number of credits entered is 50. A message box is displayed informing the user that the student is ineligible and thus will not be added to the list. The user must then click the OK button in the message box before he or she can enter more names.

Figure 5–35
Credits Problem (Visual Basic—Screen 2)

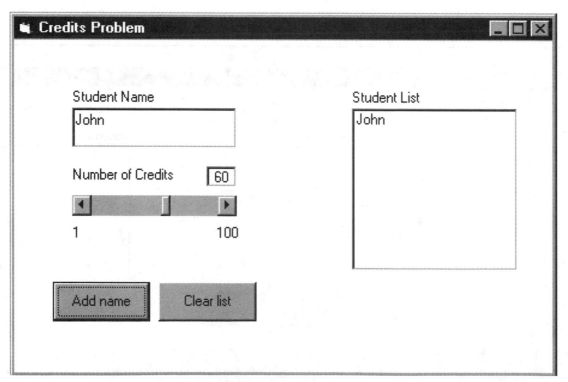

Figure 5–36
Credits Problem (Visual
Basic—Screen 3)

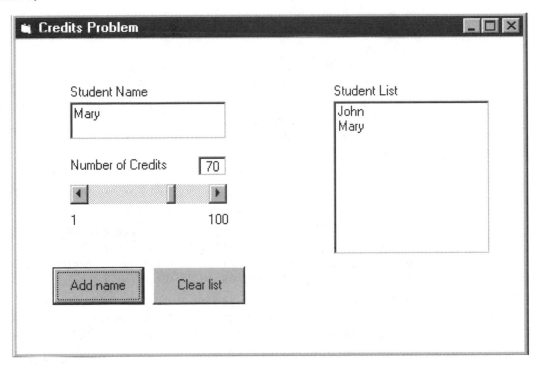

Figure 5–37
Credits Problem (Visual
Basic—Screen 4)

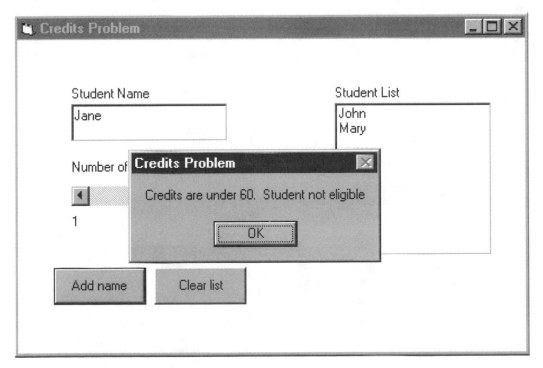

Figure 5–38 illustrates the screen after the user has entered several more names and credit amounts. Note that each name is added to the list box on a new line.

Figure 5–39 illustrates the screen after the user has clicked the Clear list button. As you can see, all the names have been removed from the list box.

Figure 5–40 illustrates the program that is associated with the click event of the Add name button. A simple IFTHENELSE statement checks the value of credits, which is represented by the value property of the horizontal scroll bar. The standard name for this type of scroll bar begins with *hsb*. In Visual Basic a test for greater than or equal to is represented by the logical operators > and =, side by side as >=.

The true path of the IFTHENELSE statement causes a name to be added to the list box. The standard name for a list box begins with *lst*. The AddItem method adds the value of the text box to the end of the list box on a separate line. A *method* is a prewritten program that performs some special function. There are many methods in Visual Basic. Methods are invoked using the same dot notation that is used to specify properties. The false path of the IFTHENELSE statement causes the message box to be displayed.

Figure 5–41 illustrates the program that is associated with the click event of the Clear list button. The Clear method is used to delete all items (names in this case) from the list box.

Figure 5–38
Credits Problem (Visual Basic—Screen 5)

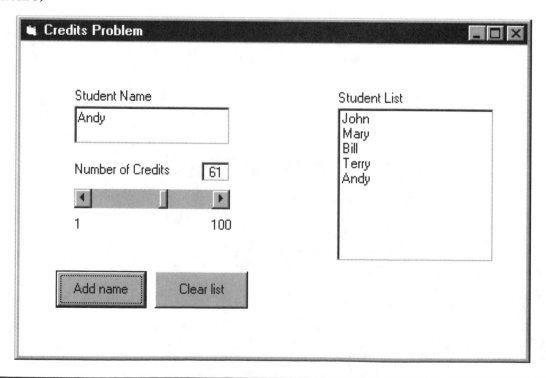

Figure 5–39
Credits Problem (Visual
Basic—Screen 6)

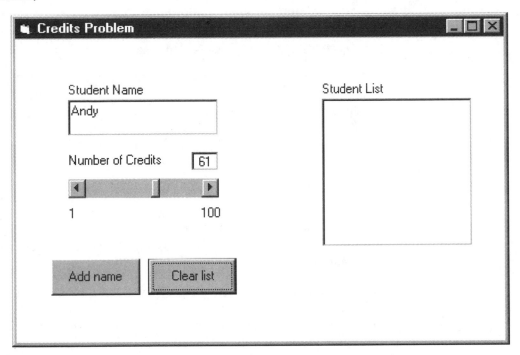

Figure 5–40
Credits Problem (Visual
Basic—cmd_ADD_Click)

```
Private Sub cmd_ADD_Click()

If hsb_CREDITS.Value >= 60 Then
        1st_NAMES.AddItem txt_NAME.Text
Else
        MsgBox "Credits are under 60. Student not eligible",,"Credits Problem"
End If

End Sub
```

Figure 5–41
Credits Problem (Visual
Basic—cmd_CLEAR_Click)

```
Private Sub cmd_CLEAR_Click()

1st_NAMES.Clear

End Sub
```

Key Terms

trailer record logic	heading line	loop read
trailer record	detail line	automatic end-of-file
dummy data value	total line	facility
(sentinel value)	priming read	empty file condition

Exercises

1. State in your own words the difference between header record logic and trailer record logic. How are the loops controlled in each type of logic?

2. Explain the differences between a heading line, a detail line, and a total line. Where should the WRITE statements associated with each type of line be positioned in reference to the main processing loop?

   For the remainder of these exercises, include report and column headings as well as a page number on every page, with 55 detail lines per page, unless directed otherwise. Output an appropriate message if the input contains no records, include descriptive messages in the total lines, and use a modular design. Construct a structure chart as well as flowcharts and pseudocode for each module.

3. Redo the solution to Sample Problem 3.1 to process data for any number of employees. Use the automatic end-of-file facility to control end-of-loop processing. Output a report heading, a column heading, and a page number on each page of the payroll report. Construct flowcharts and pseudocode for your solution.

4. Redo Sample Problem 5.4 to include two total lines showing a count of the total number of students for which data was input and the total number of accumulated credits for all students. Construct flowcharts and pseudocode for your solution.

5. Redo Exercise 16 in Chapter 2 but process multiple records. Assume that a length of 0 will be used to indicate the end of the input.

6. Redo Exercise 17 in Chapter 2 but process multiple records. Use automatic end-of-file logic to signal the end of the input.

7. Redo Exercises 5 and 6 to include the steps to compute and output the total number of input records processed.

8. Design an algorithm to read an arbitrary number of data records, each containing a name, age, and code. A code of 1 will indicate female, a code of 2 will indicate male, and a code of 0 will indicate that the end of file has been reached. For each record, write a detail line listing the person's name and age. In addition, compute and output the following values:

   - Number of males less than or equal to 21 years old.
   - Number of females less than or equal to 21 years old.
   - Average age of all persons over 21.
   - Total number of people.

9. Design an algorithm to input student records; each record contains a student name, registration code, and credits field. A code of 1 indicates that the student is a resident, and a code of 2 indicates that the student is a nonresident. Output a detail line for each student, containing the student's name and a tuition amount computed as follows (12 or more credits means full-time status):

   - FT resident $600.00 flat fee
   - PT resident $50.00 per credit

- FT nonresident $1,320.00 flat fee
- PT nonresident $110.00 per credit

Five total lines are also to be output as follows:

- Total number of FT resident students.
- Total number of PT resident students.
- Total number of FT nonresident students.
- Total number of PT nonresident students.
- Total number of students.

Use automatic end-of-file logic to signal the end of the input.

10. Design an algorithm to prepare a daily hotel charge report. Input consists of a series of records that contain a room number, the customer name, the cost of the room, and the cost of meals charged to the room. Output is a hotel charge report that will contain the room number, customer name, room charge, meal charges, and total charges. After all records have been processed, the total number of rooms rented, the total room charges, total meal charges, and a final total of all charges are to be printed. A room number of 000 will be used to signal the end of the input.

11. Design an algorithm to prepare a report of real estate sales and commissions. Input consists of a series of records that contain the address, city, selling price of houses that have been sold during the month, and the percentage used to compute the commission that the real estate company received. Output is to consist of a real estate sales and commissions report that will contain the address, city, selling price, and commission paid for each of the houses. After all records have been processed, the total number of houses sold, the total selling price of all houses, the average price of all houses sold, and the total commission are to be printed. Use automatic end-of-file logic to signal the end of the input.

12. Design an algorithm to prepare a job applicant report. Input consists of a series of records that contain the Social Security number, last name, first name, middle initial, verbal test score, science test score, CIS test score, and logic test score of each job applicant. Output is to consist of detail lines containing the contents of each input record as well as the average of the four test scores. In addition, averages for each of the four test score categories should be output at the end of the report. Use automatic end-of-file logic to signal the end of the input.

13. Design an algorithm to prepare a monthly report for a legal clinic. Input consists of a series of records that contain the name of the client, name of the attorney, and hours worked by the attorney on the case. Output is a monthly legal clinic report that lists the client's name, attorney, hours worked by the attorney on the case, and fee. The fee charged by the attorney is based upon the hours worked. The first 20 hours are charged at the rate of $50.00 per hour. Hours in excess of 20 are charged at the rate of $40.00 per hour. After all records have been processed, the final totals are to be printed. Include the total clients,

total hours billed, total hours billed at $50.00 per hour, total hours billed at $40.00 per hour, and total fees. End of file will be indicated when the hours worked input is 0.

14. Design an algorithm to compute and print the average earnings, lowest earnings, and highest earnings of a group of employees. Each input record will contain the name and earnings of one employee. No headings or page numbers are required. Use automatic end-of-file logic to signal the end of the input.

15. Design an algorithm for the following problem. You are a cashier in a department store. Each of your customers buys exactly 1 item costing $1.00 or less. Each customer pays for the item with exactly $1.00. Your job is to give each customer the correct amount of change in some combination of pennies, nickels, dimes, and quarters. The combination must be the minimum amount of coins. For example, if the item cost is $.38, the charge would be 2 quarters, 1 dime, 0 nickels, and 2 pennies ($.62). The input is composed of customer records, each containing customer name and item cost. The output is composed of lines, each containing customer name, item cost, change, number of quarters, number of dimes, number of nickels, and number of pennies. A cost of $0.00 will be used to signal the end of the input.

16. Design an algorithm to prepare a property tax report. Input consists of a series of records that contain the property type field, which indicates the type of property owned (H—home; C—commercial), the name of the property owner, the home type field (N—nonresidence; R—residence), the commercial property type (L—commercial land; B—commercial building), the tract parcel number, and the assessed value. Output is to consist of the property owner, parcel number, assessed value, tax rate, and property tax for each property in the input. In addition, totals for the following fields are to be printed at the end of the report:

   Home—primary residence
   Home—nonresidence
   Commercial building
   Commercial land
   Total property taxes

The property tax is determined in the following manner:

- If the property is a home, is used as the primary residence of the owner, and has an assessed value greater than $150,000.00, the tax rate is 2 percent of the assessed value.
- If the property is a home, is used as the primary residence of the owner, and has an assessed value equal to or less than $150,000.00, the tax rate is 1.4 percent of the assessed value
- If the property is a home, but it is not the primary residence of the owner, and the assessed value is greater than $95,000.00, the tax rate is 2 percent of the assessed value.

- If the property is a home, but it is not the primary residence of the owner, and the assessed value is equal to or less than $95,000.00, the tax rate is 1.4 percent of the assessed value.
- If the property is a commercial building and the assessed value is greater than $200,000.00, the tax rate is 2.5 percent of the assessed value.
- If the property is a commercial building and the assessed value is equal to or less than $200,000.00, the tax rate is 2 percent of the assessed value.
- If the property is commercial land and the assessed value is greater than $60,000.00, the tax rate is 2.5 percent of the assessed value.
- If the property is commercial land and the assessed value is equal to or less than $60,000.00, the tax rate is 2 percent of the assessed value.

Use automatic end-of-file logic to signal the end of the input; assume all the input values are valid.

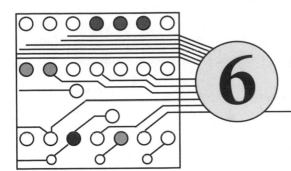

6 CASE Control Structure

Objectives

Upon completion of this chapter you should be able to

- Distinguish between a master file and a transaction file.
- Identify, and use in program design, the CASE control structure.
- Distinguish between numeric and alphabetic data.

Introduction

Often, a computer program must be designed and coded to handle a wide variety of inputs. We must provide flexibility in a solution algorithm, incorporating within the program an ability to process not only a variable number of inputs, but also whatever type of input is provided.

In business applications such as accounts receivable or employee payroll, large numbers of records are kept for reference purposes as relatively permanent data. Such data is not highly subject to change. Usually, it is needed for numerous business operations of the firm. Together, the data records constitute a **master file.** Current activities, or transactions, to be processed against the master file are called a **transaction file** or a **detail file.**

Assume, for example, that a firm's customer master file contains customer records. Each customer record contains several fields. The fields are customer number, name, address, telephone number, and credit rating. Customer transaction records to be processed against this file include fields containing address changes, corrections to telephone numbers, and the like.

Inventory Control Example

As another example, consider an inventory-control master file that contains stock status records of the numbers of various kinds of parts available for manufacturing planning. Each record contains several data items, located in specific fields of the record. These data items indicate quantity in stock, quantity on order, and so on.

Transactions to be processed against this master file originate daily. They are assigned transaction numbers and grouped together to form a transaction file. A transaction file is a temporary file containing data that is used to update a master file. In some applications, transactions are collected and processed as a group, say at the end of each day. In other applications, transactions are entered directly, as they occur, through any number of online input devices. In our example, a one-digit code is placed in a field of each transaction record to indicate the type of activity, as follows:

Code	Activity
1	Receipts (parts that arrive in response to previous orders)
2	Orders (requests for additional parts to be included in stock)
3	Withdrawals (also called issues; depletions from stock)
4	Adjustments (changes to stock levels for reasons other than those above; for example, transfers of parts to other manufacturing locations)

Our task is to design, code, and test a program to process the transaction records against the inventory-control master file. A part of the program flowchart and corresponding pseudocode that we might construct in developing a solution algorithm are shown in Figures 6–1 and 6–2.

Figure 6–1
Master File Update Using Nested IFs (Partial Flowchart)

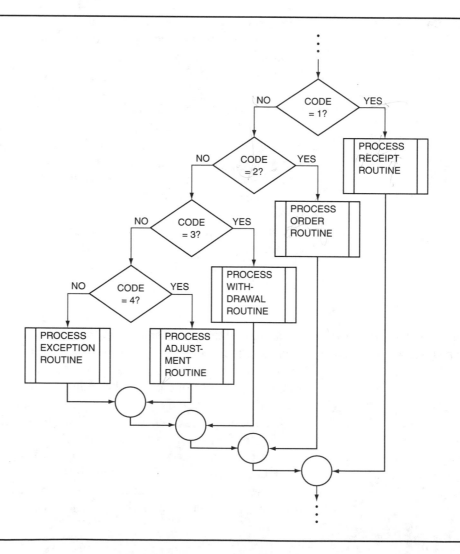

**Figure 6–2
Master File Update
Using Nested IFs
(Partial Pseudocode)**

```
.
.
.
IF CODE = 1 THEN
   Process receipt routine
ELSE
   IF CODE = 2 THEN
      Process order routine
   ELSE
      IF CODE = 3 THEN
         Process withdrawal routine
      ELSE
         IF CODE = 4 THEN
            Process adjustment routine
         ELSE
            Process exception routine
         ENDIF
      ENDIF
   ENDIF
ENDIF
.
.
.
.
```

Solution 1: Nested IFTHENELSE Control Structure

Do you recognize which control structure is being used? You should see a nested IFTHENELSE pattern. If one of the tests for the activity type (specified as CODE) yields a true outcome, the routine or module for that activity type is executed. No additional tests are made (they're obviously unnecessary). Instead, the entire nested IFTHENELSE control structure is exited. Program execution continues with the processing step that follows the nested IFTHENELSE. The number of tests performed depends on the activity type. Only if all four tests are made and yield false outcomes is the exception routine (error routine) executed. (Recall that not executing all tests each time is a key difference between the nested IFTHENELSE pattern and a sequence of separate IFTHENELSEs, which we called the sequential IFTHENELSE pattern.)

Although the nested IFTHENELSE pattern seems to meet our decision-making needs, it is often difficult to work with. In this example we have to make four tests, which amounts to a nesting level of four. What will happen if we inadvertently omit a program statement corresponding to one of the closing ENDIFs? Or if we want to remove just one of the tests of activity type at a later time? Suppose we need to add a test for another activity type within the nested IFTHENELSE structure. The program coding to implement this structure must be done very carefully, or errors will most certainly occur. And what if there are 10, or even 100, possible activity types to be tested? Obviously, many pages of flowcharting, or an unmanageable number of pseudocode indentions, will be required.

Solution 2: CASE Control Structure

Fortunately, another option is available. We can replace the nested IFTHENELSE structure with a **CASE control structure.** CASE generalizes the basic IFTHENELSE pattern, extending it from a two-valued operation to a multiple-valued one. With one CASE control structure, we can represent all of the tests shown in Figure 6–1 (see Figure 6–3). Once we understand how this structure is derived, and see that it consists only of basic patterns, we can use it where we might otherwise resort to a nested IFTHENELSE.

One note of caution is warranted. Although the CASE control structure serves as an alternative for the nested IFTHENELSE control structure, it cannot be used in place of a sequential IFTHENELSE pattern. Both sequential and nested IFTHENELSE patterns were initially discussed in Chapter 3. Make sure you remember the difference between them, and consider the CASE control structure only when the logic needed in an algorithm is the nested IFTHENELSE pattern.

Another point worth mentioning is that you should not confuse the use of the term *CASE* here with our earlier use of the letters *CASE* as an acronym for the phrase *computer-assisted software engineering*. Here CASE is simply the name of a particular kind of control structure.

Figure 6–3
Master File Update Using CASE (Partial Flowchart)

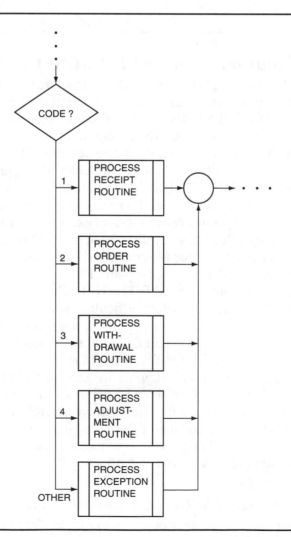

The program logic in Figure 6–3 is the same as that shown in Figure 6–1, but it appears in a much more understandable form. By the simple use of parallel flowlines, the same possible outcomes are documented. Generally, when this documentation technique is used, the first test to be made should be shown by the topmost flowline on the flowchart (or the leftmost one, if the parallel flowlines are vertical rather than horizontal). For processing efficiency, the test most likely to reveal a true outcome should be made first, the next most likely one second, and so on; this helps to minimize the number of tests actually carried out on any one pass through this portion of the program. In most cases, the word *other* appears by the last (bottom or rightmost) flowline to indicate what processing should occur if none of the preceding conditions is true. This path usually involves some type of error processing.

We express the CASE control structure in pseudocode form using the keywords CASENTRY, CASE, and ENDCASE, as shown in Figure 6–4. Notice that three levels of indention are used, no matter how many tests are made. The text following the keyword CASENTRY identifies the variable data on which tests are to be made. Each CASE keyword is then slightly indented from the position of CASENTRY. The text following each CASE keyword indicates the details of a particular test. For example, CASE 1 in Figure 6–4 represents a test to see whether the variable CODE is equal to 1. The statement(s) following each CASE line are then indented a few spaces from the position of the CASE line. These statements specify what processing is to be done in a particular case. For example, the receipt routine will be executed when CODE is equal to 1.

The keyword ENDCASE is specified at the physical end of the CASE structure to denote that all required tests (cases) have been stated. It is lined up with the keyword CASENTRY. This positioning is consistent with the positioning of the keywords ENDIF and ENDDO in other structures we've

Figure 6–4
Master File Update Using CASE (Partial Pseudocode)

```
   •
   •
   •
CASENTRY CODE
   CASE 1
      Process receipt routine
   CASE 2
      Process order routine
   CASE 3
      Process withdrawal routine
   CASE 4
      Process adjustment routine
   CASE other
      Process exception routine
ENDCASE
   •
   •
   •
```

already learned. Note that, in the flowchart, the exit point of the structure is shown by the connector symbol, as was done with the IFTHENELSE structure. Even though the CASE structure implies several tests, only one exit connector (or one ENDCASE) is indicated, because we are representing only one CASE control structure. The top-to-bottom arrangement of the conditions or tests in the CASE structure dictates the actual order that will be used by the computer to make the tests.

We should make one final note before leaving this example. We have illustrated the CASE control structure with an example of part of the logic required to process a master file. In Chapter 11, we will expand this discussion and show a complete modular design for a master file update procedure.

Sample Problem 6.1 (Op Code Problem)

Problem:

Design an algorithm to accept three values as input. The first input value will be one of four operation codes, either "A" (addition), "S" (subtraction), "M" (multiplication), or "D" (division). The other two input values will be numbers. The computer is to perform a computation on the two numbers as determined by the operation code. The result of the computation, as well as the original inputs, is to be written as output. An error message should be output if the operation code is invalid.

Solution:

A plan for the solution to this problem is given in flowchart and pseudocode forms in Figures 6–5 and 6–6, respectively.

For simplicity, this solution is written to process only one set of input; that is, we have not included loop processing logic. A modular design including the handling of several inputs is provided as an exercise.

In this example, values for three variables are input. One is an operation code (OP), and two are numbers (N1 and N2). In previous examples, most of the variables were numeric quantities such as N1 and N2 in this example. The variable OP is used to represent one of four operation codes. The operation codes are not numbers; they are the letters "A," "S," "M," and "D." A variable can hold only one type of data; that is, we cannot use a single variable name to represent both numeric quantities and alphabetic data. Alphabetic data cannot be used in computations. Alphabetic data values are called **character strings.** We usually designate the value of a character string by enclosing it in single or double quotes, thereby distinguishing it from a variable name. "A" (character string), then, is very different from A (variable name).

There are several types of variables besides numeric and character variables. We will not address those other variable types in this text. However, it is important for you to understand that most programming languages require that each variable used in a program be defined to the computer as being of a specific type. In practice, the programmer names each variable in the program and "declares" it to be of a specific type.

Figure 6–5
Op Code Problem
(Flowchart)

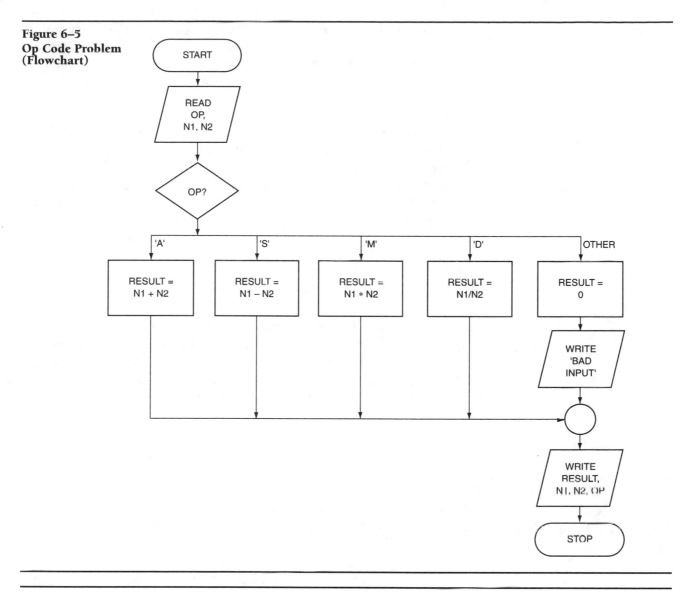

Figure 6–6
Op Code Problem
(Pseudocode)

```
Start
Read OP,N1,N2
CASENTRY OP
   CASE 'A'
      RESULT = N1 + N2
   CASE 'S'
      RESULT = N1 - N2
   CASE 'M'
      RESULT = N1 * N2
   CASE 'D'
      RESULT = N1 / N2
   CASE other
      RESULT = 0
      Write 'Bad Input'
ENDCASE
Write RESULT, N1, N2, OP
Stop
```

Now look again at Figure 6–5. After the data is input, a CASE control structure is used to determine which computation needs to be done. There are five paths shown, one for each operation code and one "other" path to handle the case where the operation code input is invalid. For example, someone may key in an "E" instead of an "S" since the E and S keys are close together on the keyboard. Notice the order in which the tests will be made. If the operation codes are evenly distributed in the input file, the order in which the tests are made will not matter. In this example, the natural order is used. When dealing with simple arithmetic, most people think in order of add, subtract, multiply, and divide. We do, however, need to place the "other" path last. All the tests must fail before we conclude that the code is invalid.

The variable RESULT is used in all five cases to hold the answer. It may seem strange that RESULT is given a value of 0 when the operation code is invalid. If you look at the second WRITE statement in this algorithm (the one after ENDCASE), you will see why. The value of RESULT is output, regardless of which path is taken. If we do not give RESULT some "dummy" value in the "other" path, then RESULT will be undefined to the computer when an invalid record is processed. If an attempt is made to output a variable with an undefined value, an error will occur. Notice also that if the operation code is invalid, two lines of output will be written: first, the "Bad Input" line and then the detail line, which contains a 0 in the RESULT field.

Sample Problem 6.2 (Sales Problem Without Modules)

Problem:

Redo Sample Problem 3.4 using the CASE control structure.

Solution:

A solution to this problem is shown in flowchart and pseudocode forms in Figures 6–7 and 6–8, respectively.

In this solution we replace the nested IFTHENELSE control structure with the CASE control structure to determine the value of CLASS. There are four possible valid values for class (1,2,3,4), and these values are tested in order within the CASE structure. The "other" path represents the processing required if CLASS is invalid. This example illustrates how several structures can be contained within each path of the CASE control structure. For example, the CASE 1 path contains a nested IFTHENELSE structure, and the CASE 2 path contains a simple IFTHENELSE structure. It is even possible to have a DOWHILE control structure within one or more of the CASE paths. As you can see, the problem solution can become very complex and hard to follow unless the steps within each CASE path are grouped together in a separate module, as was shown in Figures 6–3 and 6–4. This modular breakdown is certainly desirable, though not always required. Now let's look at the next problem to see how we might modularize the same solution.

Figure 6–7
Sales Problem without
Modules (Flowchart)

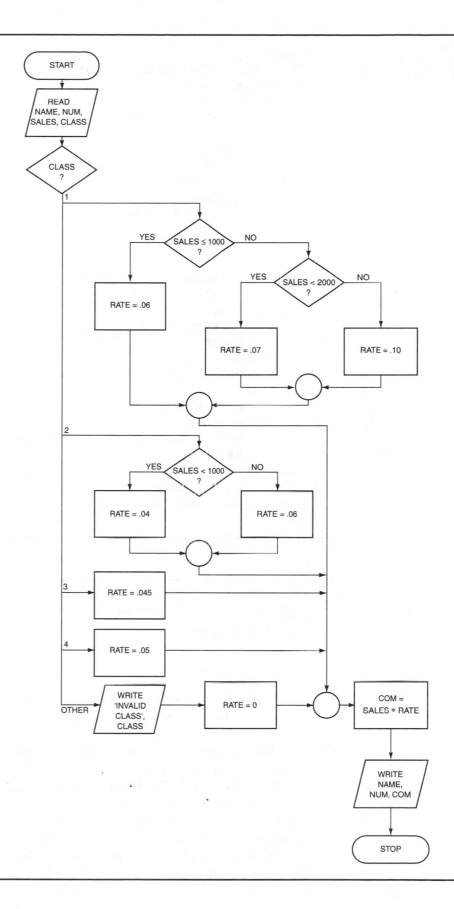

Figure 6–8
Sales Problem without
Modules (Pseudocode)

```
Start
Read NAME, NUM, SALES, CLASS
CASENTRY CLASS
    CASE 1
        IF SALES ≤ 1000 THEN
            RATE = .06
        ELSE
            IF SALES < 2000 THEN
                RATE = .07
            ELSE
                RATE = .10
            ENDIF
        ENDIF
    CASE 2
        IF SALES < 1000 THEN
            RATE = .04
        ELSE
            RATE = .06
        ENDIF
    CASE 3
        RATE = .045
    CASE 4
        RATE = .05
    CASE other
        Write 'Invalid Class', CLASS
        RATE = 0
ENDCASE
COM = SALES * RATE
Write NAME, NUM, COM
Stop
```

Sample Problem 6.3 (Sales Problem Using Modules)

Problem:

Redo Sample Problem 6.2 and place all the steps within each CASE path in separate modules.

Solution:

A structure chart for this problem is shown in Figure 6–9. There are five level-2 modules, each representing the steps to process one value of CLASS.

The overall control module (A000) is shown in flowchart and pseudocode forms in Figures 6–10 and 6–11, respectively.

You can see that the problem solution appears simpler with a modular design; it allows us to focus more clearly on the CASE control structure and not on the complex details within each path. These details are shown in modules B000 (Figure 6–12), B010 (Figure 6–13), B020 (Figure 6–14), B030 (Figure 6–15), and B040 (Figure 6–16). Each module represents the processing for a specified value of CLASS.

Figure 6–9
Sales Problem Using
Modules (Structure Chart)

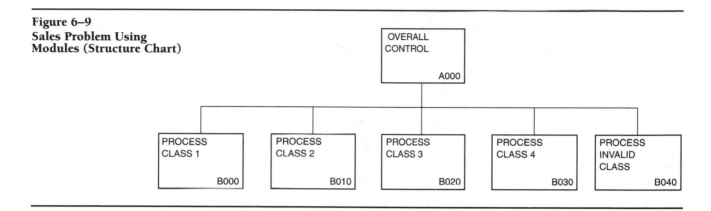

Figure 6–10
Sales Problem Using
Modules—Overall Control
(Flowchart)

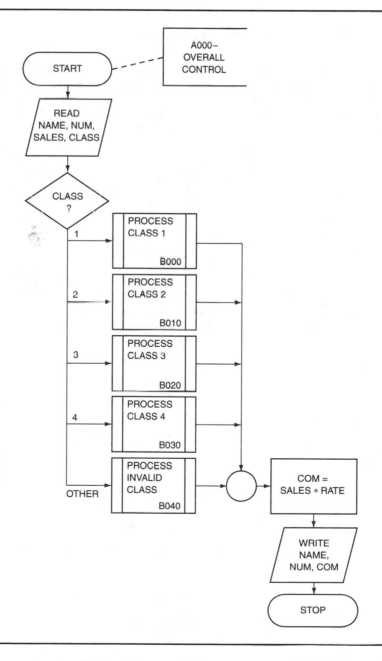

Figure 6–11
Sales Problem Using
Modules—Overall Control
(Pseudocode)

```
A000
Start
Read NAME, NUM, SALES, CLASS
CASENTRY CLASS
    CASE 1
        Process class 1 (B000)
    CASE 2
        Process class 2 (B010)
    CASE 3
        Process class 3 (B020)
    CASE 4
        Process class 4 (B030)
    CASE other
        Process invalid class (B040)
ENDCASE
COM = SALES * RATE
Write NAME, NUM, COM
Stop
```

Figure 6–12
Sales Problem Using
Modules—Process Class 1

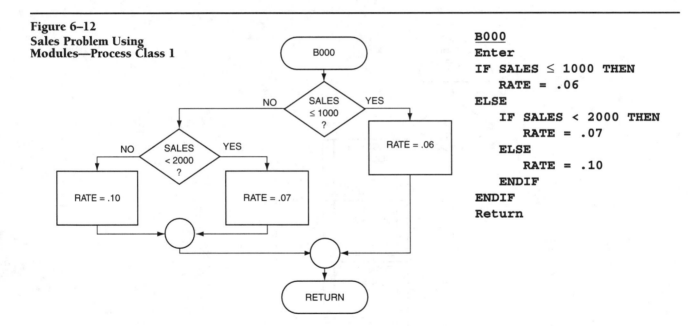

```
B000
Enter
IF SALES ≤ 1000 THEN
    RATE = .06
ELSE
    IF SALES < 2000 THEN
        RATE = .07
    ELSE
        RATE = .10
    ENDIF
ENDIF
Return
```

Figure 6–13
Sales Problem Using
Modules—Process Class 2

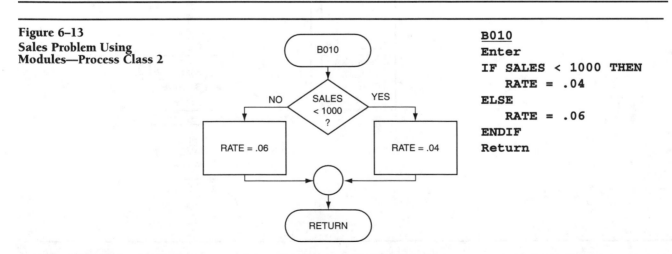

```
B010
Enter
IF SALES < 1000 THEN
    RATE = .04
ELSE
    RATE = .06
ENDIF
Return
```

Figure 6–14
Sales Problem Using
Modules—Process Class 3

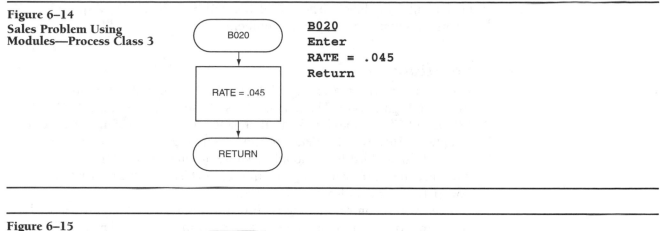

```
B020
Enter
RATE = .045
Return
```

Figure 6–15
Sales Problem Using
Modules—Process Class 4

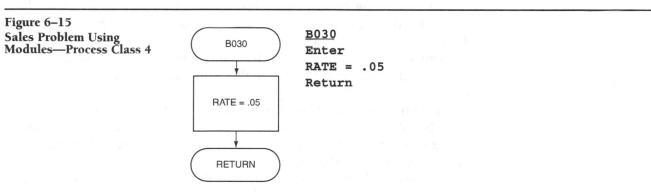

```
B030
Enter
RATE = .05
Return
```

Figure 6–16
Sales Problem Using
Modules—Process Invalid
Class

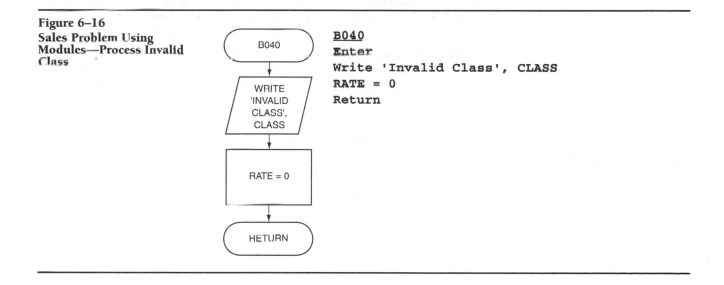

```
B040
Enter
Write 'Invalid Class', CLASS
RATE = 0
Return
```

Sample Problem 6.4 (Sales Problem with Totals)

Problem:

Redo Sample Problem 6.3 to process several records. Detail lines are to be output on a daily sales commission report. In addition, report and column headings are to be output on every page of the report. The pages are to be numbered, and up to 55 detail lines are to be included on a page. Five total lines are to be output on the last page of the report. These lines are to specify the total number of records containing a class of 1, 2, 3, and 4, as well as the total number of records containing an invalid class. All totals should have identifying labels. The end-of-file will be indicated by a special record containing an employee number of 0000.

Solution:

A structure chart representing all the modules used in this solution is shown in Figure 6–17. The relationships of modules A000, B000, B010, B020, and C000 should look familiar, since this same design was used in Chapter 5. However, the detail-processing module is now broken into several additional third-level modules. These modules represent the steps within each CASE path. As you will see, the CASE control structure is now part of the detail-processing module.

The overall control module is shown in Figures 6–18 and 6–19, and is, again, consistent with the general requirements of trailer record logic. There is no indication, however, of a CASE structure in this module. Remember, A000 specifies only the main processing loop. The details of the solution (using the CASE in this example) are placed in another module.

The initialization module (Figure 6–20) contains no unusual processing, so it should look somewhat familiar to you. Notice that, in B000, we initialize five variables to 0. These variables are used to accumulate the total number of records within each class.

Now look at the detail-processing module (Figures 6–21 and 6–22). First, a check is made to see if the headings need to be output and a new page started. Then CLASS is checked using a CASE control structure. Four paths (1,2,3,4) process all the valid values of CLASS, and the fifth path handles invalid class records. The processing steps within each CASE path are handled in separate modules as before. After the appropriate third-level module is executed, commission is computed by multiplying the sales (input in A000) by the commission rate (computed in one of the previous

Figure 6–17
Sales Problem with Totals
(Structure Chart)

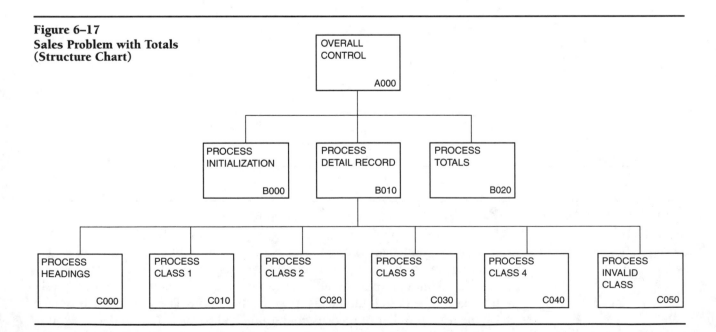

modules). The actual detail line is then output in all five cases and LINECNT is updated.

**Figure 6–18
Sales Problem with Totals—
Overall Control (Flowchart)**

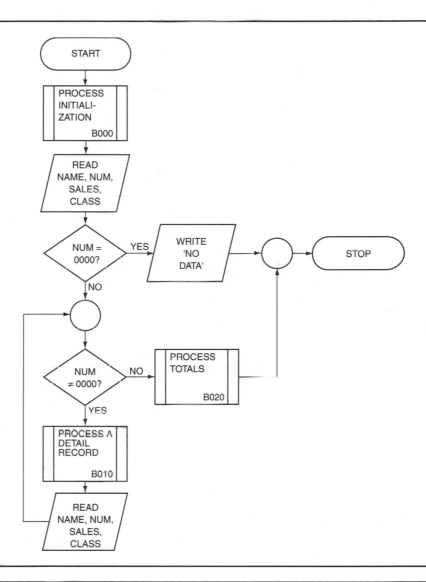

**Figures 6–19
Sales Problem with Totals—
Overall Control
(Pseudocode)**

```
A000
Start
Process initialization (B000)
Read NAME, NUM, SALES, CLASS
If NUM = 0000 THEN
   Write 'No data'
ELSE
   DOWHILE NUM ≠ 0000
      Process a detail record (B010)
      Read NAME, NUM, SALES, CLASS
   ENDDO
   Process totals (B020)
ENDIF
Stop
```

Figure 6–20
Sales Problem with Totals—
Process Initialization

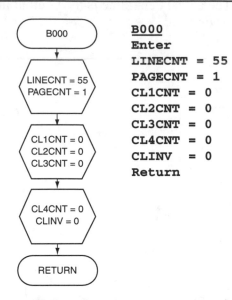

```
B000
Enter
LINECNT = 55
PAGECNT = 1
CL1CNT = 0
CL2CNT = 0
CL3CNT = 0
CL4CNT = 0
CLINV  = 0
Return
```

Figure 6–21
Sales Problem with Totals—
Process a Detail Record
(Flowchart)

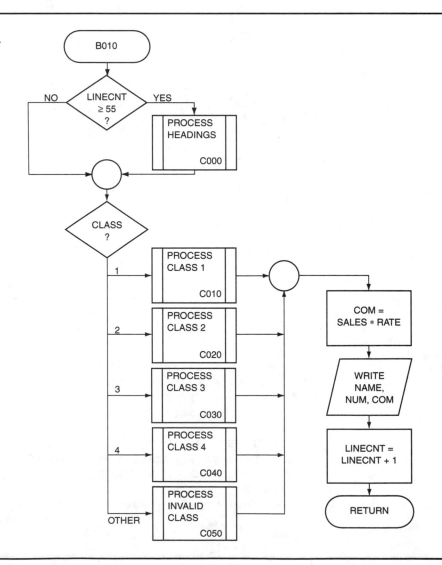

The headings module (C000), shown in Figure 6–23, contains no unusual processing, so you should find it likewise familiar.

Figure 6–22
Sales Problem with Totals—
Process a Detail Record
(Pseudocode)

```
B010
Enter
IF LINECNT ≥ 55 THEN
    Process headings (C000)
(ELSE)
ENDIF
CASENTRY CLASS
    CASE 1
        Process class 1 (C010)
    CASE 2
        Process class 2 (C020)
    CASE 3
        Process class 3 (C030)
    CASE 4
        Process class 4 (C040)
    CASE other
        Process invalid class (C050)
ENDCASE
COM = SALES * RATE
Write NAME, NUM, COM
LINECNT = LINECNT + 1
Return
```

Figure 6–23
Sales Problem with Totals—
Process Headings

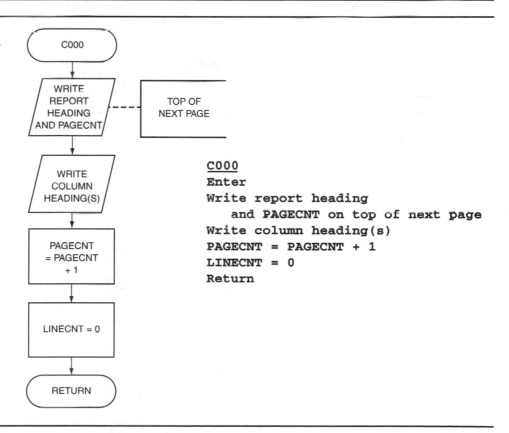

```
C000
Enter
Write report heading
    and PAGECNT on top of next page
Write column heading(s)
PAGECNT = PAGECNT + 1
LINECNT = 0
Return
```

Modules C010 (Figure 6–24), C020 (Figure 6–25), C030 (Figure 6–26), C040 (Figure 6–27), and C050 (Figure 6–28) contain the steps required to compute the commission rate for each class. Each module begins by incrementing a counter (set to 0 in B000) to keep track of the number of records within the particular class. The rest of the steps within these modules are identical to modules B000, B010, B020, B030, and B040 in Sample Problem 6.3.

Figure 6–24
Sales Problem with Totals—
Process Class 1

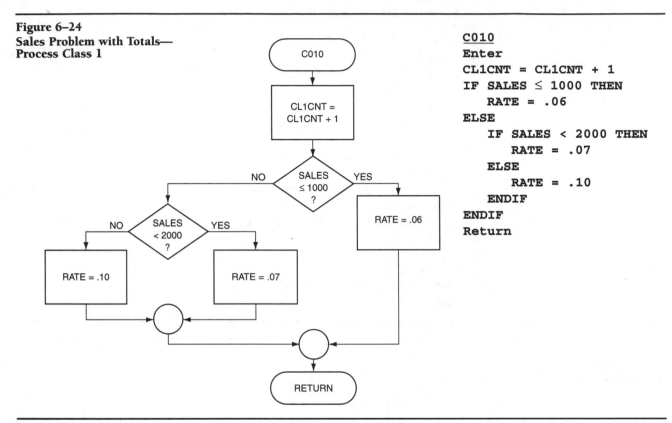

```
C010
Enter
CL1CNT = CL1CNT + 1
IF SALES ≤ 1000 THEN
    RATE = .06
ELSE
    IF SALES < 2000 THEN
        RATE = .07
    ELSE
        RATE = .10
    ENDIF
ENDIF
Return
```

Figure 6–25
Sales Problem with Totals—
Process Class 2

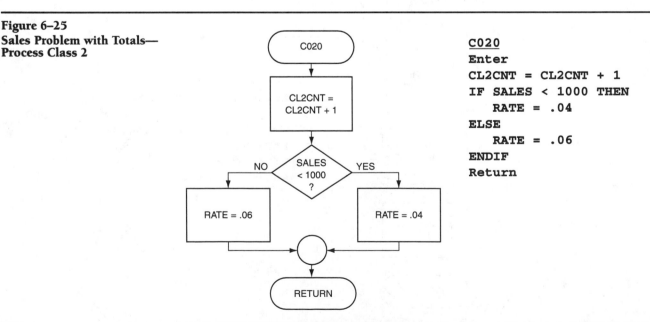

```
C020
Enter
CL2CNT = CL2CNT + 1
IF SALES < 1000 THEN
    RATE = .04
ELSE
    RATE = .06
ENDIF
Return
```

Figure 6–26
Sales Problem with Totals—
Process Class 3

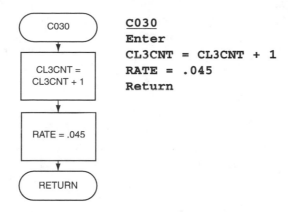

```
C030
Enter
CL3CNT = CL3CNT + 1
RATE = .045
Return
```

Figure 6–27
Sales Problem with Totals—
Process Class 4

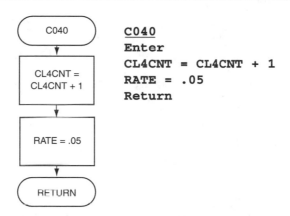

```
C040
Enter
CL4CNT = CL4CNT + 1
RATE = .05
Return
```

Figure 6–28
Sales Problem with Totals—
Process Invalid Class

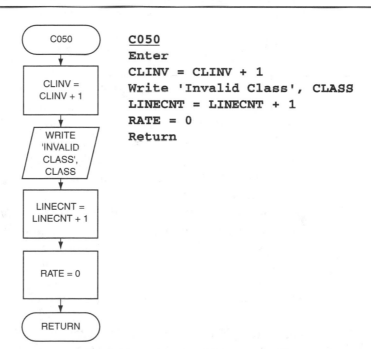

```
C050
Enter
CLINV = CLINV + 1
Write 'Invalid Class', CLASS
LINECNT = LINECNT + 1
RATE = 0
Return
```

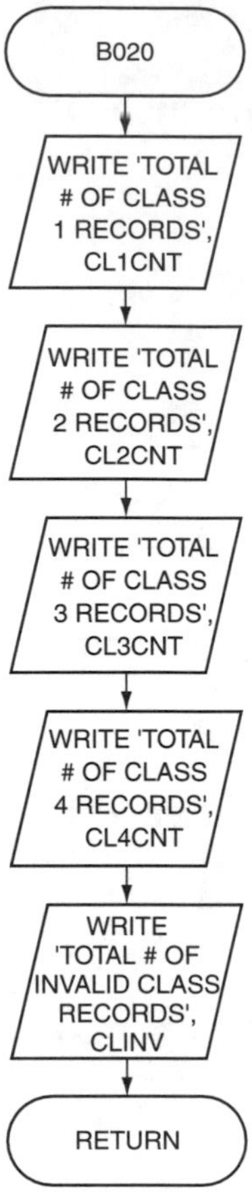

Figure 6–29
Sales Problem with Totals—
Process Totals

```
B020
Enter
Write 'Total # of Class 1 Records',
        CL1CNT
Write 'Total # of Class 2 Records',
        CL2CNT
Write 'Total # of Class 3 Records',
        CL3CNT
Write 'Total # of Class 4 Records',
        CL4CNT
Write 'Total # of Invalid Class
        Records', CLINV
Return
```

The totals module (B020), shown in Figure 6–29, simply writes out the values of the five counters with appropriate labels.

Enrichment (Basic)

Figure 6–30 illustrates a listing of the program that solves the Op Code Problem (Figures 6–5 and 6–6). In this example, the Input statement is used to request the op code and the two numbers from the user. Two separate Input statements are used for clarity. Note that the variable name for the op code is OP$ since this variable will be holding alphabetic data ("A", "S", "M", or "D"). As you can see, the Basic program is very similar to the pseudocode in Figure 6–6. One difference, however, is the syntax used in Basic for the CASE control structure. The keywords SELECT CASE and END SELECT are used in place of the pseudocode keywords CASENTRY and ENDCASE. In addition, the keyword ELSE replaces the word *other* in the last CASE path. We do, however, employ the same indention standards within the SELECT CASE structure as we do in the pseudocode. The four output values have been labeled and have been written on separate lines for readability.

Figure 6-31 illustrates the output that will be produced when the program is executed and the user enters a valid op code, "A" in this case.

Figure 6–30
Op Code Problem
(Basic List)

```
PRINT "Enter an operation code - A, S, M or D";
INPUT OP$
PRINT "Enter two numbers, separated by a comma";
INPUT N1,N2
SELECT CASE OP$
     CASE "A"
          RESULT = N1 + N2
     CASE "S"
          RESULT = N1 - N2
     CASE "M"
          RESULT = N1 * N2
     CASE "D"
          RESULT = N1 / N2
     CASE ELSE
          RESULT = 0
          PRINT
          PRINT "Bad input"
END SELECT
PRINT
PRINT "The answer is "; RESULT
PRINT "The two numbers are "; N1; "and "; N2
PRINT "The operation code is "; OP$
END
```

Figure 6–31
Op Code Problem
(Basic Run—Valid Data)

```
Enter an operation code - A, S, M, or D? A
Enter two numbers, separated by a comma? 5,7

The answer is  12
The two numbers are  5 and  7
The operation code is A
```

Figure 6–32
Op Code Problem
(Basic Run—Invalid Data)

```
Enter an operation code - A, S, M, or D? B
Enter two numbers, separated by a comma? 3,8

Bad input

The answer is  0
The two numbers are  3 and  8
The operation code is B
```

Figure 6–32 illustrates the output that will be produced when the program is executed and the user enters an invalid op code, "B" in this case. Note that an extra line of output is printed—the error message—and that a dummy value of 0 is printed for the result.

Enrichment (Visual Basic)

Figure 6–33 illustrates the graphical interface for the Op Code Problem (Figures 6–5 and 6–6). In this example, three text boxes are created to accept user input. A command button is created to compute the result, and a label is created to hold the computed result.

Figure 6–34 illustrates the screen after the user has entered the input values in each of the text boxes.

Figure 6–33
Op Code Problem (Visual Basic—Screen 1)

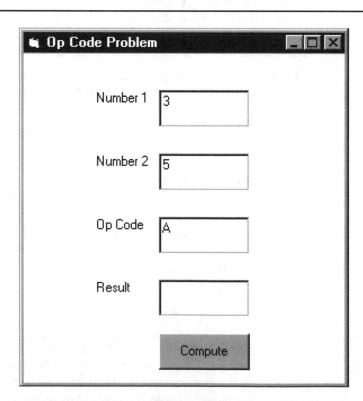

Figure 6–34
Op Code Problem (Visual Basic—Screen 2)

Figure 6–35 illustrates the screen after the user has clicked the Compute button. The value for the result is displayed in the label.

Figure 6–36 illustrates the screen after the user has entered an invalid op code. Note that the label control still contains an "8," the result of the last computation.

Figure 6–37 illustrates the screen after the user has clicked the Compute button. A message box is displayed indicating that the op code was invalid.

Figure 6–38 illustrates the screen after the user has read the error message and has clicked the OK button within the message box. Note that the label control holding the old result has been cleared. Note also that the insertion point is now located in the third text box. This will make it easier for the user to delete the invalid op code and key in a new one. A special method is used to reposition the insertion point. This method will be discussed shortly.

Figure 6–39 illustrates the program that is associated with the click event of the Compute button. As you can see, the Visual Basic code is very similar to the pseudocode in Figure 6–6. One difference, however, is the syntax used in Visual Basic for the CASE control structure. The keywords SELECT CASE and END SELECT are used in place of the pseudocode keywords CASENTRY and ENDCASE. In addition, the keyword ELSE replaces the word *other* in the last CASE path. We do, however, employ the same indention standards within the SELECT CASE structure as we do in the pseudocode.

The appropriate computation is done in each path of the SELECT CASE structure. Since the two numbers to be used in the computation are located in text boxes, the text property of each text box is used to reference the

Figure 6–35
Op Code Problem (Visual Basic—Screen 3)

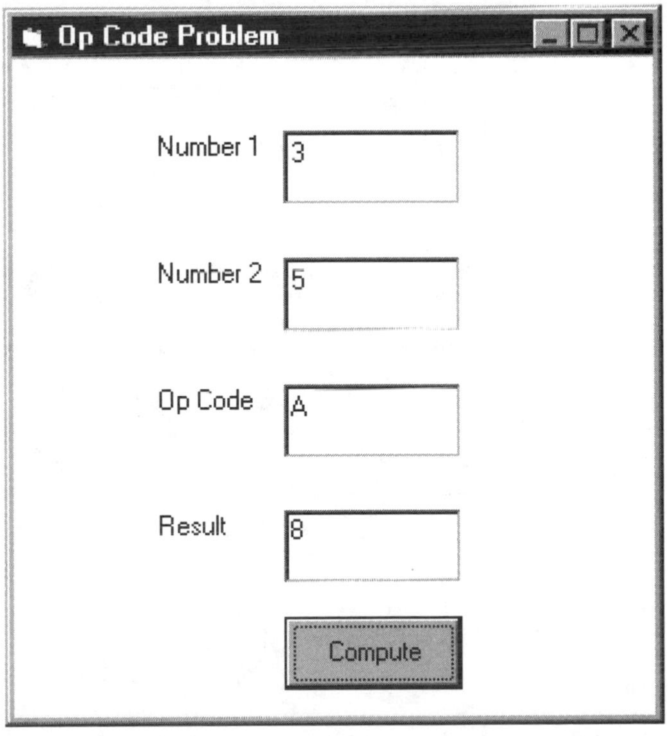

Figure 6–36
Op Code Problem (Visual Basic—Screen 4)

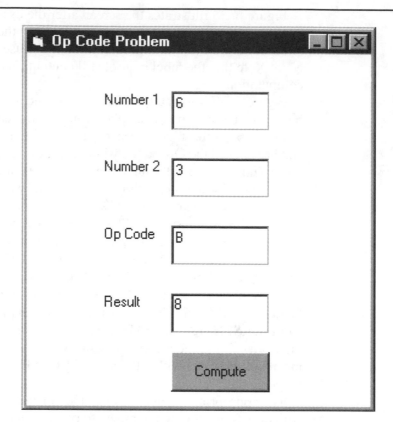

Figure 6–37
Op Code Problem (Visual Basic—Screen 5)

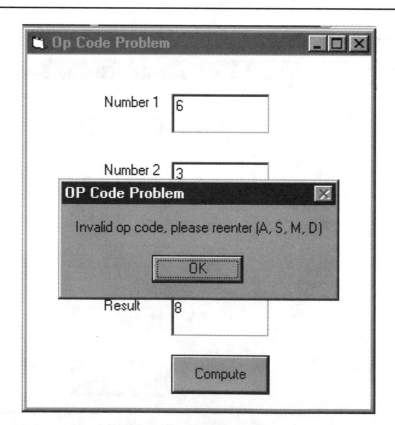

Figure 6–38
Op Code Problem (Visual Basic—Screen 6)

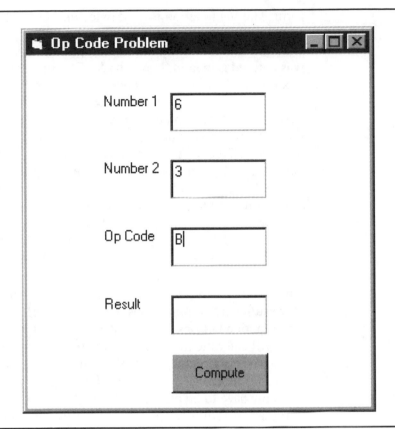

Figure 6–39
Op Code Problem (Visual Basic— cmd_COMPUTE_Click)

```
Private Sub cmd_COMPUTE_Click()

Select Case txt_OPCODE.Text
    Case "A"
        lbl_RESULT.Caption = Val(txt_NUMBER1.Text) + Val(txt_NUMBER2.Text)
    Case "S"
        lbl_RESULT.Caption = Val(txt_NUMBER1.Text) - Val(txt_NUMBER2.Text)
    Case "M"
        lbl_RESULT.Caption = Val(txt_NUMBER1.Text) * Val(txt_NUMBER2.Text)
    Case "D"
        lbl_RESULT.Caption = Val(txt_NUMBER1.Text) / Val(txt_NUMBER2.Text)
    Case Else
        MsgBox "Invalid op code, please reenter (A, S, M, D)",,"OP Code Problem"
        txt_OPCODE.SetFocus
        lbl_RESULT.Caption = ""
End Select

End Sub
```

value entered in the text box. However, data that is entered into a text box is stored as a string and cannot always be used in computations. A special function, *Val*, is needed to convert the data from string form to numeric form. The Val function is used twice in each of the four assignment statements to facilitate this conversion.

In the CASE ELSE path, a message box is displayed if the op code that was entered is invalid. Next, the *SetFocus* method is executed for the text box control holding the op code. This method causes the *focus* (the insertion point in this case) to be placed in the text box—txt_OPCODE. The SetFocus method can be executed for any control that can receive the focus. For example, the statement cmd_COMPUTE.SetFocus would place the focus on the Compute button. In this case, the border of the command button would be darkened, since command buttons do not have insertion points. Finally, the label holding the old result is cleared by assigning the *null string* (" ") to the caption property of the label control.

Now let's look at another solution to this same problem. Figure 6–40 illustrates a different graphical interface for the Op Code Problem. In this solution, two text boxes are used to input the numbers as before. The third text box (used to input the op code) and the command button have been replaced by four option buttons. Each option button represents one of the four arithmetic computations that will be performed on the two numbers. These option buttons will be used to accept the user input for op code. The user will enter the numbers into the two text boxes and then click the appropriate option button. At this point the computation will be done and the result displayed in the label. Note that appropriate program statements will now have to be placed in the click event of each option button.

Figure 6–41 illustrates the screen after the user has entered the two numbers. No option button has been selected and no result computed.

Figure 6–42 illustrates the screen after the user has clicked the first option button (Add). As soon as the Add option was selected, the click event of the first option button was executed. This event caused the two numbers to be added and the result to be placed in the label. If the user now selects the

Figure 6–40
Op Code Problem (Visual Basic—Screen 7)

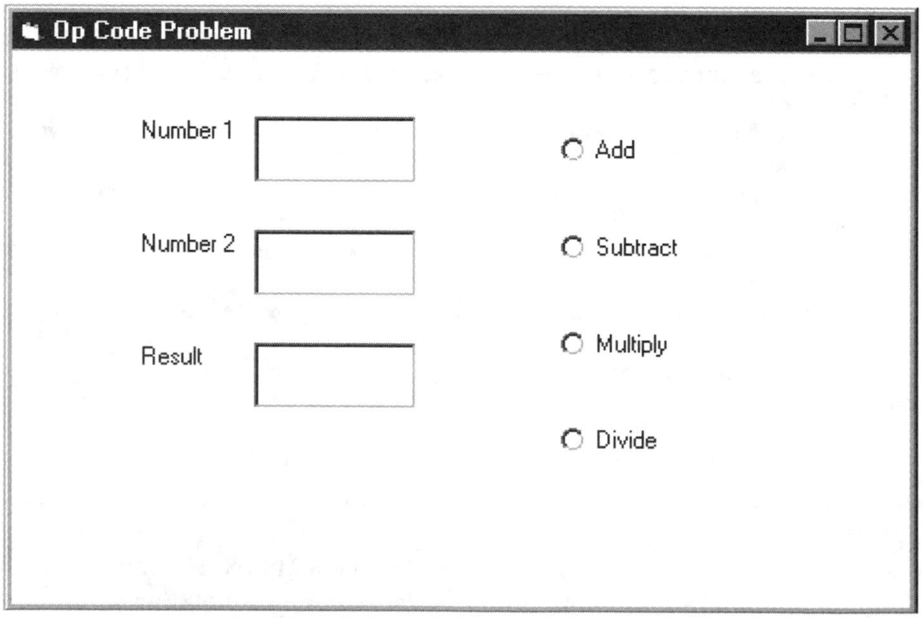

Figure 6–41
Op Code Problem (Visual Basic—Screen 8)

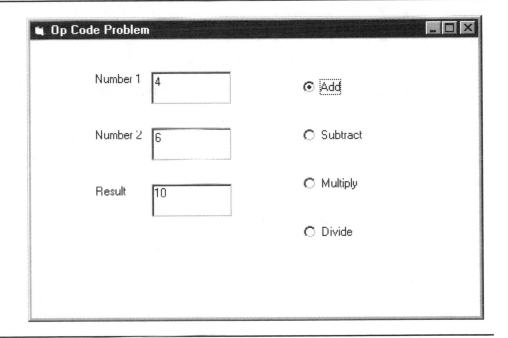

Figure 6–42
Op Code Problem (Visual Basic—Screen 9)

Subtract option, the label will immediately display a –2, since the click event of the second option button will execute. The code in this event subtracts the two numbers. Similar events will occur for Multiply and Divide. Remember, option buttons should be used only to represent mutually exclusive choices.

Figures 6–43, 6–44, 6–45, and 6–46 illustrate the program that is associated with the click event of each option button. This example illustrates how we can change the interface to simplify the program. Notice that we did not need to use the SELECT CASE control structure in this solution. Do you see why?

Figure 6–43
Op Code Problem (Visual Basic—opt_ADD_Click)

```
Private Sub opt_ADD_Click()

lbl_RESULT.Caption = Val(txt_NUMBER1.Text) + Val(txt_NUMBER2.Text)

End Sub
```

Figure 6–44
Op Code Problem (Visual Basic— opt_SUBTRACT_Click)

```
Private Sub opt_SUBTRACT_Click()

lbl_RESULT.Caption = Val(txt_NUMBER1.Text) - Val(txt_NUMBER2.Text)

End Sub
```

Figure 6–45
Op Code Problem (Visual Basic— opt_MULTIPLY_Click)

```
Private Sub opt_MULTIPLY_Click()

lbl_RESULT.Caption = Val(txt_NUMBER1.Text) * Val(txt_NUMBER2.Text)

End Sub
```

Figure 6–46
Op Code Problem (Visual Basic—opt_DIVIDE_Click)

```
Private Sub opt_DIVIDE_Click()

lbl_RESULT.Caption = Val(txt_NUMBER1.Text) / Val(txt_NUMBER2.Text)

End Sub
```

Key Terms

master file
transaction (detail) file

CASE control structure
character string

Exercises

1. (a) Distinguish between master files and transaction files.
   (b) Describe in detail some examples of each.

2. Describe three types of flowcharting situations where use of connector symbols is necessary or advisable.

3. **(a)** Using ANSI-approved flowcharting symbols, sketch the logic of a CASE control structure.
   (b) State the logic of the CASE control structure in pseudocode form.
   (c) What pseudocode keywords did you use in your response to Exercise 3(b)?
   (d) What indentations did you use in your response to Exercise 3(b)? Why?

4. Does the order of the tests specified in a CASE control structure matter? If so, why?

5. **(a)** Using a modular design, redo Sample Problem 6.1 to process any number of input records. Print a report heading and column headings on every page, as well as a page number, with 55 detail lines per page. Assume the first record input will specify how many records are to follow. Construct a structure chart. Create a flowchart and pseudocode for each module in the design.
   (b) Use automatic end-of-file processing instead of a header record to solve Exercise 5(a).

6. Simulate the execution of the solution to Exercise 5(b) assuming the following input values:

OP	N1	N2
'A'	3	5
'M'	2	7
'A'	4	3
'S'	3	1
'D'	10	5
'D'	12	3
'B'	1	4
'S'	4	4
'A'	8	2

   What will the computer provide as output?

7. Redo Sample Problem 6.4 to compute and output the total sales within each class, as well as the total records within each class. Also compute and output the total number of records processed.

8. Construct a structure chart, as well as a flowchart and pseudocode, for the following problem. Assume each input record contains a taxpayer's name, the value of a personal property belonging to the taxpayer, and a code defining the type of personal property owned. Each type of property is taxed at a unique rate. The codes, property types, and tax rates follow:

Code	Property Type	Tax Rate
1	Bike	2 percent of value
2	Car	4 percent of value
3	Truck	5 percent of value

Your program is to compute the tax for each property and to output a line specifying the taxpayer's name, value of property, and tax. The program should output counts of the numbers of bikes, cars, and trucks for which taxes are computed, with appropriate labels. Include a report heading and column headings, as well as a page number on every page, with 55 detail lines per page. Also include an initial IF and a modular design. Write an error message if the input contains an invalid code value. Assume a code of 0 indicates the end of the input file.

9. Simulate the execution of the solution to Exercise 8 assuming the following input values:

Name	Value	Code
J. GREENE	350.00	1
A. SMITH	9750.00	3
P. WOOLEY	10500.00	3
M. MANLEY	500.00	1
B. COURTNEY	15000.00	2
C. JONES	12225.00	2
L. BLACK	100.00	1
F. KINGSMAN	300.00	1
V. HENLEY	8250.00	4
T. MORROW	6000.00	3
END-OF-FILE	0.00	0

What will the computer provide as output?

10. Construct a structure chart, as well as a flowchart and pseudocode, for the following problem. The NVCC National Bank needs a program to compute the monthly balances in customers' checking accounts. Each customer input record contains customer name, account number, previous account balance, transaction amount, and a code specifying the type of transaction. The code can be interpreted as follows:

CODE	TYPE OF TRANSACTION
D	deposit
W	withdrawal

Any other value of CODE is invalid. Use the CASE control structure to check CODE, and output an error message if CODE is invalid. Compute the new monthly balance for each customer by adding the transaction amount to the previous account balance if the transaction is a deposit, or subtracting the transaction amount from the previous account balance if the transaction is a withdrawal. Output the customer name, account number, previous monthly balance, and new computed monthly balance. Include a report heading and column headings, as well as a page number, on every page, with 50 detail lines per page. Also include an initial IF and a modular design. A code of "S" will be used to signal the end of the input.

11. Construct a structure chart, as well as a flowchart and pseudocode, for the following problem, which is a modification of Exercise 10. The NVCC National Bank needs a program to compute the monthly balances in customers' checking accounts. Each customer input record contains customer name, account number, previous account balance, and number of transactions. The customer record is then followed by the transaction records for that customer. Each transaction record contains the amount of the actual transaction and a code specifying the type of transaction. The code can be interpreted as follows:

CODE	TYPE OF TRANSACTION
1	deposit
2	withdrawal

Any other value of CODE is invalid. Use the CASE control structure to check CODE, and output an error message if CODE is invalid. Compute the new monthly balance for each customer by adding the transaction amount to the previous account balance if the transaction is a deposit (CODE = 1), or subtracting the transaction amount from the previous account balance if the transaction is a withdrawal (CODE = 2). Complete this processing for each transaction. Finally, output the customer name, account number, previous monthly balance, and new computed monthly balance. If the number of transactions is less than or equal to 0, the new balance will be equivalent to the previous balance. Also, assume that the proper number of transaction records always follows the customer name record. Include a report heading and column headings, as well as a page number, on every page, with 50 detail lines per page. Also include an initial IF and a modular design. Use automatic end-of-file to signal the end of the input.

12. Construct a program flowchart and corresponding pseudocode to prepare automobile liability insurance estimates for customers. The input consists of a series of records that contain the name of the customer, the amount of liability coverage (which is fixed at $100,000), the age of the customer, and a risk code. A code of 1 indicates a high-risk driver with recent moving violations. A code of 2 indicates a low-risk driver with no recent moving violations. If a record does not contain a code of 1 or a code of 2, the code is invalid, and an error message is to be printed on the report. The output is to consist of insurance estimates for $100,000 liability insurance. The report is to contain the customer's name, age, risk code, a message identifying the customer as a high insurance risk or a low insurance risk, and the cost of the insurance coverage. If the customer is less than 25 years of age and has a risk code of 1 (high risk), the cost of insurance is $280.00. If the customer is 25 years of age or more and has a risk code of 1 (high risk), the cost of the insurance is $250.00. If the customer is 25 years of age or more and has a risk code of 2 (low risk), the cost of insurance is $200.00. If the customer is less than 25 years of age and has a risk code of 2 (low risk), the cost of insurance is $225.00. If the risk code is invalid, the message "RISK CODE IS INVALID" should appear on the report.

After all records have been processed, the total number of customers, the total number of low-risk drivers, the total number of high-risk drivers, and the total number of invalid risk types should be printed. A sample format of the report is illustrated below.

```
                         INSURANCE REPORT

NAME                  AGE    RISK      RISK        INSURANCE
                             CODE      TYPE        COST

T. L. ELTON           42     1         HIGH RISK      250.00
C. C. FOX             18     2         LOW RISK       225.00
L. R. GUMM            26     2         LOW RISK       200.00
M. M. MATT            23     1         HIGH RISK      280.00
C. R. NUMIS           21     RISK CODE IS INVALID

TOTAL CUSTOMERS   05
TOTAL LOW RISK    02
TOTAL HIGH RISK   02
TOTAL INVALID RISK TYPE    01
```

Include a report heading and column headings, as well as a page number, on every page, with 45 detail lines per page. Also include an initial IF and a modular design. Use automatic end-of-file to signal the end of the input and use the CASE control structure to check the risk code.

DOUNTIL Control Structure

Objectives

Upon completion of this chapter you should be able to

- Identify, and use in program design, the DOUNTIL control structure.
- Distinguish between the logic of a DOWHILE pattern and the logic of a DOUNTIL pattern.

Introduction

By now you have acquired some familiarity with the three basic patterns of structured programming: SIMPLE SEQUENCE, IFTHENELSE, and DOWHILE. You can express these patterns in flowchart and pseudocode forms.

In Chapter 6 we saw how a series of tests may be set up as a nested IFTHENELSE control structure, and we learned a shorthand notation to substitute in its place: the CASE control structure. The CASE structure more conveniently describes the decision-making logic used in a nested IFTHENELSE. Since the CASE structure consists entirely of basic structured-programming patterns, we can use it with confidence that we are maintaining structure in our solution algorithms. The computer-program representation of the algorithm, then, will be a well-structured program.

Another common combination of the basic patterns of structured programming is a SIMPLE SEQUENCE followed by a DOWHILE. This combination is shown in its general form in Figure 7–1. First, statement e is executed. Then we enter a DOWHILE loop. We test for the condition "not q" (indicated by q with a line over it, or $\overline{q}$). We execute statement e while condition $\overline{q}$ is true. Note that when condition $\overline{q}$ is false, we have not $\overline{q}$—which is the same as q. We exit the loop at that time. If you find this negative logic confusing, don't be discouraged—many system designers and programmers also find it confusing. Remember, negative logic is frequently found when a DOWHILE loop is used, because the loop steps can be executed only when the tested condition is true.

Because of the difficulties that may arise when using negative logic, many programmers prefer to use the **DOUNTIL control structure,** which is represented in Figure 7–2. This program logic can be summarized as follows: Do statement e until the condition q is known to be true.

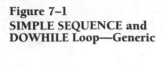

Figure 7–1
SIMPLE SEQUENCE and
DOWHILE Loop—Generic

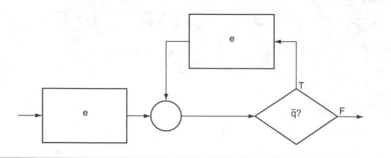

Figure 7–2
DOUNTIL Loop—Generic

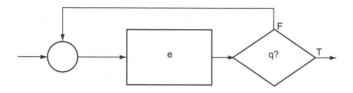

To demonstrate the differences between DOWHILE logic and DOUNTIL logic, let's consider how they might apply to a real-life situation. Suppose, for example, that you are employed as a sandwich maker in a neighborhood delicatessen. Your employer may say: "Make one beef sandwich. Continue to make (do) beef sandwiches while you are not too tired to do so." This is the pattern of logic shown in Figure 7–1. Alternatively, your employer may say: "After you have made one beef sandwich, continue to make (do) beef sandwiches until you are too tired to do so." This is the pattern of logic shown in Figure 7–2.

What is the significant difference between the DOWHILE pattern that we have learned to use and this combination of SIMPLE SEQUENCE and DOWHILE known as DOUNTIL? We saw earlier that the DOWHILE pattern is a **leading-decision program loop:** The test for the loop-terminating condition is made immediately upon entering the loop. In contrast, the DOUNTIL pattern is a **trailing-decision program loop:** The test for the loop-terminating condition is not made until the other processing steps in the loop have been executed. This means that no matter what the outcome of the test within the loop, the processing steps that precede the test will always be performed at least once before the test is made. So before using DOUNTIL we must be sure that we want to perform the functions within the loop at least once. How many more times we perform the functions within a trailing-decision loop depends on the outcomes of any successive tests. The execution of the processing steps in the loop and subsequent condition testing continue until the tested condition is known to be true. Then the loop is exited.

Note that a DOWHILE control structure is exited when the tested condition is false, but a DOUNTIL is exited when the tested condition is true. It is essential to set up all loop constructs in a solution algorithm using either a DOWHILE or DOUNTIL control structure. Otherwise, the computer-program representation of the algorithm will not be a well-structured program.

DOUNTIL Counter Loops

In Chapter 4 we discussed numerous DOWHILE loops that were executed once, reexecuted, or exited on the basis of the current value of a loop counter. (See the tests for COUNT < 6 in Figure 4–4, for COUNT < 10 in Figure 4–8, or any of the other examples in that chapter.) The execution of a DOUNTIL loop can be controlled in a similar manner. We initialize the loop counter to its starting value before entering the loop. With each execution of the loop, we increase (or decrease) the value of the counter; then we test its value to determine whether or not the processing steps within the loop should be reexecuted.

The flowchart in Figure 7–3 shows how to use a DOUNTIL loop to read six data values, add them together in an accumulator, and write their sum. The corresponding pseudocode is shown in Figure 7–4.

Figure 7–3
Adding Six Numbers Using DOUNTIL (Flowchart)

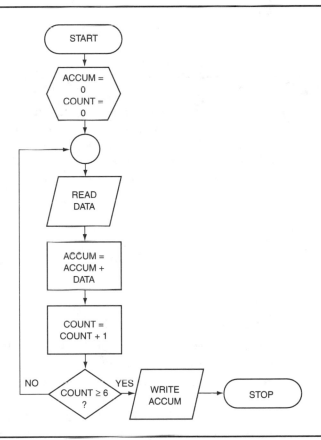

Figure 7–4
Adding Six Numbers Using DOUNTIL (Pseudocode)

```
Start
ACCUM = 0
COUNT = 0
DOUNTIL COUNT ≥ 6
    Read DATA
    ACCUM = ACCUM + DATA
    COUNT = COUNT + 1
ENDDO
Write ACCUM
Stop
```

We achieved exactly the same result using a DOWHILE program loop in Figure 4–4. Compare the tests for loop termination in these algorithms. As mentioned earlier, the DOWHILE program loop is exited when the tested condition is false; the DOUNTIL program loop is exited when the tested condition is true. It is for this reason that the test in Figure 7–3 (COUNT ≥ 6) is the negation of the test in Figure 4–4 (COUNT < 6). Look at the test in Figure 7–3 again. Do you think it could be made even simpler?

Now look at the pseudocode in Figure 7–4. It may appear that the condition (COUNT ≥ 6) is being tested before the loop steps are executed. However, this is not the case. In pseudocode, the tested condition is placed next to the keyword DOUNTIL, which precedes the loop steps. It's important to understand that even though the test is written before the loop steps, it is not actually made until the loop steps have been executed one time.

Sample Problem 7.1 (Property— Counter-Controlled)	**Problem:** With computer help, a table is to be generated that shows the storage costs for personal property at a large warehouse. The table covers property values from $1,000 through $20,000, in increments of $100. Storage costs are computed at 5 percent of property values. Each table entry is to consist of a property value and a corresponding storage cost, as follows:

$1,000 $50
$1,100 $55
$1,200 $60
    ⋮   ⋮
    ⋮   ⋮

Solution:

A program flowchart of an algorithm to solve this problem is given in Figure 7–5. It contains a DOUNTIL pattern and numerous examples of SIMPLE SEQUENCE. The same algorithm is shown in pseudocode form in Figure 7–6.

Here, the loop-control variable is not a specially introduced data item. Instead, it is one of the data items discussed in the problem statement: the personal property value (PROP). We initialize PROP to its starting value, $1,000, before we enter the DOUNTIL loop. Upon entering the loop, we use this value immediately in computing a storage cost, and print a table entry accordingly. Next, we increase the value of PROP by $100. Finally, we test the value of PROP to see whether it exceeds $20,000. The loop is reexecuted if the tested condition is false; it is exited if the tested condition is true. Note that one table entry has been computed and printed before the value of the loop-control variable is tested.

How do we know to set PROP to $1,000 initially, increase it by $100, and test for an upper limit of $20,000? We derive these steps from the

Figure 7–5
Property—Counter-
Controlled (Flowchart)

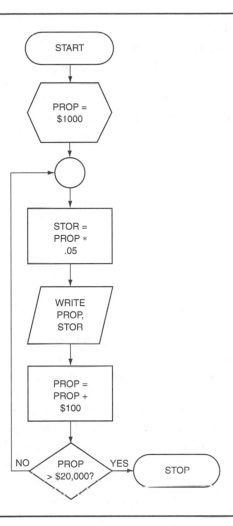

Figure 7–6
Property—Counter-
Controlled (Pseudocode)

```
Start
PROP = $1000
DOUNTIL PROP > $20,000
    STOR = PROP * .05
    Write PROP, STOR
    PROP = PROP + $100
ENDDO
Stop
```

requirements of the problem statement. Because the problem statement specified exactly which property values to process, we did not have to read any property values as input. In this example the loop steps actually generated the property values that needed to be processed. What would have happened if we had tested for PROP = $20,000, or PROP ≥ $20,000, instead of PROP > $20,000? The loop would not have been reexecuted when PROP had a value of $20,000. No table entry would have been created to show the storage cost for personal properties valued at $20,000, so the requirements of the problem statement would not have been satisfied.

Sample Problem 7.2 (Property—Header Record Logic)

Problem:

Redo the solution to Sample Problem 7.1 to accept any number of property values as input. Assume that the first input record will contain a number indicating how many property values are to be processed. Succeeding records (if any) will contain property values. Include report and column headings, as well as page numbers on every page of the output, with 55 detail lines per page. Construct a flowchart and pseudocode for this revised algorithm.

Solution:

This solution has been designed using four modules, as indicated in the structure chart in Figure 7–7. The flowchart and pseudocode for A000 are shown in Figures 7–8 and 7–9.

In this algorithm we are using header record logic to determine when the end-of-file has been reached. The main processing loop is a DOUNTIL loop. First, B000 is executed to initialize the line count and the page count. Then the header record is input, and the variable represented by N is tested to make sure it is positive—that is, to determine if additional records follow. If N proves to be greater than 0, the main processing loop is entered. Because we are using a DOUNTIL loop, the connector is followed by the actual processing steps within the loop. After one record containing a property value is processed in B010, the loop-control variable (N) is decremented by 1 and the DOUNTIL loop test is made. Remember, this test must be the last step in a DOUNTIL control structure. In terms of the logic used, a DOUNTIL test is more straightforward than typical DOWHILE tests. The DOUNTIL loop requirement specifies that the loop will be executed when the tested condition is false, and exited when the tested condition is true. In most cases, negative logic is not necessary. We would normally test for N > 0 if the DOWHILE loop was used. Because we are using the DOUNTIL loop, we test for the opposite condition, N ≤ 0. Since N must be a positive number at this point, it will get increasingly smaller and will reach 0 before it can ever become negative. Thus, we can simplify the

Figure 7–7
Property—Header Record Logic (Structure Chart)

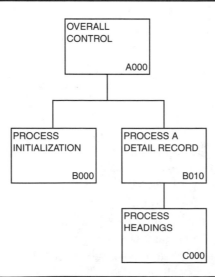

DOUNTIL Control Structure

Figure 7–8
**Property—Header Record
Logic—Overall Control
(Flowchart)**

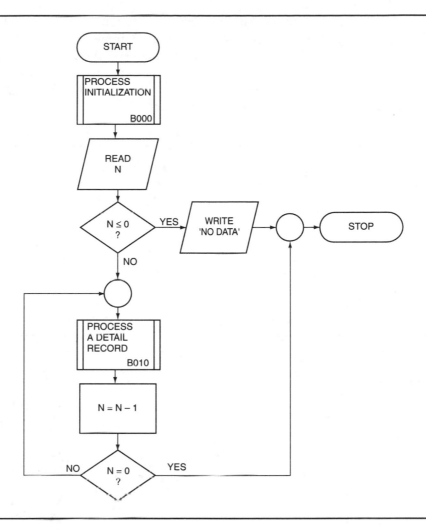

Figure 7–9
**Property—Header Record
Logic—Overall Control
(Pseudocode)**

```
A000
Start
Process initialization (B000)
Read N
IF N ≤ 0 THEN
    Write "No data"
ELSE
    DOUNTIL N = 0
        Process a detail record (B010)
        N = N - 1
    ENDDO
ENDIF
Stop
```

loop test further and change the N ≤ 0 test to an N = 0 test. Consequently, the wording within the DOUNTIL test is less confusing.

The initialization module (B000) is shown in Figure 7 -10. The detail-processing module (B010) is shown in Figure 7–11. In B010, LINECNT is first checked to determine if a new page needs to be started and headings output. An input record containing one property value is then read; the corresponding storage cost is computed; a detail line is written; and LINECNT is incremented. Notice that several steps in the original algorithm are omitted in this one. PROP is not initialized to $1,000; PROP is not increased by $100; and PROP is not tested against $20,000. Do you see why these steps are no longer necessary?

Figure 7–10
Property—Header Record Logic—Process Initialization

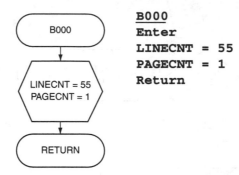

B000
Enter
LINECNT = 55
PAGECNT = 1
Return

Figure 7–11
Property—Header Record Logic—Process a Detail Record

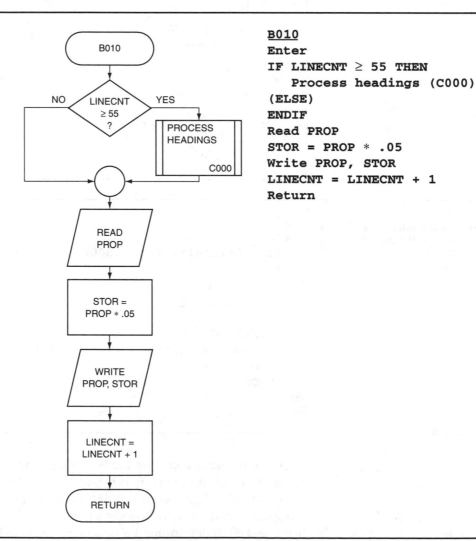

B010
Enter
IF LINECNT ≥ 55 THEN
    Process headings (C000)
(ELSE)
ENDIF
Read PROP
STOR = PROP * .05
Write PROP, STOR
LINECNT = LINECNT + 1
Return

Figure 7–12
Property—Header Record
Logic—Process Headings

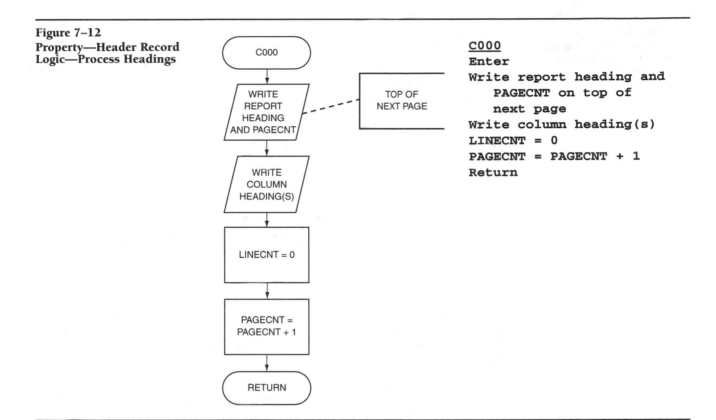

```
C000
Enter
Write report heading and
    PAGECNT on top of
    next page
Write column heading(s)
LINECNT = 0
PAGECNT = PAGECNT + 1
Return
```

The headings module (C000) is shown in Figure 7–12. This logic should look familiar to you.

Sample Problem 7.3 (Property— Trailer Record Logic)

Problem:

Redo the solution to Sample Problem 7.2 to illustrate trailer record logic instead of header record logic. A property value of 0 will serve as the trailer record, denoting end-of-file.

Solution:

A program flowchart and pseudocode for the overall control module are shown in Figures 7–13 and 7–14.

The first READ statement (priming READ) reads a property value as input. The value is checked immediately to determine whether or not the end-of-file has been reached. If not, the main processing DOUNTIL loop is executed. Notice that the loop steps are done before the condition is tested. The order of these processing steps is the same for both types of loops (DOWHILE and DOUNTIL). The second READ (loop READ) is still placed after the predefined-process symbol that references module B010. Again, the important differences between these two loops is the position of the test. In a DOWHILE loop, the test is always placed first; that is, right after the connector. In a DOUNTIL loop, the test is always placed last. The detail-processing module for this algorithm is shown in Figure 7–15. Can

Figure 7–13
Property—Trailer Record
Logic—Overall Control
(Flowchart)

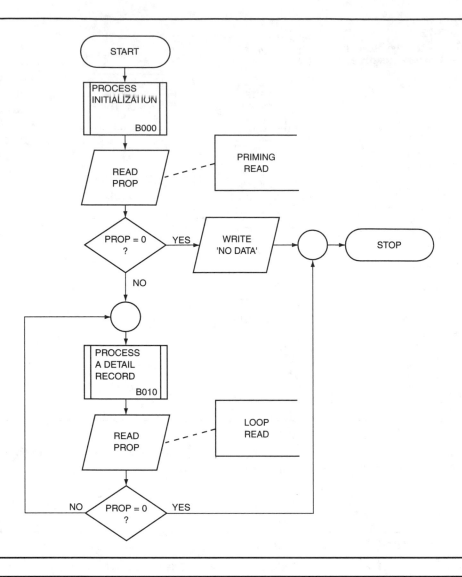

Figure 7–14
Property—Trailer Record
Logic—Overall Control
(Pseudocode)

```
A000
Start
Process initialization (B000)
Read PROP
IF PROP = 0 THEN
   Write 'No data'
ELSE
   DOUNTIL PROP = 0
      Process a detail record (B010)
      Read PROP
   ENDDO
ENDIF
Stop
```

you see why a READ statement is not needed in this module? Why was a READ statement placed in the detail-processing module in Figure 7–11? Modules B000 and C000 contain the same processing steps as they did in Sample Problem 7.2.

Figure 7–15
Property—Trailer Record
Logic—Process a Detail
Record

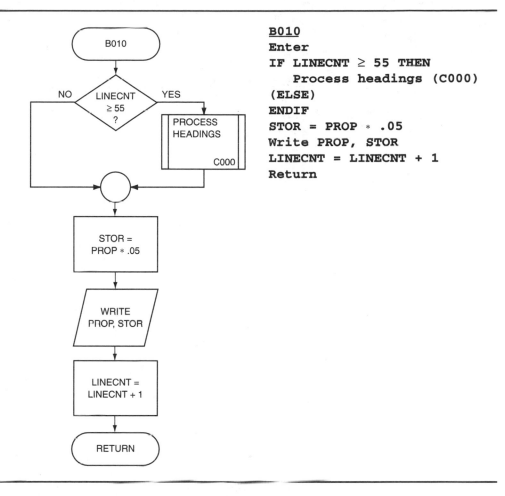

```
B010
Enter
IF LINECNT ≥ 55 THEN
    Process headings (C000)
(ELSE)
ENDIF
STOR = PROP * .05
Write PROP, STOR
LINECNT = LINECNT + 1
Return
```

DOWHILE vs. DOUNTIL

Before we leave this topic, it is important to discuss some very subtle differences between DOWHILE and DOUNTIL. Look at Figure 7–16. Two flowchart and pseudocode representations are shown. Each shows one of the loop types (DOWHILE or DOUNTIL) and how it is used in conjunction with the typical logic needed when automatic end-of-file processing is used. Both algorithms appear to work; however, only one is correct in all situations. Consider what would happen if end-of-file was reached the first time a READ was attempted. If the DOWHILE loop is used, the "NOT EOF" condition will be false the first time the test is made and the loop steps will never be executed. If the DOUNTIL loop is used, the module will be executed before the EOF test is even made. This attempt to process a normal input record will probably cause an error. If the module does successfully complete its own processing, a second READ will be attempted after control is returned to the overall control module. This attempt to read another record will most definitely generate an error condition, because we cannot read another record when end-of-file has already been reached.

In most of our examples, we have placed an IFTHENELSE statement just prior to the main processing loop to test for this condition—that is, to detect when EOF is reached on the first READ attempt. Figures 7–17 and

**Figure 7–16
DOWHILE vs. DOUNTIL—
No Initial Test**

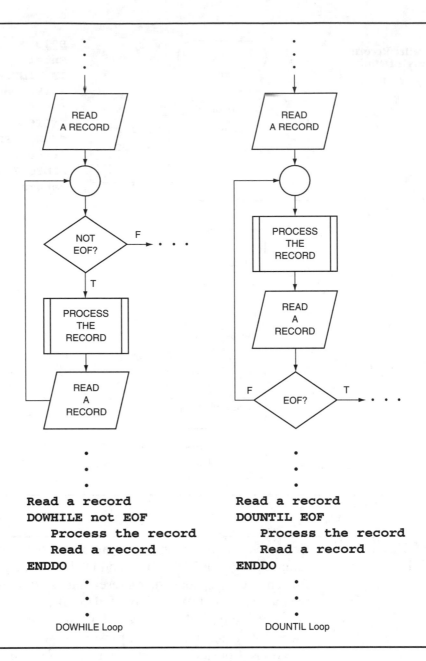

Read a record
DOWHILE not EOF
    Process the record
    Read a record
ENDDO

DOWHILE Loop

Read a record
DOUNTIL EOF
    Process the record
    Read a record
ENDDO

DOUNTIL Loop

7–18 show the two flowchart and pseudocode representations again, with the inclusion of this IFTHENELSE statement.

Although this extra step is not necessary when a DOWHILE loop is used, it does provide a convenient way to output a message indicating that no data was found. It is very important, however, to see that this additional IFTHENELSE statement is not merely helpful when it precedes a DOUNTIL loop: It is a requirement. Now if EOF is reached on the first READ attempt, the true path of the IFTHENELSE will be executed, and the loop steps will be bypassed entirely (as they should be). Make sure that you understand the limitations as well as the conveniences of using a DOUNTIL loop.

Figure 7–17
DOWHILE vs. DOUNTIL—
Initial Test (Flowchart)

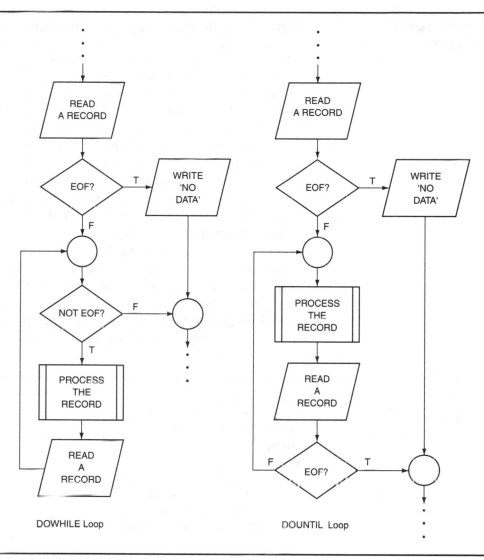

Figure 7–18
DOWHILE vs. DOUNTIL—
Initial Test (Pseudocode)

```
.
.
.
Read a record
IF EOF THEN
    Write 'No data'
ELSE
    DOWHILE not EOF
        Process the record
        Read a record
    ENDDO
ENDIF
.
.
.


            DOWHILE Loop
```

```
.
.
.
Read a record
IF EOF THEN
    Write 'No data'
ELSE
    DOUNTIL EOF
        Process the record
        Read a record
    ENDDO
ENDIF
.
.
.


            DOUNTIL Loop
```

Enrichment (Basic)

Figure 7–19 illustrates a listing of the program that solves the Property Problem (Figures 7–5 and 7–6). In this example we implement the DOUNTIL loop with a construct in Basic that is very similar to DOUNTIL pseudocode. Notice, however, that the loop test is placed at the bottom of the loop in Basic. This improves the clarity of the program by more clearly reflecting the logic of a DOUNTIL loop. Remember that the DOUNTIL loop is a trailing-decision loop. Again, the keyword LOOP is used in Basic instead of the keyword ENDDO. The same type of indentation is used in the Basic program, and the logic of the Basic DOUNTIL loop is identical to the logic of the DOUNTIL loop in pseudocode. In addition, most of the statements in the Basic program parallel the pseudocode. We did not need to include either a Read statement or an Input statement since the property values are generated by the loop steps. The Print statements are used to output the headings prior to entering the loop. Two Print statements are used to print the headings on separate lines. A final property value of 2,500 is used instead of 20,000 to limit the output to one page.

Figure 7–20 illustrates the output that will be produced when the program is executed. Note that there is one line of output (a property value and a storage cost) for every property value that is processed.

**Figure 7–19
Property Problem
(Basic List)**

```
PROP = 1000
PRINT "Property", "Storage"
PRINT "Value", "Cost"
PRINT
DO
        STOR = PROP * .05
        PRINT PROP,STOR
        PROP = PROP + 100
LOOP UNTIL PROP > 2500
END
```

**Figure 7–20
Property Problem
(Basic Run)**

Property Value	Storage Cost
1000	50
1100	55
1200	60
1300	65
1400	70
1500	75
1600	80
1700	85
1800	90
1900	95
2000	100
2100	105
2200	110
2300	115
2400	120
2500	125

Enrichment (Visual Basic)

Figure 7–21 illustrates the graphical interface for the Property Problem (Figures 7–5 and 7–6). In this example, only two command buttons are created. When the user clicks the End button, the program execution stops. When the user clicks the Begin button, an input box is presented, as illustrated in Figure 7–22. We have modified this example to allow the user to input the property values. Remember, the input box is another way (in addition to the text box control) to accept input from the user. At this point the user should enter a property value, as shown in Figure 7–23, and click the OK button. Once the user enters a property value and clicks OK, a message box displaying the property value and corresponding storage cost is presented, as shown in Figure 7–24.

When the user clicks the OK button in Figure 7–24, another message box is presented as shown in Figure 7–25. This message box displays a message asking if the user wishes to enter another property value. The user can choose Yes or No at this point. Notice that this message box contains a Yes button and a No button, not an OK button. The contents of a message box, as well as what types of buttons are displayed, are specified by the programmer. Note that we have modified this example to allow the user to determine how many property values will be processed. (Remember: The original algorithm actually generated the property values and stopped at the first property value greater than 20,000.)

Figure 7–21
Property Problem (Visual Basic—Screen 1)

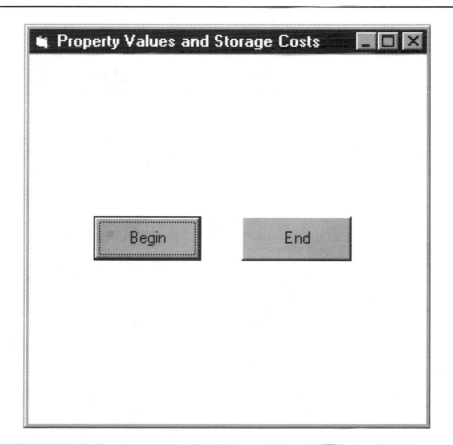

Figure 7–22
Property Problem (Visual Basic—Screen 2)

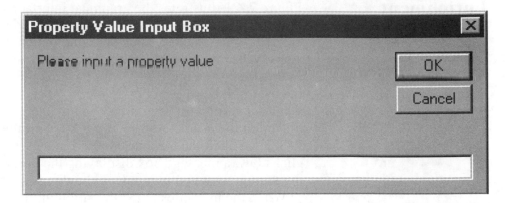

Figure 7–23
Property Problem (Visual Basic—Screen 3)

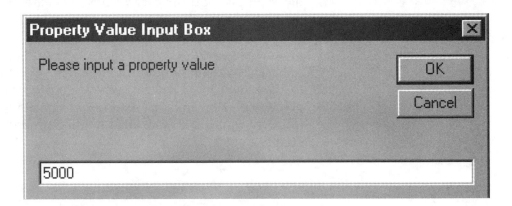

Figure 7–24
Property Problem (Visual Basic—Screen 4)

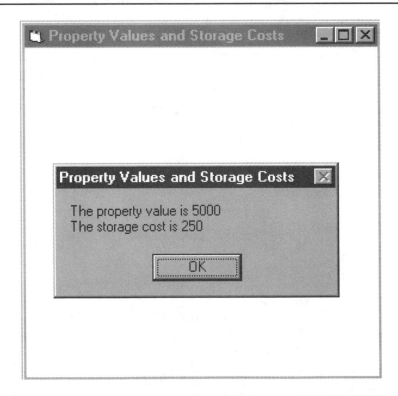

Figure 7–25
Property Problem (Visual
Basic—Screen 5)

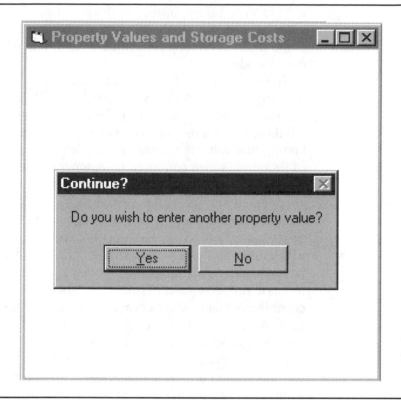

Figure 7–26 illustrates the program that is associated with the click event of the Begin button. In this example a DOUNTIL loop is used to control the processing of each property value. We implement the DOUNTIL loop with a construct in Visual Basic that is very similar to DOUNTIL pseudocode. Notice, however, that the loop test is placed at the bottom of the loop in Visual Basic. This improves the clarity of the program by more clearly reflecting the logic of a DOUNTIL loop. Remember that the DOUNTIL loop is a trailing-decision loop. Again, the keyword LOOP is

Figure 7–26
Property Problem (Visual
Basic—cmd_BEGIN_Click)

```
Private Sub cmd_BEGIN_Click()


Do

    Property = InputBox$("Please input a property value", "Property Value Input Box")
    Storage = Val(Property) * 0.05
    MsgBox "The property value is " & Property & Chr$(13) & "The storage cost is " & Storage,,_
        "Property Values and Storage Costs"
    Response = MsgBox("Do you wish to enter another property value?",vbYesNo, "Continue?")
Loop Until Response = vbNo


End Sub
```

used in Visual Basic instead of the keyword ENDDO. The same type of indentation is used in the Visual Basic program, and the logic of the Visual Basic DOUNTIL loop is identical to the logic of the DOUNTIL loop in pseudocode.

The first statement in the loop causes an input box that requests a property value from the user to be displayed. Remember, the programmer determines both the message to be displayed and the title of the input box window. When a user enters a value into the input box and clicks the OK button, that value is assigned to the variable named Property. The value of Property is then converted to a numeric value by the Val function (InputBox$ returns a string), multiplied by 0.05, and assigned to the variable named Storage. If the user clicks the Cancel button instead of the OK button, a null string (" ") will be assigned to Property. The null string will be evaluated to 0 by the Val function, resulting in a computed storage cost of 0. Although this situation will not cause an error to occur, the output will be misleading. A similar situation may occur if the user enters a non-numeric property value. Visual Basic includes additional functions and capabilities that can aid a programmer with data validation. These functions are included in any book that describes all Visual Basic capabilities, but are beyond the scope of this book.

Once the storage cost is computed, a message box displaying the property value and corresponding storage cost is presented. The message box displays the output as one long string. The string is composed of several parts—identifying labels, the variable names representing the property value and storage cost, and a special function, *Chr$(13)*. The concatenation operator, &, is used to join the parts of the string. Chr$(13) is a special function that converts the internal code of 13 to a character. A 13 represents a carriage return and is used to output the string on two separate lines. The underline character (_) is not part of the string, but rather a Visual Basic code to indicate continuation. In this case, two lines were needed to represent the message box statement in the code.

After the property value and storage cost are output, another message box is presented to the user. This time a message box function is being used. The message box function will return a value and store it in the variable named Response. This value indicates which button the user clicked—Yes or No. A special variable—*vbYesNo*—is included in the message box function to cause the buttons Yes and No to be displayed in the message box instead of the default button (the OK button). After the user clicks one of the buttons (Yes or No), the DOUNTIL loop test is made. This test determines whether or not the user wishes to enter another property value. Another special variable—*vbNo*—represents a No answer and is tested against the value of the variable Response. If the user has chosen No, the loop test will evaluate to true and the loop will be exited. If the user has chosen Yes, the loop test will evaluate to false and the loop steps will be re-executed. Note that the programmer does not need to define the special variables vbYesNo and vbNo. These variables are predefined within the Visual Basic programming system.

Figure 7–27 illustrates the program that is associated with the click event of the End button. The single statement End is used to stop program execution.

Figure 7–27
Property Problem (Visual Basic—cmd_END_Click)

```
Private Sub cmd_END_Click()

End

End Sub
```

Key Terms

DOUNTIL control structure	leading-decision program loop	trailing-decision program loop

Exercises

1. **(a)** What kind of program loop is formed in a DOWHILE pattern?
   (b) What kind of program loop is formed in a DOUNTIL pattern?
   (c) When is the difference between DOWHILE and DOUNTIL particularly important? Why?

2. **(a)** If condition q is "X is less than or equal to Y," what is condition $\overline{q}$?
   (b) If condition q is "$A + B < C$," what is condition $\overline{q}$?
   (c) If condition q is "C is greater than or equal to $A + B$," what is condition $\overline{q}$?
   (d) If condition q is "$X - Y > A + B$," what is condition $\overline{q}$?
   (e) If condition q is "$X * Y = Z$," what is condition $\overline{q}$?
   (f) If condition q is "Z not equal to A/B," what is condition $\overline{q}$?

   For the remainder of the exercises, include report and column headings, as well as a page number on every page, with 55 detail lines per page unless directed otherwise. Output an appropriate message if the input contains no records; include descriptive messages in the total lines; and use a modular design. Construct flowcharts and pseudocode for each module.

3. Modify the program flowchart and pseudocode shown in Figures 7–3 and 7–4 to make a more general-purpose algorithm. The revised algorithm should describe how to read and add *any number* of data values (not just six). A count of the number of values added should be printed along with the sum of the values. Try this with both the header record logic approach and the trailer record logic approach. Report and column headings and page numbers are not required.

4. Redo Sample Problems 7.2 and 7.3 to output the following totals:
   - total number of records processed
   - total property value of all records processed
   - total storage cost for all property records processed

5. **(a)** Construct an algorithm to solve the following problem. One data item, MULT, is to be read as input. The sum of the following operations is to be computed and printed: 1, 1 + 1 * MULT, 1 + 2 * MULT, . . . ,1 + 9 * MULT. Assume that only one value of MULT will be input; that is, there will be one and only one input record.

Headings, page numbers, the no-data test, and modules are not required.

(b) Perform a procedure execution (trace) of the solution algorithm that you constructed in your response to Exercise 5(a) to answer the following questions:

- What value is provided as output if MULT is 5?
- What value is provided as output if MULT is 10?
- What value is provided as output if MULT is 0?

(c) Redo Exercise 5(a) to process any number of input values, that is, one or more values of MULT. Use both the header record logic approach and the trailer record logic approach.

6. Construct an algorithm to show the processing steps needed to solve the following problem. Data values to be added are provided as input. The number of items to be added will be indicated by the first value provided as input (which is not to be included in the sum). A count of the number of data items whose value exceeds 30,000 is also to be accumulated. The sum of the values added and the count of those exceeding 30,000 are to be provided as output. Headings and page numbers are not required.

7. Simulate the execution of your solution to Exercise 6, assuming the following input values:

10	Header Value
2000	
10000	
45000	
31000	Other
30000	data
30001	values
29000	
5000	
50000	
1000	

What values will the computer provide as output?

8. (a) Construct an algorithm to show the processing steps needed to solve the following problem. Two data items, LOWER and UPPER, are to be read as input. The sum of all odd numbers from LOWER to UPPER, inclusive, is to be computed and printed. Assume that LOWER is less than UPPER and that only one input record exists. Headings, page numbers, the no-data test, and modules are not required.

(b) Redo Exercise 8(a) to process any number of input values; that is, many records containing LOWER and UPPER limits. Use both the header record logic approach and the trailer record logic approach.

9. To answer the following questions, perform a procedure execution (trace) of the solution algorithm that you constructed in response to Exercise 8(a).

    (a) What value is provided as output by the algorithm if LOWER is 3 and UPPER is 18?
    (b) Is the output of the algorithm correct? If the output is not correct, examine both your solution algorithm and your procedure execution to determine where errors have occurred.

10. Repeat Exercise 9, but assume that LOWER is 3 and UPPER is 4.

11. Assume that you are given a file of records, each containing two fields, NAME and QUANTITY. The last record is a trailer record containing DUMMY in the name field and 999 in the quantity field. Two algorithms follow. (At least one is incorrect—possibly both are.)

    (a) Will algorithm A work?
    (b) Will algorithm B work?
    (c) If your answer to (a), (b), or both was no, explain why.
    (d) If either algorithm A or algorithm B is incorrect, write the pseudocode for either or both, as the case may be, to correct.

```
A.   START                              B.   START
     ACCUM = 0                               ACCUM = 0
     DOWHILE NAME not = 'DUMMY'              DOUNTIL NAME = 'DUMMY'
        READ NAME, QUANTITY                     READ NAME, QUANTITY
        ACCUM = ACCUM + QUANTITY                ACCUM = ACCUM + QUANTITY
     ENDDO                                   ENDDO
     WRITE ACCUM                             WRITE ACCUM
     STOP                                    STOP
```

12. Redo Exercise 15 from Chapter 5 using DOUNTIL loops instead of DOWHILE loops in your solution. You will need to add some additional tests in this solution.

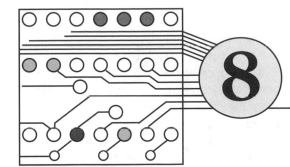

8 Introduction to Arrays

Objectives

Upon completion of this chapter you should be able to

- Distinguish between a simple variable and a subscripted variable.
- Input, output, and manipulate values stored in a list, or one-dimensional array.
- Input, output, and manipulate values stored in a table, or two-dimensional array.
- Distinguish between row-major ordering and column-major ordering and explain how each ordering affects the efficiency of processing.

Introduction

In preceding chapters we have directed our attention to the reading, processing, and writing of single values. Each value has been stored in a particular location and referred to as a **single** (or **simple**) **variable.** For each such variable, we selected and used a particular variable name (e.g., COUNT, N, A, ITEM, NUM). This need not always be the case.

Suppose a list of ten input values is to be read into ten consecutive storage locations. We could assign a unique name to each of the ten locations—say, INPUT1, INPUT2, and so on. We could also use the names to refer to the values throughout the program.

But what if the list contained 100 or even 1,000 values? The same approach might work, but it would not be convenient. Writing the program would be a tedious, time-consuming chore. With so many different values and corresponding variable names to keep track of, errors would be apt to occur.

List Structures

Suppose that, instead of treating the ten input values as ten similar but separate data items, we treat them as a group of data items. We reserve a storage area large enough for all the values, and then assign a name to the area. Various terms are used to describe data items stored and identified in this way. In COBOL this kind of data group is usually known as a **single-level table.** In Basic, Pascal, C, and C++, it may be called a **list, vector,** or **one-dimensional array.**

Only the group of data items is given a name. An individual item in the group is referred to by stating its relative position (on a left-to-right basis). This position is specified by means of a **subscript** following the group name.[1]

As an example, then, let us assume that a storage area is reserved for the ten input values mentioned above, and that the name INAREA is chosen for the area (see Figure 8–1). Use of the **unsubscripted variable name** INAREA, if permitted in the programming language, is interpreted as a reference to all the items in the group. Individual items in the group are referred to by means of the **subscripted variable names** INAREA(1), INAREA(2), and so on.

Grouping capabilities are available in numerous programming languages. Because it is to our advantage to make use of them, we will examine the program logic needed to effectively manage group data items in this chapter.

List Examples

Figures 8–2, 8–3, and 8–4 illustrate three common procedures used in the processing of one-dimensional arrays. Figure 8–2 shows the processing steps required to initialize an array. Figure 8–3 shows the steps to input values into an array. Figure 8–4 shows the steps to output values from an array. In all three examples the variable SUB is used as a subscript to point to a particular **member** (or **element**) of an array called LIST. When SUB represents a value of 1, the subscripted variable LIST(1) refers to the first element of LIST; when SUB represents a value of 2, the subscripted variable LIST(2) points to the second element; and so on. A DOUNTIL loop is executed repetitively, with the value represented by SUB increased by 1 on each execution. The loop is exited when the value represented by SUB is equal to 10. Notice that all three algorithms contain the same processing steps to control the loop. The subscript SUB plays two roles: It is used both as a counter to control the DOUNTIL loop and as a pointer into the array LIST. Note also that the READ statement in Figure 8–3 indicates the input of one data value each time through the loop. Think of that READ step as "Read a new input value into the current position of LIST." The WRITE statement in Figure 8–4 can be understood in a similar manner. Think of the WRITE step as "Write out the value in the current position of the array LIST."

Figure 8–1
One-Dimensional Array Example

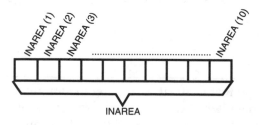

---

[1]In COBOL a distinction exists between a *subscript*, which is an integer value ("occurrence number") that may range from 1 to the total number of entries in a table, and an *index*, which is a storage displacement value from the beginning of the table. In other programming languages, the terms *subscript* and *index* are used interchangeably with respect to the identification of data items in a group. In this discussion the term *subscript* can be understood to mean either.

Figure 8–2
Initialize One-Dimensional
Array

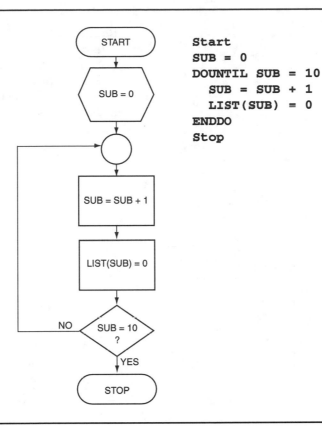

```
Start
SUB = 0
DOUNTIL SUB = 10
   SUB = SUB + 1
   LIST(SUB) = 0
ENDDO
Stop
```

Figure 8–3
Input One-Dimensional
Array

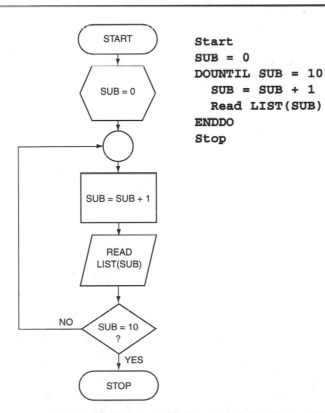

```
Start
SUB = 0
DOUNTIL SUB = 10
   SUB = SUB + 1
   Read LIST(SUB)
ENDDO
Stop
```

Figure 8–4
Output One-Dimensional Array

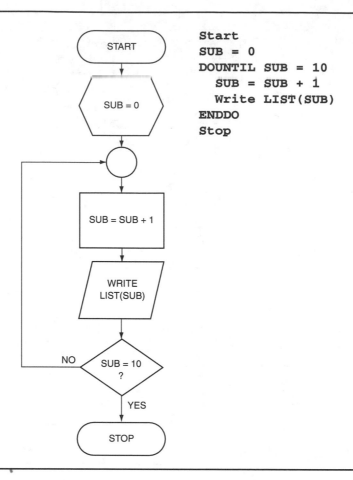

```
Start
SUB = 0
DOUNTIL SUB = 10
   SUB = SUB + 1
   Write LIST(SUB)
ENDDO
Stop
```

Sample Problem 8.1 (Finding the Smallest Number)

Problem:

Compute and output the smallest number in a ten-element array called LIST.

Solution:

Figure 8–5 shows a structure chart consisting of three modules: A000 (overall control), B000 (input array), and B010 (compute and output small). Figure 8–6 shows the logic within the overall control module A000. A000 calls upon two lower-level modules: one to read ten values into ten consecutive storage locations as a group, or array (B000); one to find and output the smallest value in the array (B010).

Module B000 contains the steps to read the ten values into LIST. This is essentially the same algorithm shown in Figure 8–3; the START and STOP steps are replaced with, respectively, an indication of entry into B000 and a RETURN to A000 when the module completes its processing.

Figure 8–7 shows the actual steps to find and output the smallest of the ten values. We begin our search for the smallest value by assuming arbitrarily that the first member of LIST, which is LIST(1), holds the smallest value. We store this value in SMALL, the location set aside for the smallest value. We also set the variable SUB to 1.

Figure 8–5
Finding the Smallest
Number (Structure Chart)

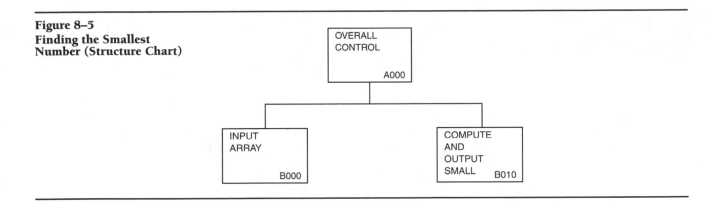

Figure 8–6
Finding the Smallest
Number—Overall Control

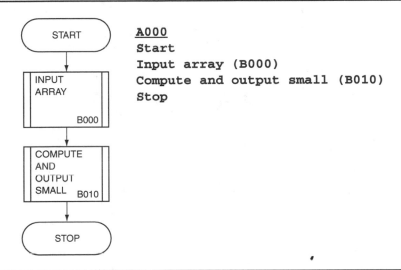

```
A000
Start
Input array (B000)
Compute and output small (B010)
Stop
```

The DOUNTIL control structure in Figure 8–7 controls subsequent processing. All succeeding members of LIST are compared with the value of SMALL by means of the IFTHENELSE nested inside the loop. Any value smaller than the current content of SMALL becomes, itself, the current content of SMALL, via the THEN clause (YES path) of the IFTHENELSE. The DOUNTIL loop is exited when SUB is known to be equal to 10—at which time the content of SMALL is the smallest value. This value is written as output, and control is returned to A000, which terminates processing.

The value 10 used in this algorithm could easily be replaced by another value. This would permit us to handle a different number of values, and therefore to find the smallest value in a different-sized group of data items or array. Changes to the program flowchart or pseudocode and to the programming-language representation of the algorithm would be minimal.

Even greater flexibility would be available if the number of values to be processed was indicated by means of the first input value (remember header record logic from Chapter 4). This value could be assigned to a variable, say N, for use in loop control. The program could be used to find the smallest of any number of values without any program modification; only the first input value would have to be changed. (See Exercise 4.)

Figure 8–7
Finding the Smallest
Number—Compute and
Output SMALL

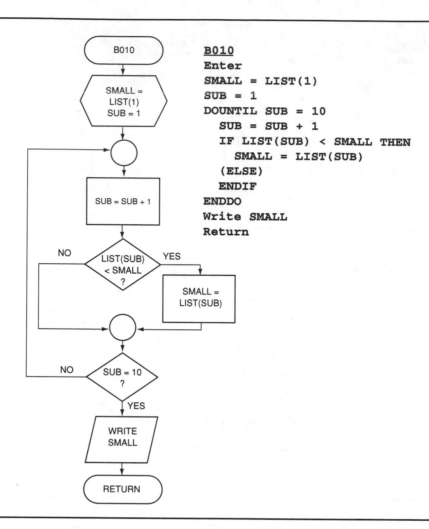

```
B010
Enter
SMALL = LIST(1)
SUB = 1
DOUNTIL SUB = 10
  SUB = SUB + 1
  IF LIST(SUB) < SMALL THEN
    SMALL = LIST(SUB)
  (ELSE)
  ENDIF
ENDDO
Write SMALL
Return
```

Sample Problem 8.2 (Finding the Average)

Problem:

Compute and output the average number in a ten-element array called LIST. Output the values in LIST as well.

Solution:

Figure 8–8 shows a structure chart consisting of four modules: A000 (overall control), B000 (input array), B010 (output array), and B020 (compute and output average). A000 calls upon three lower-level modules: one to read ten values into ten consecutive storage locations as a group, or array (B000); one to write ten values from ten consecutive storage locations (B010); and one to find and output the average of the values in an array (B020). The module A000 is much like A000 in the previous example (Figure 8–6) and is not shown here.

Modules B000 and B010 contain the steps to read the ten values into LIST and write the ten values from LIST. Again, these algorithms contain the same processing steps as shown in Figures 8–3 and 8–4. Only the beginning and ending steps need be changed to indicate the proper module entry and exit points.

Figure 8–8
Finding the Average
(Structure Chart)

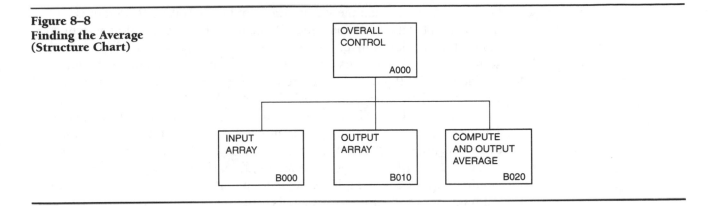

In Figure 8–9 we see the actual steps to find and output the average of the ten values. We begin by initializing the variable ACCUM to 0. ACCUM will be used to sum the values in LIST. We also set the variable POS to 0.

Figure 8–9
Finding the Average—
Compute and Output
Average

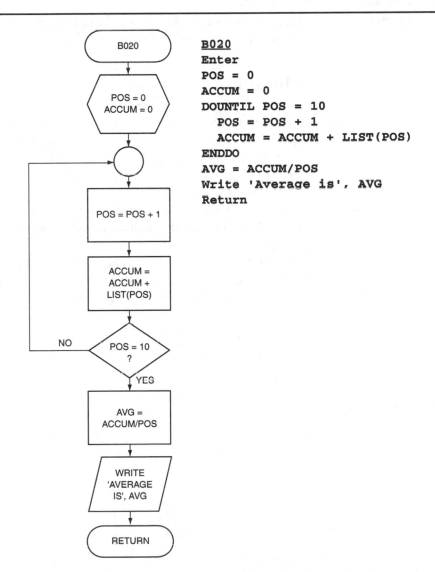

```
B020
Enter
POS = 0
ACCUM = 0
DOUNTIL POS = 10
  POS = POS + 1
  ACCUM = ACCUM + LIST(POS)
ENDDO
AVG = ACCUM/POS
Write 'Average is', AVG
Return
```

Notice that in this example we use the name POS, not SUB, to represent the subscript. Any name can generally be used, but you should try to pick names that are descriptive. For example, POS (for position), SUB (for subscript), and IND (for index) are better choices than names like I, J, and K.

The DOUNTIL control structure in Figure 8–9 controls subsequent processing. Each member of LIST is added to ACCUM during one iteration of the loop. The DOUNTIL loop is exited when the value of POS is equal to 10—at which time the average is computed. Notice that the current value of POS is used in the computation of the average, not the constant 10. This makes the algorithm somewhat more flexible. (Fewer program changes would be necessary, then, if we decided to compute the average of a different number of values.) The average is written as output and control is returned to A000, which terminates processing.

Sample Problem 8.3 (Counting Words)

Problem:

Compute and output the number of occurrences of the word 'CAT' in a 100-element array called BOOK.

Solution:

Figure 8–10 shows a structure chart consisting of three modules: A000 (overall control), B000 (input array), and B010 (count words and output). Figure 8–11 shows the logic within the overall control module A000. A000 calls upon two lower-level modules: one to read 100 values into 100 consecutive storage locations as a group, or array (B000); another to compute the number of occurrences of the word 'CAT' in the array BOOK (B010).

Module B000 (Figure 8–12) contains the steps to read the 100 values into BOOK. Notice again that this module contains the same general processing steps shown in Figure 8–3.

Figure 8–13 (flowchart) and Figure 8–14 (pseudocode) show the actual steps to compute the number of times 'CAT' is found in the array BOOK. We use a counter (COUNT) to keep track of each word 'CAT' that we find. The variables COUNT and POS are set to 0 as we begin.

The DOUNTIL control structure in Figures 8–13 and 8–14 controls subsequent processing. All members of BOOK are compared with 'CAT' by

Figure 8–10
Counting Words (Structure Chart)

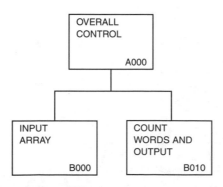

Figure 8–11
Counting Words—Overall
Control

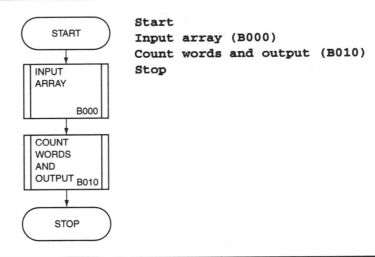

```
Start
Input array (B000)
Count words and output (B010)
Stop
```

Figure 8–12
Counting Words—Input
Array

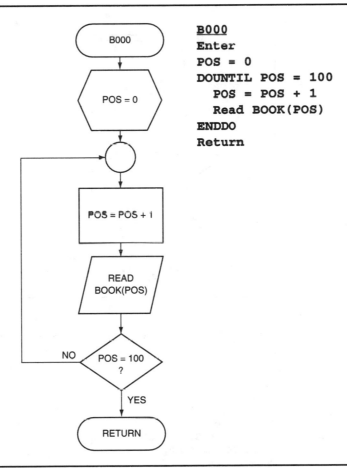

```
B000
Enter
POS = 0
DOUNTIL POS = 100
  POS = POS + 1
  Read BOOK(POS)
ENDDO
Return
```

means of the IFTHENELSE nested inside the loop. Any value equal to 'CAT' will cause the counter to be incremented by 1 via the THEN clause (YES path) of the IFTHENELSE. The DOUNTIL loop is exited when POS is equal to 100. At that time the counter is tested to determine whether the word 'CAT' was found. An appropriate message is output, and control is returned to A000, which terminates processing.

Figure 8–13
Counting Words—Count
Words and Output
(Flowchart)

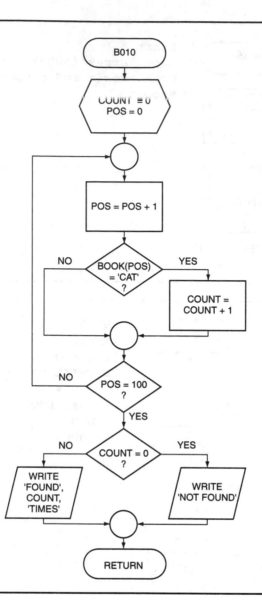

Figure 8–14
Counting Words—Count
Words and Output
(Pseudocode)

```
B010
Enter
COUNT = 0
POS = 0
DOUNTIL POS = 100
   POS = POS + 1
   IF BOOK(POS) = 'CAT' THEN
      COUNT = COUNT + 1
   (ELSE)
   ENDIF
ENDDO
IF COUNT = 0 THEN
   Write 'Not found'
ELSE
   Write 'Found', COUNT, 'times'
ENDIF
Return
```

Sample Problem 8.4 (Doubling an Array)

Problem:

Input 50 values into an array called SINGLE. Create an array called DOUBLE that will contain the values in the array SINGLE, doubled. Output both arrays, SINGLE and DOUBLE.

Solution:

Figure 8–15 shows a structure chart consisting of six modules: A000 (overall control), B000 (input array), B010 (create array DOUBLE), B020 (output arrays), C000 (output array SINGLE), and C010 (output array DOUBLE).

Module B000 contains the steps to read the 50 values into the array SINGLE. Modules C000 and C010 contain the steps to write the 50 values from the arrays SINGLE and DOUBLE. Again, these modules contain processing steps equivalent to the algorithms shown in Figures 8–3 and 8–4. Module B020 simply calls upon C000 and C010 to output each array separately; it is therefore not shown here.

Figure 8–16 shows the actual steps to create the array DOUBLE. Notice that the values for DOUBLE do not need to be input; rather, they are generated from the values already input into the array SINGLE.

Sample Problem 8.5 (Squaring and Cubing an Array)

Problem:

Create and output two arrays containing the squares and cubes of the numbers from 1 to 100.

Solution:

Figure 8–17 shows a structure chart consisting of five modules: A000 (overall control), B000 (create arrays SQUARE and CUBE), B010 (output arrays), C000 (output array SQUARE), and C010 (output array CUBE).

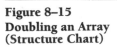

Figure 8–15
Doubling an Array
(Structure Chart)

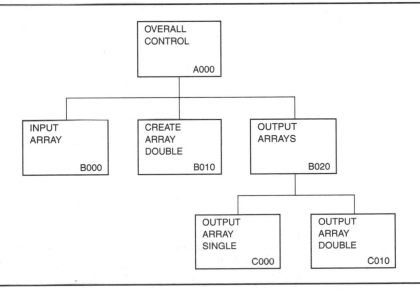

Figure 8–16
Doubling an Array—Create
Array DOUBLE

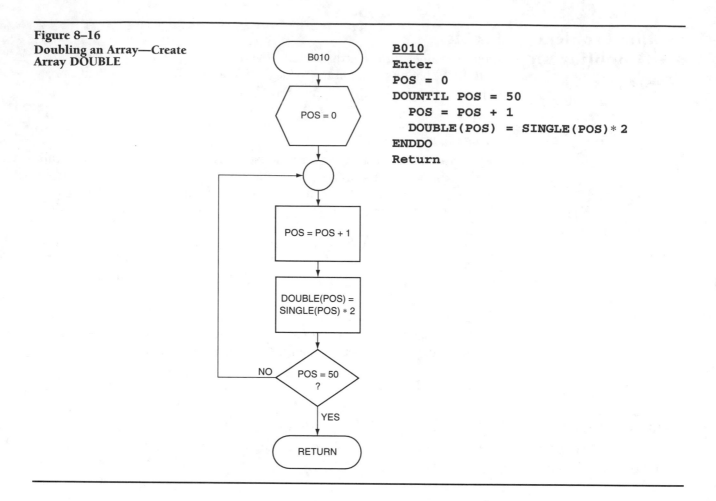

```
B010
Enter
POS = 0
DOUNTIL POS = 50
  POS = POS + 1
  DOUBLE(POS) = SINGLE(POS) * 2
ENDDO
Return
```

Figure 8–17
Squaring and Cubing an
Array (Structure Chart)

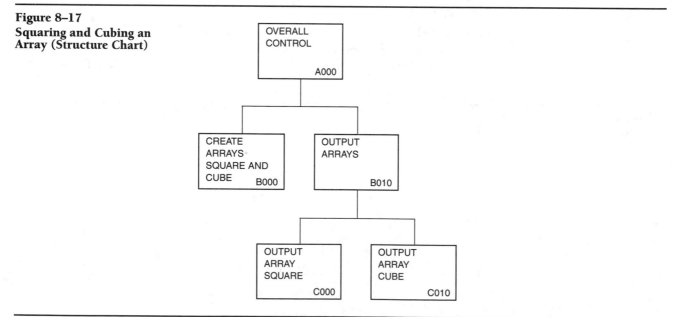

Modules C000 and C010 contain the steps to write the 100 values from the arrays SQUARE and CUBE. Again, these modules contain processing steps equivalent to the algorithm shown in Figure 8–4. Module B010 simply

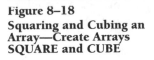
Figure 8–18
Squaring and Cubing an
Array—Create Arrays
SQUARE and CUBE

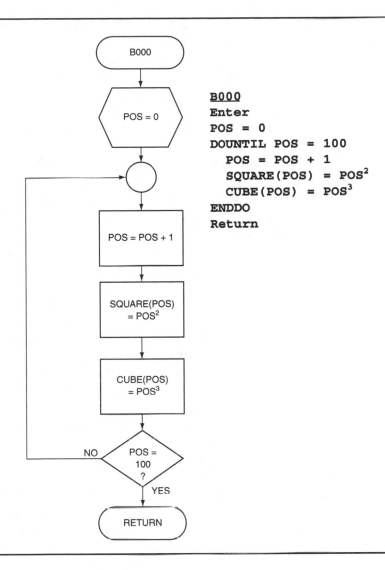

```
B000
Enter
POS = 0
DOUNTIL POS = 100
   POS = POS + 1
   SQUARE(POS) = POS²
   CUBE(POS) = POS³
ENDDO
Return
```

calls upon C000 and C010 to output each array separately, as module B020 did in the previous example.

Figure 8–18 shows the actual steps to create the arrays SQUARE and CUBE. Notice that the values for SQUARE and CUBE do not need to be input. Rather, they are generated from the value of the subscript represented by the variable POS.

The DOUNTIL control structure in Figure 8–18 controls subsequent processing, as it has in all the previous examples. It might be worth mentioning at this point that a DOWHILE loop also could have been used to control the processing in any of our examples. You may wish to convert the DOUNTIL loops in some of the modules to DOWHILE loops.

Table Structures

To refer to a specific element in any of the data groups discussed thus far, we have used a subscripted variable name containing only a single subscript [INAREA(1), INAREA(2), LIST(POS), where POS = 1,2, . . . ,n].

One subscript was sufficient to identify a particular element because each group had a very simple structure; it could be treated as a list. We say that such a group has one **dimension.**

In some problem situations it is convenient to treat a group of values as though it has more than one dimension. For example, instead of storing values as a list, we can store them as a **table.** Such a data group has two dimensions: **rows** and **columns.** A specific member of the group is identified by a subscripted variable name having two subscripts. The first subscript identifies a particular row; the second identifies a particular column. Here again, the terminology used for the data group varies. In COBOL, this kind of group is called a **two-level,** or **multilevel, table.** In Basic, Pascal, C, and C++, it may be called a **table, matrix, two-dimensional array,** or **multidimensional array.**

Tables are widely used in problem solving. To determine how much sales tax is owed on items purchased at a local supermarket, a checkout clerk may refer to sales tax tables. When preparing annual income tax returns, we refer to other types of tax tables. An insurance representative refers to rating tables to determine the premiums to be charged for insurance policies. Postal clerks refer to tables showing weights and distances to determine mailing costs. The results of market research and statistical analyses are often displayed in tabular form. To convert temperatures from Fahrenheit to Celsius, or to convert English measurements (inches, feet, yards, etc.) to metric units, we use tables. It should not surprise us, then, that tables are used widely in the computer-program representations of solution algorithms.

The table in Figure 8–19 contains numerical values arranged in four rows and five columns. M is the name of the table. Double-subscripted variables are used to refer to specific members of the table. For example, M(2,3) refers to the value in the second row and third column of the table, or 8. Similarly, M(4,1) refers to the value in the fourth row and first column, or 9. Multiplying the number of rows by the number of columns (4 × 5, in this example) gives the total number of elements in the table.

Figure 8–19
Two-Dimensional Array
Example

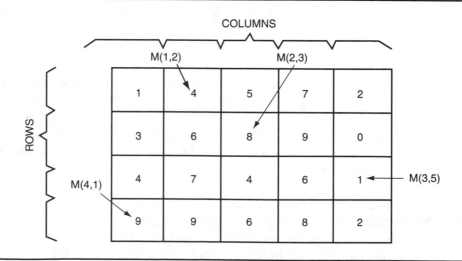

Table Examples

Figures 8–20, 8–21, and 8–22 illustrate three common procedures used in the processing of two-dimensional arrays. Figure 8–20 shows the processing steps required to initialize an array. Figure 8–21 shows the steps to input values into an array; and Figure 8–22 shows the steps to output values from an array. In all three examples the variables ROW and COL are used as subscripts to point to a particular member (or element) of an array called GRID. These algorithms use **row-processing logic:** All members of row 1 are

Figure 8–20
Initialize Two-Dimensional Array

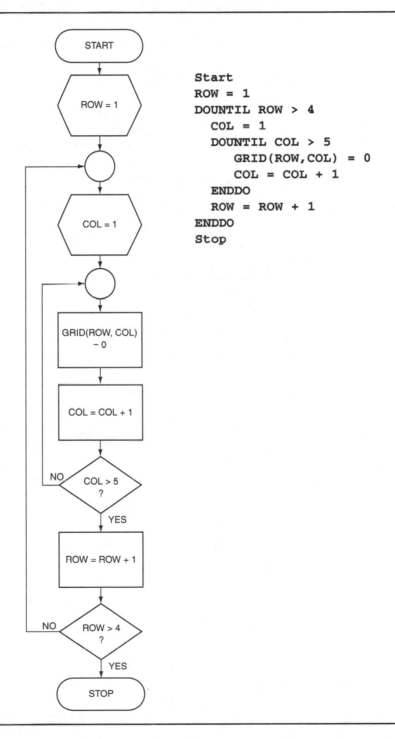

```
Start
ROW = 1
DOUNTIL ROW > 4
   COL = 1
   DOUNTIL COL > 5
      GRID(ROW,COL) = 0
      COL = COL + 1
   ENDDO
   ROW = ROW + 1
ENDDO
Stop
```

accessed first, starting with the value in the first column and proceeding to the value in the last (fifth) column. Then all members of row 2 are accessed, and so on. Nested DOUNTIL loops are used to set up the processing logic required. The inner DOUNTIL loop controls the initializing, reading, or writing of values into or from specific columns; the outer DOUNTIL loop controls the row in which these columns are located. Notice that all three algorithms contain the same processing steps to control the loop. The subscripts ROW and COL play two roles. They are used both as counters to control the DOUNTIL loops and as pointers into the array GRID.

Figure 8–21
Input Two-Dimensional Array

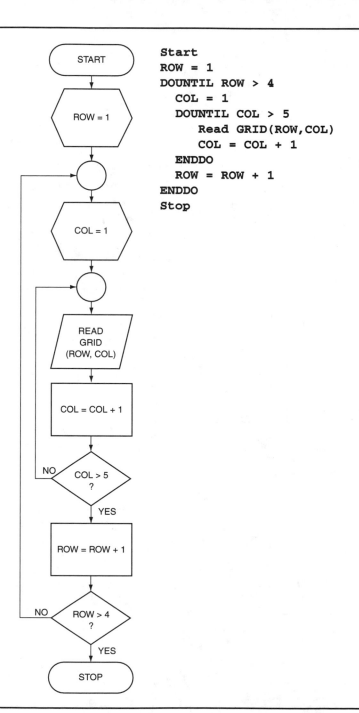

```
Start
ROW = 1
DOUNTIL ROW > 4
   COL = 1
   DOUNTIL COL > 5
      Read GRID(ROW,COL)
      COL = COL + 1
   ENDDO
   ROW = ROW + 1
ENDDO
Stop
```

Figure 8–22
Output Two-Dimensional Array

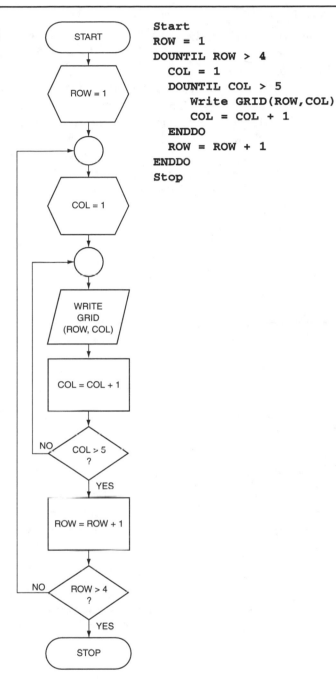

```
Start
ROW = 1
DOUNTIL ROW > 4
  COL = 1
  DOUNTIL COL > 5
     Write GRID(ROW,COL)
     COL = COL + 1
  ENDDO
  ROW = ROW + 1
ENDDO
Stop
```

**Sample Problem
8.6 (Two-
Dimensional
Array
Computation)**

Problem:

Input values into a two-dimensional array called A. A header record will contain two numbers representing the number of rows (M) and the number of columns (N) in the array A. Also, input N values into a one-dimensional array called V. Create and output an array called T that will be generated by multiplying each element in every row of A by the list element in the corresponding position in V.

Solution:

The structure chart shown in Figure 8–23 consists of four modules to do array processing. Figure 8–24 shows the logic within the overall control module.

The first module that is executed reads values into consecutive storage locations as a two-dimensional group, Table A. The flowchart and pseudocode representations of the algorithm are shown in Figure 8–25. The first pair of values submitted as input indicates the number of rows (M) and the number of columns (N) to be read. Specific members (elements) of the table are entered row by row, one member at a time. The algorithm uses row-processing logic and contains the same processing steps as shown in Figure 8–21.

After all members of the table have been read into storage (i.e., when both the inner DOUNTIL and the outer DOUNTIL have been exited), control is returned to the overall control module. Specific values from the table can now be used in subsequent processing.

Figure 8–23
Two-Dimensional Array
Computation (Structure
Chart)

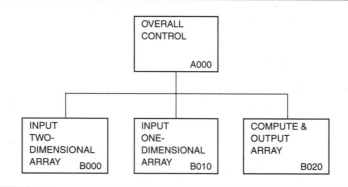

Figure 8–24
Two-Dimensional Array
Computation—Overall
Control

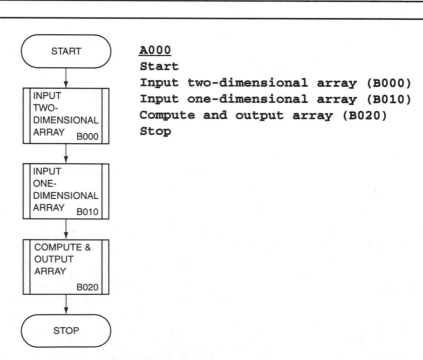

The next module that is executed reads a second group of data items—a list having N elements. Figure 8–26 shows the reading of input into the list V in flowchart and pseudocode forms. Note the similarities and differences between this part of the algorithm and the logic in Figure 8–3.

Figure 8–25
Two-Dimensional Array
Computation—Input
Two-Dimensional Array

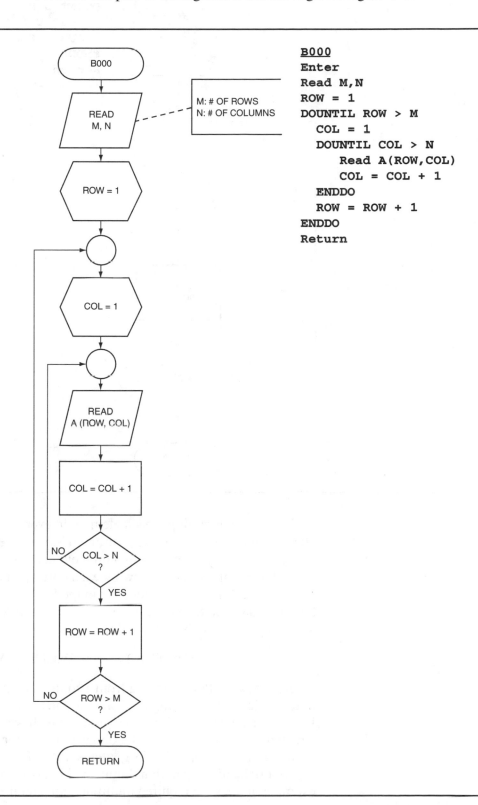

```
B000
Enter
Read M,N
ROW = 1
DOUNTIL ROW > M
   COL = 1
   DOUNTIL COL > N
      Read A(ROW,COL)
      COL = COL + 1
   ENDDO
   ROW = ROW + 1
ENDDO
Return
```

Figure 8–26
Two-Dimensional Array
Computation—Input
One-Dimensional Array

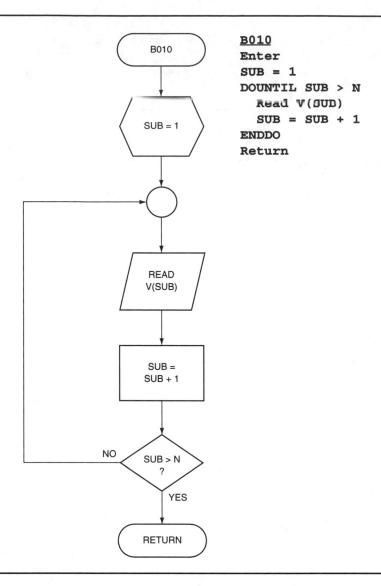

```
B010
Enter
SUB = 1
DOUNTIL SUB > N
  Read V(SUB)
  SUB = SUB + 1
ENDDO
Return
```

We are now to multiply each element in every row of the table by the list element in the corresponding position in V. First we multiply each element of the first row by each corresponding element of the list; then we multiply each element of the second row by each corresponding element of the list; and so on. The number of elements in the list must be the same as the number of columns in the table. In our example, with A representing the table and V representing the list, we find

$$T(ROW,COL) = A(ROW,COL) * V(COL)$$

repeatedly, with ROW ranging from 1 to the total number of rows (M) in the table, and COL ranging from 1 to the total number of columns (N). In effect, a new two-dimensional group, which we have called T, is constructed element by element. Its dimensions are the same as the dimensions of the original table, A, but its contents differ. Each value in T is the result of a multiplication operation. Figure 8–27 shows module B020 in this example; it does the required multiplication and the printing of the new table, T. Documentation within the annotation symbols helps to explain some of the steps.

Figure 8–27
Two-Dimensional Array
Computation—Compute
and Output Array

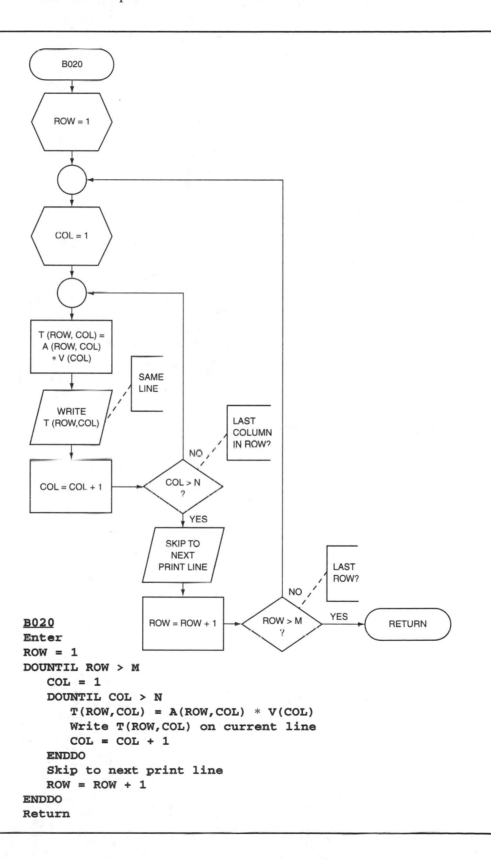

```
B020
Enter
ROW = 1
DOUNTIL ROW > M
    COL = 1
    DOUNTIL COL > N
        T(ROW,COL) = A(ROW,COL) * V(COL)
        Write T(ROW,COL) on current line
        COL = COL + 1
    ENDDO
    Skip to next print line
    ROW = ROW + 1
ENDDO
Return
```

Multidimensional Structures

Some programming languages allow specification of data groups with 200 or more dimensions. In all cases, the number of a group's dimensions determines the number of subscripts needed to refer to a particular element of the group. Although groups with many dimensions are difficult or impossible for us to visualize, they may be extremely useful in computation. The same kind of program logic—loops within loops—can be used repetitively for all data groups.

The system designer or programmer who develops an algorithm involving multidimensional data groups should be aware of the programming language that will be used to express the algorithm in computer-program form. Some programming languages read, write, and store the data items in a group in **row-major order** (with the first subscript varying least rapidly, and the last subscript varying most rapidly). We assumed such logic was used in our example above. However, some programming languages read, write, and store the data items in a group in **column-major order** (with the first subscript varying most rapidly, and the last subscript varying least rapidly). The logic within the solution algorithm must be set up according to the specifications of the language being used—otherwise, the computer cannot process the data efficiently. To understand why, consider a simple analogy. Assume you are shopping at a local supermarket. Do you try to select all the items you want from aisle 1, then all from aisle 2, then all from aisle 3, and so on? Or do you prefer to select oranges from the fruits/vegetables section, then syrup from aisle 3, then bacon from the meat counter, then onions (which are, in fact, positioned right next to the oranges), and then return to aisle 3 for strawberrry jam?

Now look at Figure 8–28. If row-major ordering is used, the table shown in Figure 8–19 is processed as shown in the first column of Figure 8–28. In con-

**Figure 8–28
Two-Dimensional Array
Ordering**

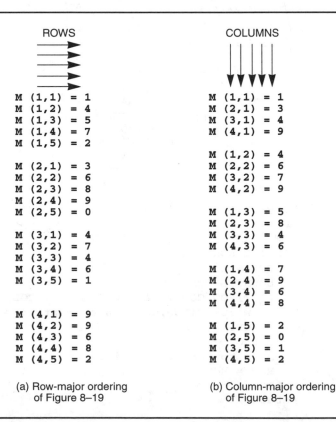

(a) Row-major ordering
of Figure 8–19

(b) Column-major ordering
of Figure 8–19

trast, the second column of Figure 8–28 shows column-major ordering of the same table. Pascal, C, Basic, and COBOL are designed to store and process data groups in row-major order as in Figure 8–28a. Some implementations of Basic, however, may store and process data groupings in column-major order. It is important to find out which of the two orderings has been used in the Basic implementation available to you. FORTRAN uses column-major ordering as in Figure 8–28b. In either approach, the total numbers of elements in the various dimensions of the data groups are often specified as loop controls.

Enrichment (Basic)

Figure 8–29 illustrates a listing of the program for the Finding the Smallest Number Problem (Figures 8–6 and 8–7). We have modified this example to include an additional module—Output Array (B020).

Figure 8–29
Finding the Smallest Number (Basic List)

```
DECLARE SUB ComputeAndOutputSmall ()
DECLARE SUB OutputArray ()
DECLARE SUB InputArray ()

REM A000 - Overall Control Module
DIM SHARED LISTOFVALS(10)
CALL InputArray
CALL OutputArray
CALL ComputeAndOutputSmall
END

REM B000
SUB InputArray
SUBVAL = 0
PRINT "Enter ten numbers, one per line"
DO
        SUBVAL = SUBVAL + 1
        INPUT LISTOFVALS(SUBVAL)
LOOP UNTIL SUBVAL = 10
END SUB

REM B010
SUB ComputeAndOutputSmall
SMALL = LISTOFVALS(1)
SUBVAL = 1
DO
        SUBVAL = SUBVAL + 1
        IF LISTOFVALS(SUBVAL)< SMALL THEN
                SMALL = LISTOFVALS(SUBVAL)
        END IF
LOOP UNTIL SUBVAL = 10
PRINT
PRINT "The smallest number in the list is "; SMALL
END SUB

REM B020
SUB OutputArray
SUBVAL = 0
PRINT
PRINT "The numbers in the list are:"
DO
        SUBVAL = SUBVAL + 1
        PRINT LISTOFVALS(SUBVAL);
LOOP UNTIL SUBVAL = 10
END SUB
```

Figure 8–30
Finding the Smallest
Number (Basic Run)

```
Enter ten numbers, one per line
?6
?8
?5
?3
?9
?7
?6
?9
?4
?8

The numbers in the list are:
6 8 5 3 9 7 6 9 4 8
The smallest number in the list is  3
```

The program begins with three declaration statements specifying the name of each subprogram that will be invoked during program execution. The overall control module is very similar to the pseudocode in Figure 8–6. In this example, however, we invoke an additional module—B020—to output the values of the array. The first statement in the overall control module is a *Dim* statement that specifies the size of the array. In this case, ten memory locations are specified to hold the values of the array named LISTOFVALS. In addition, since the array is global in scope, the keyword Shared must also be included in the Dim statement. Remember that in Basic we must include a Shared statement for each global variable. In this example, the Shared statement is placed in the overall control module because the shared variable is an array. It is not necessary to include the Shared statement within each subprogram as we did in Chapter 5.

The program statements for each module or subprogram are listed after the overall control module. The statements in B000, B010, and B020 are very similar to the pseudocode in Figures 8–3, 8–4, and 8–7. Note that the variable SUBVAL is used in the three subprograms. SUBVAL holds the value of the index, or subscript, of the array LISTOFVALS. There is no Shared statement included for SUBVAL because SUBVAL is not a global variable. SUBVAL is local to each subprogram. We could just as easily have used three different variables to represent the index of the array LISTOFVALS in each of our three subprograms.

Figure 8–30 illustrates the output that will be produced when the program is executed. The user is prompted to enter the ten numbers, one per line. Each of these numbers is stored in one location in the array LISTOF-VALS. After all ten numbers are input, the contents of the array are output. Note that all the numbers are printed on one line. Placing a semicolon at the end of the Print statement in module B020 prevents a linefeed from occurring each time the Print statement is executed. Finally, the smallest value in the list is output with an identifying label.

Enrichment (Visual Basic)

Arrays can be used to represent data in a program as we saw in this chapter. They can also be used to group controls created in a Visual Basic program.

An array that is used to group controls is called a *control array*. The following example (Shape Problem) illustrates the concept of a control array. The graphical interface for the Shape Problem is shown in Figure 8–31.

In this example, four command buttons are created and grouped together into a control array. A control array is created for a group of controls by giving all controls the same name. Each command button is given the name cmd_SHAPE. Each individual array item is actually one of the command buttons and is uniquely identified by an index. This index is similar to the index or subscript used with an array of data. The index is automatically assigned by Visual Basic when each control in a control array is created. In this example the index is assigned as follows:

Command Button	Index Value
Rectangle	0
Square	1
Oval	2
Circle	3

The Rectangle command button can be referenced in code as cmd_SHAPE(0), the Square command button can be referenced in code as cmd_SHAPE(1), and so on. Note that Visual Basic assigns a value of 0 to the first index in each control array. Zero is the default value and can be changed by the programmer. Although the names of the command buttons in the control array must be identical, the caption of each command button can be unique. For example, the caption of the first command button is "Rectangle." The caption is simply a way to label the control on the interface.

Figure 8–31
Shape Problem
(Visual Basic—
Screen 1)

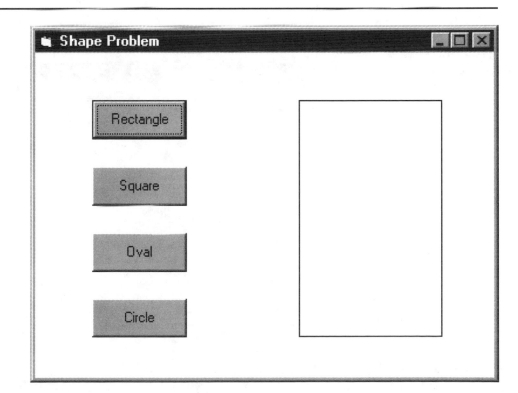

When the user clicks the first command button (Rectangle), a rectangle shape appears on the right of the interface, as shown in Figure 8–31. Similarly, when the user clicks any of the other command buttons, the corresponding shape is displayed, as shown in Figures 8–32, 8–33, and 8–34.

Figure 8–32
Shape Problem (Visual Basic—Screen 2)

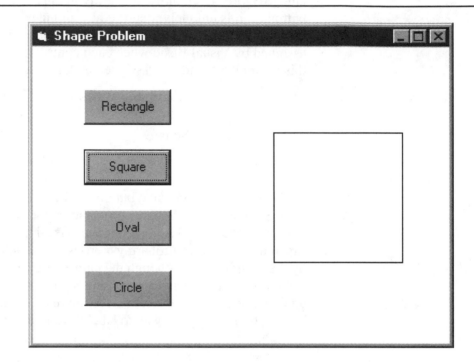

Figure 8–33
Shape Problem (Visual Basic—Screen 3)

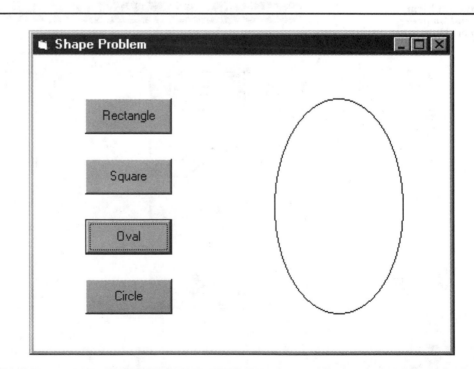

Figure 8–34
Shape Problem (Visusal Basic—Screen 4)

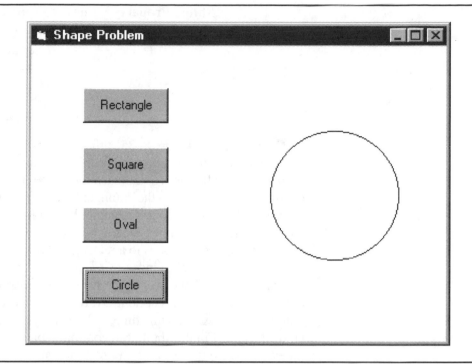

Figure 8–35
Shape Problem (Visual Basic—cmd_SHAPE_Click)

```
Private Sub cmd_SHAPE_Click(Index As Integer)

shp_SHAPE.Shape = Index

End Sub
```

Figure 8–35 illustrates the program that is associated with the click event of each command button. Since the four command buttons constitute a control array, only one click event is written. The first statement in this event includes a parameter (Indcx As Integer), an integer variable automatically generated by Visual Basic. This variable identifies which command button was actually clicked by the user. If thc user clicked the Rectangle button, the value of Index will be 0 when the event code is executed. If the user clicked the Square button, the value of Index will be 1 when the event code is executed. If the user clicked the Oval button, the valuc of Index will be 2 when the event code is executed. Finally, if the user clicked the Circle button, the value of Index will be 3 when the event code is executed. The programmer can then refer to the value of Index. In this example, the value of Index is assigned to the *shape* property of a *shape* control named shp_SHAPE.

A shape control is used in Visual Basic to display various shapes. The name of a shape control begins with *shp* as specified by standard naming conventions. The shape control in this example is named shp_SHAPE and is used to display one of four different shapes. The shape property of a shape control defines the type of shape that will be displayed as follows:

Shape Property Value	Type of Shape
0	Rectangle
1	Square
2	Oval
3	Circle
4	Rounded Rectangle
5	Rounded Square

The program in Figure 8–35, although simple, is quite powerful. The command buttons were created in a specific sequence to ensure that the index of each command button would match the shape property value of the shape control corresponding to the command button's caption. For example, the first command button (caption: Rectangle) has an index of 0 since it was the first button created. Remember, indices begin at 0. At the same time, a shape property value of 0 corresponds to a rectangle shape. The second command button (caption: Square) has an index of 1 since it was the second button created. At the same time, a shape property value of 1 corresponds to a square shape. The third command button (caption: Oval) has an index of 2 since it was the third button created. At the same time, a shape property value of 2 corresponds to an oval shape. Finally, the fourth command button (caption: Circle) has an index of 3 since it was the fourth button created. At the same time, a shape property value of 3 corresponds to a circle shape. Clearly, our choice to use a control array for the command buttons and relate the index to the shape property of the shape control greatly simplified the program. A well-thought-out interface is essential in the design of a Visual Basic program.

Key Terms

single (simple) variable
single-level table
list
vector
one-dimensional array
subscript
index
unsubscripted variable
   name

subscripted variable
   name
member (of an array)
element (of an array)
dimension
table
row
column
two-level table

multilevel table
matrix
two-dimensional array
multidimensional
   array
row-processing logic
row-major order
column-major order

Exercises

1. (a) What is a data group?
   (b) Give some examples of data for which grouping capabilities are likely to be appropriate.

2. Using the term *COLOR(I)*, distinguish between an array name, a subscript, and a subscripted variable name.

3. E is an eight-member one-dimensional array. Its contents are shown as follows:

57	12	03	48	34	16	50	22

(a) What is the content of E(4)?

(b) Write the subscripted variable name that should be used to refer to the location containing 57.

(c) Write the subscripted variable name that should be used to refer to the Rth position in the array E.

(d) The variable R, in (c) above, must have a value within a range between what two numbers?

4. Refer to Figures 8–3 through 8–7. Modify either the program flowchart or the pseudocode as suggested in this chapter to show how to find the smallest of any number of values.

5. Modify either the program flowchart or the pseudocode in Figure 8–7 to keep track of which position in LIST contains the smallest value. The position of the smallest value and the value itself should be provided as output.

6. A is a 30-member two-dimensional array with six rows and five columns. S is a simple variable. The contents of these locations have been set to 0; they appear as follows:

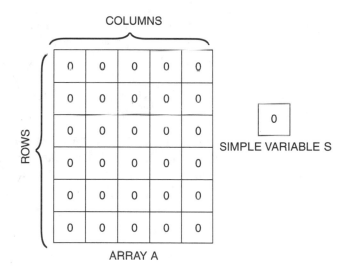

Show the contents of these locations after the following statements have been executed:

$$S = 5$$
$$A(2,4) = 40$$
$$A(1,2) = 67$$
$$A(6,2) = A(4,3) + A(2,4)$$
$$A(S,1) = 99$$
$$A(5,4) = A(1,2) - A(2,S-1)$$

7. **(a)** Construct a program flowchart and corresponding pseudocode to show the logic required in the following problem situation. Read a two-level table called SALES into storage. The table has three rows and each row contains 18 values. Compute the total value of the elements in each row. Provide three computed totals and a grand total, which is the sum of all values, as output. Be sure to plan a well-structured, modular program.

   (b) Modify your solution to the problem in (a) to total the values of the elements in each column. Provide the column totals as well as the grand total as output. Note that only one of the two solutions to this exercise will be efficient. The other solution will be very inefficient, depending on which programming language is used.

   (c) Modify your solutions to the problems in (a) and (b) to compute and output averages instead of totals.

8. Construct a program flowchart and corresponding pseudocode to show the logic required in the following problem. Read into storage a two-level table, called MATRIX, that has five rows and five columns. Compute and output the sum of the elements on each of the two diagonals in the table MATRIX. Be sure to plan a well-structured, modular program. Remember to keep efficiency in mind when designing the order in which the elements will be processed.

9. Construct a program flowchart and corresponding pseudocode to show the logic required in the following problem. Read numbers into a ten-element one-dimensional array called LIST. Create another ten-element one-dimensional array called REVERSE that is to contain the same elements as LIST but in reverse order. For example, the first element in LIST will be placed in the last position in REVERSE; the second element in LIST will be placed in the second-to-last position in REVERSE; and so on. After REVERSE has been created, output the contents of both arrays. Be sure to plan a well-structured, modular program.

10. Construct a program flowchart and corresponding pseudocode for an algorithm that searches a 4×5 table named M (to be input) and counts all the occurrences of the items that match the value of MVAL, which will also be input. Output table M in row-order fashion and output a line at the end identifying how many times MVAL was found in table M. Be sure to plan a well-structured, modular program.

11. A, B, and C are one-dimensional arrays of size 100, 50, and 200, respectively. Construct a program flowchart and corresponding pseudocode for an algorithm to store the first 100 numbers (1,2,3,4,5, . . . ,100) into array A, the first 50 positive odd numbers (1,3,5,7, . . .) into array B, and the reciprocal of each position [C(5) = 1/5] into array C. After

all the arrays have been defined, output each array. Notice that no input is required. Be sure to plan a well-structured, modular program.

12. Construct a program flowchart and corresponding pseudocode to solve the following problem. Read the items for two ten-element arrays named I1 and I2. Each item can be assumed to be on a separate record. Multiply the items in array I1 by the items in corresponding positions in array I2. For example, I1(1) is multiplied by I2(1); I1(2) is multiplied by I2(2); and so on. The resulting products are to be stored in the corresponding item positions in a ten-element array called I3. When the multiplication process is complete, output the items for each array. Be sure to plan a well-structured, modular program.

9 Object-Oriented Programming Concepts

Objectives

Upon completion of this chapter you should be able to

- Distinguish between object-oriented design and procedure-oriented design.
- Define the terms *class* and *object.*
- Distinguish between a data member and a method.
- Define the term *encapsulation.*
- Explain the purpose of a driver program.
- Define the term *instantiation.*
- Explain the purpose of a constructor and a destructor.
- Distinguish between parameters and arguments.
- Define the terms *overloading* and *overriding.*
- Explain what is meant by inheritance.
- Explain what is meant by polymorphism.
- Distinguish between a base class and a derived class.

Introduction

In traditional procedure-oriented design of programs, the emphasis is on doing things, that is, on performing actions and on the sequence of those actions—the data is secondary. As procedure-oriented programs increase in complexity, they become increasingly difficult for programmers to understand and thus more expensive to maintain. In addition, as graphical user interfaces have gained popularity, programming issues are changing. Programs must be designed to allow users to interact frequently with computers. The programs must be easy to use. Thus, the emphasis today is on developing window-based programs. It is difficult if not impossible, however, to design programs that handle multiple windows using a procedure-oriented approach. Therefore, development teams are looking for alternatives.

Object-oriented programming is a methodology that bases the design of an application around the data to be manipulated and the operations to be performed on the data. The general characteristics of a window (the data) are defined in abstract form. A single program may include many windows that assist users in interacting with the system. The window

213

abstraction is usually implemented by means of a construct called a **class.** Many types of classes may be used when designing a program.

Classes

Object-oriented design is based upon organizing a program around a collection of classes. A class represents a template from which **objects** can be created. Thus, you could design a general Window class from which individual objects (windows) could be created. A class definition contains both **data** and **behavior.** The data describes what an object looks like, and the behavior describes what an object does. The data that defines a class can also be referred to as **properties, data members** (of the class), or **instance variables.** The behaviors can also be referred to as **methods** or **member functions.** We will use the terms *data members* and *methods* from this point forward.

GradeBook Class

As an example, you could define a class called GradeBook, which could contain five data members—Name, Grade1, Grade2, Grade3, and Average. In addition, the GradeBook class could contain a method to input a student's name and three grades (GetStudent), a method to compute the average of the three grades (ComputeAverage), and a method to output the student's name and average (ShowStudent). Figure 9–1 illustrates the class GradeBook.

As you can see, Figure 9–1 clearly shows the data members and methods associated with the class GradeBook. Both the data members and the methods are encapsulated within the class. The term **encapsulation** means that a data member can be accessed and manipulated only using one of the methods defined for it as part of the class definition. Encapsulation is also called **data hiding.** Figure 9–2 illustrates pseudocode used to represent the class GradeBook.

The title statement (Class GradeBook) identifies and names the class. The End Class statement simply defines the end of the statements that make up the class. All statements inside the class are indented for readability. The first part of the class definition specifies the data members and their range of accessibility. Since all the data members are defined as

**Figure 9–1
GradeBook Class
Abstraction**

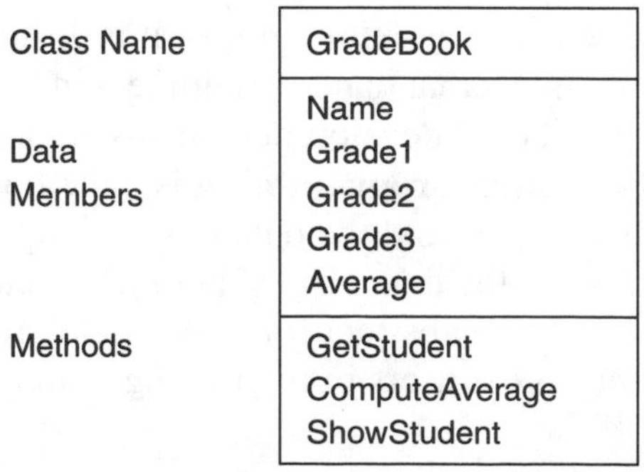

Class Name	GradeBook
Data Members	Name Grade1 Grade2 Grade3 Average
Methods	GetStudent ComputeAverage ShowStudent

**Figure 9–2
GradeBook Class
Implementation 1**

```
Class GradeBook
        private Name
        private Grade1
        private Grade2
        private Grade3
        private Average
        public GetStudent
                Input Name, Grade1, Grade2, Grade3
        End
        public ComputeAverage
                Average = (Grade1 + Grade2 + Grade3)/3
        End
        public ShowStudent
                Display Name, Average
        End
End Class
```

private, they cannot be accessed from anywhere outside the class. That is, only the methods within the class can access these data members. The next group of statements shows the implementation of the three methods defined for the class. Since these methods are defined as *public*, they can be accessed from anywhere in the program, within or outside the class. The code within each method is simple and should be familiar to you at this point.

Once a class is defined, it can be used when building a program. A program begins by creating an instance of the class, called an object. An object is a tangible representation of the data members and methods of the class to which it belongs. For example, a program could create two grade books, that is, two objects belonging to the GradeBook class. Each object has its own set of data members and methods as defined in the GradeBook class. Note that the class is simply a template or an interface with the programmer. It is not until a programmer creates an object of that class that a representation of a real grade book exists. This concept is illustrated in Figure 9–3.

Driver Program— GradeBook Example

Now let's take a look at pseudocode (Figure 9–4) for a program that actually creates and interfaces with the objects we've discussed. This type of program is sometimes referred to as a **driver program;** it is, the program that gets things going. Our example illustrates one type of driver program, a relatively simple one. On a larger scale, driver programs can be fairly complex and are used in a wide range of contexts. This driver program is the program that actually creates and manipulates the objects of a particular class. The process of creating an object, or more precisely, of creating an instance of an object, is called **instantiation.**

In this example, the first two statements cause two objects to be created from the class GradeBook—GradeBook1 and GradeBook2. Each statement consists of a class name and a colon followed by an object name.

Figure 9–3
GradeBook Class Objects

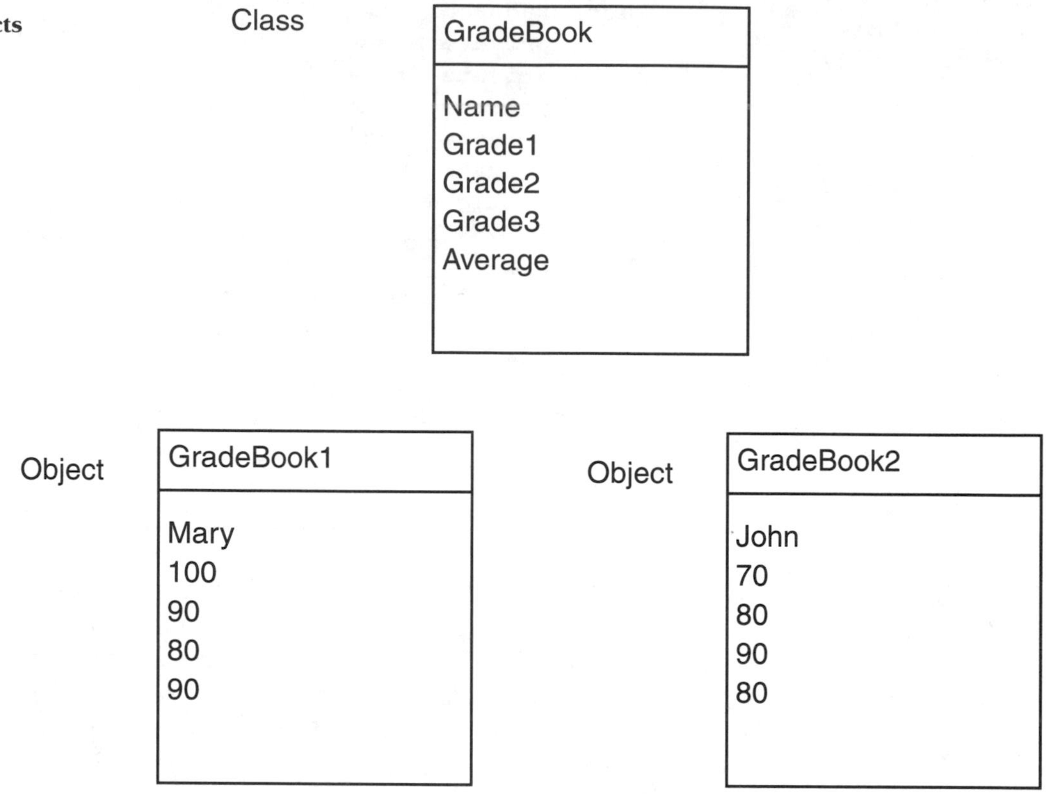

Class

```
GradeBook

Name
Grade1
Grade2
Grade3
Average
```

Object
```
GradeBook1

Mary
100
90
80
90
```

Object
```
GradeBook2

John
70
80
90
80
```

Figure 9–4
GradeBook Class Driver—
Example 1

```
Start
GradeBook: GradeBook1
GradeBook: GradeBook2
GradeBook1.GetStudent
GradeBook2.GetStudent
GradeBook1.ComputeAverage
GradeBook2.ComputeAverage
GradeBook1.ShowStudent
GradeBook2.ShowStudent
Stop
```

Subsequent statements show how methods are invoked for the objects. As you can see, in our pseudocode, methods are invoked using the notation

object.method.

This notation expresses the notion that we are sending a message to an object. The statement GradeBook1.GetStudent sends a message to the object GradeBook1 to execute the code in the method GetStudent. When the method GetStudent executes, the user of the program will be prompted to enter a name and three grades. The entries will be stored in the variables named Name, Grade1, Grade2, and Grade3 associated with the object GradeBook1 by the input method within the object. Similarly, the next statement causes four more input values to be stored in the variables named Name, Grade1, Grade2, and Grade3 associated with the object GradeBook2.

You might wonder how two different values can be stored in what appears to be the same variable—Name. Remember, each object has its own set of data members. Thus the user may have input "Mary" the first time and "John" the second time. In that case, we could use a similar "dot" notation to say that GradeBook1.Name is now equal to "Mary" and GradeBook2.Name is now equal to "John". Note, however, that we would get an error message if we included the statement GradeBook1.Name in our driver program. Name is a private variable and cannot be referred to outside the object. In contrast, since the methods are public, they can be invoked from outside the object, as shown in our driver program.

After the data for each object is input, the ComputeAverage method for each object is invoked, as is the ShowStudent method. Note that when the ShowStudent method is invoked, Name and Average are displayed, but which name and average? The object invoking the method determines which set of data will be accessed. When GradeBook1.ShowStudent is invoked, GradeBook1.Name and GradeBook1.Average are displayed. When GradeBook2.ShowStudent is invoked, GradeBook2.Name and GradeBook2.Average are displayed.

Constructors

When an object is created in the driver routine, memory is allocated automatically for that object. This memory allocation is done by a special program that we will refer to as a **constructor.** A default constructor is called every time an object is created. However, this constructor does not necessarily initialize any of the data members. For example, if the Compute-Average method were invoked before the GetStudent method, the data members representing the three grades would be undefined. When the computer attempted to add the three grades, an error would occur. To prevent this problem, we can define our own constructor. The constructor will be just another method in the class except that it will have the same name as the class. This name will identify it as a constructor.

Unlike other methods, a constructor is executed automatically for an object when that object is created. Constructors do not need to be explicitly invoked as other methods do. Figure 9–5 illustrates a simple constructor for the GradeBook class. As you can see, this constructor simply sets all the data members to initial values. In this way, all the data will be defined as soon as the object is created.

Although this constructor solves the problem of undefined data, it is not very interesting. Consider a different constructor, as shown in Figure 9–6.

Figure 9–5
GradeBook Class Constructor (no parameters)

```
public GradeBook
        Name = "Any Student"
        Grade1 = 0
        Grade2 = 0
        Grade3 = 0
        Average = 0
End
```

**Figure 9–6
GradeBook Class
Constructor (Four
Parameters)**

```
public GradeBook(AnyName,AnyGr1,AnyGr2,AnyGr3)
        Name = AnyName
        Grade1 = AnyGr1
        Grade2 = AnyGr2
        Grade3 = AnyGr3
        Average = 0
End
```

This constructor makes use of a list of **parameters** placed in parentheses after the constructor name. The parameters are simply a list of four variable names that act as placeholders. We will modify the driver program so that when a new object is created, the driver program will provide initial values for the first four data members in the list as follows:

GradeBook: AnotherBook("Sally", 100, 90, 80)

This statement causes a new object called AnotherBook to be created. When the constructor is executed, the four values (called **arguments**) in the parentheses are assigned to the four variables in the constructor parameter list as follows:

AnyName = "Sally"

AnyGr1 = 100

AnyGr2 = 90

AnyGr3 = 80

This constructor is more flexible because now the initial values of the first four data members can be determined when the object is created. Of course, the user can still invoke the GetStudent method to input new values for the name and three grades during program execution. Note that the average is still initialized to 0 by the constructor since there is no variable in the parameter list that corresponds to it.

Overloading

Figure 9–7 shows the complete class description of GradeBook with both constructors included. You'll note that both constructors have the same name—the name of the class. How, then, does the computer know which one to execute? When an object is created, the number and type of arguments determine which constructor will be called. For example, the statement GradeBook:MyGradeBook (no arguments) will call the first constructor, and the statement GradeBook:YourGradeBook("Tom", 70, 80, 80) (four arguments) will call the second constructor. The ability to use the same method name to invoke different methods that perform different actions based on the number or type of arguments in the method invocation is called **overloading.**

Another example of overloading can be seen in some computer languages. In some languages, the plus (+) operator will *add* two numbers or *concatenate* (put together) two strings as follows: 3 + 4 = 7 but "3" + "4" = 34. In this example it is the type of argument (numeric or string) that determines whether to add or to concatenate.

Figure 9–7
GradeBook Class
Implementation 2

```
Class GradeBook
        private Name
        private Grade1
        private Grade2
        private Grade3
        private Average
        public GradeBook
                Name = "Any Student"
                Grade1 = 0
                Grade2 = 0
                Grade3 = 0
                Average = 0
        End
        public GradeBook(AnyName,AnyGr1,AnyGr2,AnyGr3)
                Name = AnyName
                Grade1 = AnyGr1
                Grade2 = AnyGr2
                Grade3 = AnyGr3
                Average = 0
        End
        public GetStudent
                Input Name, Grade1, Grade2, Grade3
        End
        public ComputeAverage
                Average = (Grade1 + Grade2 + Grade3)/3
        End
        public ShowStudent
                Display Name, Average
        End
End Class
```

Now let's take a look at a new driver program, shown in Figure 9–8. This program creates three objects of the GradeBook class. When objects GradeBook1 and GradeBook2 are created, the first constructor for each object is called because no arguments are included in the object creation statement. When the object GradeBook3 is created, the second constructor is called since there are four arguments in the object creation statement. Note that in this example the GetStudent method is invoked only for GradeBook1 and the ComputeAverage method is invoked only for GradeBook2 and GradeBook3.

Let us assume that when the GetStudent method is invoked for the object GradeBook1, the user enters the data "Pat", 100, 100, 100. Figure 9–9 shows the output when the ShowStudent method is invoked for each object. The data members of GradeBook1 are initialized by the constructor and then reset to the specific values entered by the user when the method GetStudent is called. Note, however, that the average is never computed for GradeBook1 since the ComputeAverage routine isn't called for that object. Thus an average of 0 is displayed on the first line. Although the ComputeAverage method is invoked for GradeBook2, the values for Grade1, Grade2, and Grade3 are still 0. (Remember that they were set to 0

Figure 9–8
GradeBook Class Driver—
Example 2

```
Start
GradeBook: GradeBook1
GradeBook: GradeBook2
GradeBook: GradeBook3("Sally",100,90,80)
GradeBook1.GetStudent
GradeBook2.ComputeAverage
GradeBook3.ComputeAverage
GradeBook1.ShowStudent
GradeBook2.ShowStudent
GradeBook3.ShowStudent
Stop
```

by the constructor.) Thus an average of 0 is displayed on the second line. Can you see why the name "Any Student" is displayed? The third object is created using the second constructor. Since no additional data is input, the ComputeAverage routine uses the values for Grade1 (100), Grade2 (90), and Grade3 (80) that were set up when the constructor executed. The average is computed to be 90 in the ComputeAverage method and the name is "Sally" as set up by the constructor. Make sure that you understand how each object manipulates its own data. Write some variations of the driver program and see what output results.

Destructors

Just as constructors may be executed when objects are created, **destructors** may be executed when objects are destroyed. In our examples so far, a default destructor is executed for each object. The destructor de-allocates the memory for that object. As with constructors, we can write our own destructors. Since destructors are less commonly specified explicitly, they will not be covered in this book.

Inheritance

One of the powers of object-oriented design is class reusability. Once a class is tested and ready for use, it can be included in a class library. Other programmers can incorporate these preexisting classes into their own programs without "reinventing the wheel." In this way, the amount of required testing and debugging is limited to that needed for the new parts of the program created by the programmer.

Suppose, however, that a programmer wanted to use a class that was very close to what he or she needed but was missing some key data or

Figure 9–9
GradeBook Class Driver
Output

Pat	0
Any Student	0
Sally	90

Figure 9–10
Inheritance Diagram—
Employee Example

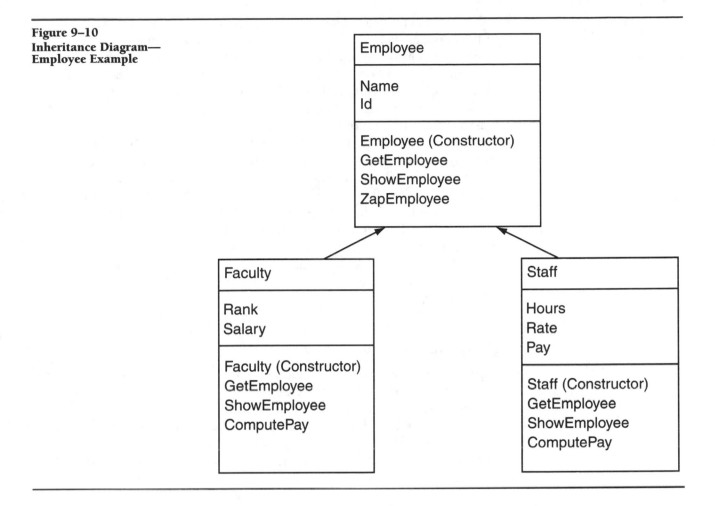

behavior necessary to accomplish the task. Rather than rewrite the entire class, the programmer could derive a subclass from the original class. This subclass would contain all the data members and methods of the original class (from the class library), as well as any additional data members and methods that the programmer incorporates. This mechanism, called **inheritance,** is a means by which one class acquires the data and methods of another class. The concept of inheritance is shown in Figure 9–10.

Base and Derived Classes

Figure 9–10 illustrates an inheritance diagram showing an original class named Employee and two subclasses named Faculty and Staff. The Employee class is the **base class** containing data members and methods that apply to a general employee. For example, all employees have a name and an id. The base class is also called a **parent class** or a **super class.** The Faculty and Staff classes are both derived from the base class Employee. A **derived class** is also called a **child class** or a **subclass.** The Faculty class, for example, includes two additional data members—Rank and Salary— and the Staff class includes three additional data members—Hours, Rate, and Pay. Name and Id are inherited from the Employee class and do not have to be restated in the subclass definitions.

Notice also that each class has a constructor, identified by the name of the class, as well as several other methods. You'll notice that all three classes have two methods of the same name—GetEmployee and ShowEmployee. Even though a subclass inherits all the methods from its base class, that subclass can reimplement or redesign any inherited method. The process of reimplementing a method inherited from a base class is called **overriding.** In this example, each subclass has its own implementation of the two methods GetEmployee and ShowEmployee. In contrast, the method ZapEmployee has not been reimplemented by either subclass. Therefore, the original implementation specified in the Employee class will be reused by each subclass. Note also that both sub-classes include a ComputePay method not included in the design of the original class. This method was not inherited from the Employee class, but rather was added to each subclass as an additional function. The method is implemented differently for each subclass. This ability of a method to be implemented differently for different classes is an example of **polymorphism.**

Employee Class

Figure 9–11 shows the implementation of the Employee class. The makeup of this class is straightforward. A single constructor initializes the data members Name and Id. The methods GetEmployee and ShowEmployee simply input and display the Name and Id. The method ZapEmployee displays a message that a particular employee is no longer employed. This method is included to illustrate a method that is inherited and not reimplemented by either subclass.

**Figure 9–11
Employee Class
Implementation**

```
Class Employee
      private Name
      private Id
      public Employee
            Name = "Any Employee"
            Id = 9999
      End
      public GetEmployee
            Display "Please enter employee name and id"
            Input Name, Id
      End
      public ShowEmployee
            Display Name, Id
      End
      public ZapEmployee
            Display Name, "no longer works here"
            Name = "Former Employee"
            Id = 9999
      End
End Class
```

Faculty Class

Figure 9–12 shows the implementation of the Faculty class. The first statement defines the class name, as before, but indicates in the parentheses that this class is a subclass of the base class Employee. A single constructor initializes the data members Rank and Salary. The methods GetEmployee and ShowEmployee are reimplemented in this class to input Rank and to display Rank and Salary. Notice that both of these methods invoke the original GetEmployee and ShowEmployee methods defined in the Employee class. This technique is often used to take advantage of previously written code. The method ComputePay is an additional method included in the Faculty class to assign a specific salary based on the rank of the faculty member. A simple CASE control structure implements this design.

Staff Class

Figure 9–13 shows the implementation of the Staff class. The first statement defines the class name and, again, indicates in the parentheses that

Figure 9–12
Faculty Class
Implementation

```
Class Faculty (base Employee)
        private Rank
        private Salary
        public Faculty
                Rank = "No rank assigned"
                Salary = 0
        End
        public GetEmployee
                Employee.GetEmployee
                Display "Please enter rank"
                Input Rank
        End
        public ShowEmployee
                Employee.ShowEmployee
                Display Rank, Salary
        End
        public ComputePay
                CASENTRY Rank
                    CASE "Instructor"
                            Salary = 25000
                    CASE "Assistant Professor"
                            Salary = 30000
                    CASE "Associate Professor"
                            Salary = 40000
                    CASE "Professor"
                            Salary = 50000
                    CASE other
                            Salary = 0
                            Display "Invalid rank"
                ENDCASE
        End
End Class
```

this class is a subclass of the base class Employee. A single constructor initializes the data members Hours, Rate, and Pay. The methods Get-Employee and ShowEmployee are reimplemented in this class as well to input Hours and Rate and to display Pay. Notice, again, that both of these methods invoke the original GetEmployee and ShowEmployee methods defined in the Employee class. The method ComputePay is an additional method included in the Staff class to compute the pay based on hours and rate. A simple IFTHENELSE control structure implements this design.

Figures 9–12 and 9–13 illustrate the two subclasses Faculty and Staff by listing all the data members and methods defined for each subclass. These figures do not, however, show the two data members, Name and Id, and the four methods, Employee, GetEmployee, ShowEmployee, and ZapEmployee, that are inherited from the base class Employee. It can become difficult, especially in more complex programs, to trace back up the inheritance chain to find the definition of a derived method. We can alleviate this problem by providing a fully instantiated view of an object. This is done by showing not only the data members and methods of the derived class but also the data members and methods inherited from the base class. Figure 9–14 illustrates the fully instantiated view of the Faculty class, and Figure 9–15 illustrates the fully instantiated view of the Staff class.

Figure 9–13
Staff Class Implementation

```
Class Staff (base Employee)
        private Hours
        private Rate
        private Pay
        public Staff
                Hours = 0
                Rate = 0
                Pay = 0
        End
        public GetEmployee
                Employee.GetEmployee
                Display "Please enter hours and rate"
                Input Hours, Rate
        End
        public ShowEmployee
                Employee.ShowEmployee
                Display Pay
        End
        public ComputePay
                IF Hours > 40 THEN
                        Pay = (40 * Rate) + ((Hours - 40) * (1.5 * Rate))
                ELSE
                        Pay = Hours * Rate
                ENDIF
        End
    End Class
```

Figure 9–14
Faculty Class
Implementation—Fully
Instantiated View

```
Class Faculty (base Employee)
        private Name (inherited from base class - Employee)
        private Id (inherited from base class - Employee)
        private Rank
        private Salary
        public Employee (inherited from base class - Employee)
                Name = "Any Employee"
                Id = 9999
        End
        public Faculty
                Rank = "No rank assigned"
                Salary = 0
        End
        public GetEmployee (inherited from base class - Employee)
                Display "Please enter employee name and id"
                Input Name, Id
        End
        public ShowEmployee (inherited from base class - Employee)
                Display Name, Id
        End
        public GetEmployee
                Employee.GetEmployee
                Display "Please enter rank"
                Input Rank
        End
        public ShowEmployee
                Employee.ShowEmployee
                Display Rank, Salary
        End
        public ZapEmployee (inherited from base class - Employee)
                Display Name, "no longer works here"
                Name = "Former Employee"
                Id = 9999
        End
        public ComputePay
                CASENTRY Rank
                        CASE "Instructor"
                                Salary = 25000
                        CASE "Assistant Professor"
                                Salary = 30000
                        CASE "Associate Professor"
                                Salary = 40000
                        CASE "Professor"
                                Salary = 50000
                        CASE other
                                Salary = 0
                                Display "Invalid rank"
                ENDCASE
        End
End Class
```

**Figure 9–15
Staff Class
Implementation—Fully
Instantiated View**

```
Class Staff (base Employee)
        private Name (inherited from base class - Employee)
        private Id (inherited from base class - Employee)
        private Hours
        private Rate
        private Pay
        public Employee (inherited from base class - Employee)
                Name = "Any Employee"
                Id = 9999
        End
        public Staff
                Hours = 0
                Rate = 0
                Pay = 0
        End
        public GetEmployee (inherited from base class - Employee)
                Display "Please enter employee name and id"
                Input Name, Id
        End
        public ShowEmployee (inherited from base class - Employee)
                Display Name, Id
        End
        public GetEmployee
                Employee.GetEmployee
                Display "Please enter hours and rate"
                Input Hours, Rate
        End
        public ShowEmployee
                Employee.ShowEmployee
                Display Pay
        End
        public ZapEmployee (inherited from base class - Employee)
                Display Name, "no longer works here"
                Name = "Former Employee"
                Id = 9999
        End
        public ComputePay
                IF Hours > 40 THEN
                        Pay = (40 * Rate) + ((Hours - 40) * (1.5 * Rate))
                ELSE
                        Pay = Hours * Rate
                ENDIF
        End
    End Class
```

Driver Program—Employee Example

Figure 9–16 illustrates a driver program that creates two objects, one of class Faculty and one of class Staff. When an object is created from a derived class, the constructor for the base class is first called, followed by the constructor for the derived class. Thus, when the object Faculty1 is

Figure 9–16
Employee Class Driver

```
Start
Faculty: Faculty1
Staff: Staff1
Faculty1.GetEmployee
Faculty1.ComputePay
Faculty1.ShowEmployee
Staff1.GetEmployee
Staff1.ComputePay
Staff1.ShowEmployee
Faculty1.ZapEmployee
Stop
```

created, the constructor for the Employee class executes first, initializing Name to "Any Employee" and Id to 9999. The constructor for the Faculty class executes next, initializing Rank to "No rank assigned" and Salary to 0. Similar actions occur when the object Staff1 is created. When the GetEmployee method is invoked for the Faculty1 object, the code in the GetEmployee method of the Faculty class calls another GetEmployee method, the method associated with the Employee class. A similar dot notation is used within the Faculty GetEmployee method (Employee.GetEmployee) to resolve the class to which the method belongs. The GetEmployee method (from the Employee class) requests the name and id from the user. When it finishes executing, control is returned to the Display statement in the GetEmployee method within the Faculty class, which then requests the rank from the user.

Next, the ComputePay method is executed and the salary for the faculty member is computed based on his or her rank. The ShowEmployee method is then executed and, again, the code in the ShowEmployee method of the Faculty class calls another ShowEmployee method, the method associated with the Employee class. The ShowEmployee method (from the Employee class) displays the name and id of the employee. When it finishes executing, control is returned to the Display statement in the ShowEmployee method within the Faculty class, which displays the rank and salary of the employee. A similar series of events occurs in the next three steps in the driver program when the methods are invoked for the Staff1 object.

Finally, the ZapEmployee method is invoked for the Faculty1 object. Since no ZapEmployee method exists in the Faculty class, the base class (Employee) method is invoked at this point. Note that a derived class object can invoke a method from the base class. Remember, all methods from the base class are inherited, that is, become part of the derived class. However, a base class object cannot invoke a method solely defined in the derived class. For example, if Employee1 was an object of the Employee class (Employee: Employee1), then the statement Employee1.ComputePay would be illegal since the method ComputePay is not defined in the base class Employee.

Figure 9–17 shows the output that would result from execution of the driver program. Assume the user entered "Joe", 1234, and "Professor" in response to the prompts for input in the GetEmployee method for the

Figure 9–17 Employee Class Driver Output	Joe	1234	Professor	50000
	Mary	4321	400	
	Joe no longer works here			

Faculty1 object and "Mary", 4321, 40, and 10 in response to the prompts for input in the GetEmployee method for the Staff1 object. Make sure that you understand how each line of output was generated.

Write some variations of the driver program and see what output results.

Object-Oriented Programming Benefits

Many benefits can be gained from object-oriented design and programming. Although some of these benefits were mentioned in previous sections, it may be worthwhile at this point to discuss the advantages of object-oriented programming over procedure-oriented programming in more detail. Object-oriented programs are easier to maintain. If a class definition is changed, that change will be picked up in any program that incorporates an object of that class. There is no need to scan through programs searching for all uses of the class and then change each occurrence individually.

Another advantage of object-oriented programming is higher productivity. Since class libraries containing many prebuilt (and thus working and reliable) classes exist, much of the design and programming for an application may be already done. These class libraries often provide many of the technical details needed in a program. Thus, the programmer need not work at that level of technical detail, but can concentrate on the business requirements of the application instead. As another example, objects can be defined in easy-to-use scripting languages. It is much easier to work with widgets as objects than to have to define pixel locations on the screen. Since class libraries provide prebuilt classes, programmers can use these classes as basic building blocks in program design.

Object-oriented programming facilitates design and code reuse. Even if a class definition doesn't completely fit the programmer's needs, the programmer can reuse much of the class and tailor it to his or her needs through overriding.

Object-Oriented Programming Tools

Tools to aid in object-oriented analysis and design are becoming commonly available. A standard for documentation of object-oriented design is being devised by Grady Booch and Jim Rumbaugh, two of the early "fathers" of design methodologies. This documentation standard is called the **Unified Modeling Language,** or **UML.** Paradigm Plus from Platinum Technology is a popular object-oriented analysis and design tool that implements UML. Other object-oriented analysis and design tools are also available. Likewise, tools for object creation, object assembly into components, and object management are also becoming widely available.

Object-Oriented Programming Languages

C++ and Smalltalk are object-oriented third-generation languages (3GLs) that can be used to write object-oriented programs, much as COBOL and Pascal have been and are being used to write procedure-oriented programs. Java, introduced to facilitate writing programs for use on the Internet, is also object-oriented. Visual Basic, although event-driven, is not object-oriented. Programmers can create and manipulate objects in Visual Basic, but Visual Basic does not support inheritance. Visual Basic is considered object-based, not object-oriented.

Key Terms

object-oriented programming	encapsulation	parent class
class	data hiding	super class
object	driver program	derived class
data	instantiation	child class
behavior	constructor	subclass
property	parameters	overriding
data member	arguments	polymorphism
instance variable	overloading	Unified Modeling
method	destructor	Language (UML)
member function	inheritance	
	base class	

Exercises

1. Distinguish between object-oriented design and procedure-oriented design.

2. Distinguish between a class and an object.

3. Name and define the two parts of a class definition.

4. What is meant by encapsulation?

5. What is one purpose of a driver program?

6. What is meant by instantiation?

7. What is meant by overloading?

8. Given the following driver program and the class definition shown in Figure 9–7, what output would result?

```
Start
GradeBook: MyGradeBook("Rynn", 80, 70, 100)
GradeBook: YourGradeBook
YourGradeBook.ComputeAverage
MyGradeBook.ShowStudent
YourGradeBook.ShowStudent
Stop
```

9. Given the following driver program and the class definition shown in Figure 9–7, what output would result?

```
Start
GradeBook: MyGradeBook("Rynn", 80, 70, 100)
GradeBook: YourGradeBook
MyGradeBook.ComputeAverage
MyGradeBook.ShowStudent
YourGradeBook.ShowStudent
Stop
```

10. Define a class that captures the logic of the Temperature Conversion Problem shown in Figure 2–9.

11. What is meant by inheritance?

12. Distinguish between a base class and a derived class.

13. What is meant by overriding?

14. Given the following driver program and the class definitions shown in Figures 9–11, 9–12, and 9–13, what output would result? Assume that the user entered "Harry", 5567, and "Instructor" in response to the prompts for input in the GetEmployee method for the NewFaculty object and "Joan", 7833, 50, and 15 in response to the prompts for input in the GetEmployee method for the NewStaff object.

```
Start
Faculty: NewFaculty
Staff: NewStaff
NewFaculty.GetEmployee
NewFaculty.ComputePay
NewFaculty.ShowEmployee
NewStaff.GetEmployee
NewStaff.ComputePay
NewStaff.ShowEmployee
Stop
```

15. Given the following driver program and the class definitions shown in Figures 9–11 and 9–12, what output would result?

```
Start
Faculty: AnotherFaculty
AnotherFaculty.ComputePay
AnotherFaculty.ShowEmployee
AnotherFaculty.ZapEmployee
Stop
```

16. List some benefits of object-oriented programming.

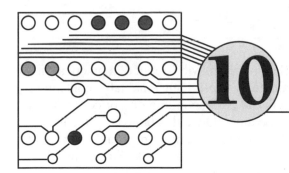

10 Array Applications

Upon completion of this chapter you should be able to

- Design an algorithm to load values into a table.
- Design an algorithm that searches a table using a sequential search.
- Design an algorithm that searches a table using a binary search.
- Design an algorithm that makes use of one or more program switches.
- Design an algorithm that sorts values in a table.

Introduction

In Chapter 8 we saw that it is sometimes useful to read, process, and write collections of similar data items as a data group rather than as separate data items. We saw how subscript notation can be used to refer to specific elements of a group. We developed solution algorithms to find and print the smallest of a set of values, average a set of values, multiply the elements in a table by the elements in corresponding positions of a list, and so on. (In mathematical problem-solving, the last of these algorithms is usually referred to as multiplying a matrix by a vector.)

Table Lookups

In programming terminology, reading a table into computer storage is often referred to as **loading a table.** This step usually occurs soon after program execution is initiated, that is, in the initialization portion of the program. After a table has been loaded, it can be referred to repeatedly during subsequent processing steps. Often another input value is read and used in a search of the table. For example, a payroll application may accept a table showing wage classes and corresponding pay rates as one of its inputs. Then, an employee time record that contains the hours worked and wage class of a particular employee may be submitted as a later input. In order to determine what pay rate to use in calculating the employee's pay, the class/rate table must first be searched. This operation is called a **table lookup.**

Sample Problem 10.1 (Table-Lookup Example)

Problem:

To understand how tables and table lookups may be applied in practical situations, consider the following example. A two-dimensional table containing a master list of unique item numbers and corresponding unit prices for registered pharmaceutical products will be input. Once this table is input, additional records will be input, each containing an item number and quantity for one of these products. The item number input will be looked up in the table. If the item number is found, the corresponding price in the table will be used to compute the total price for the particular item. If the item number input is not found in the table, an appropriate message will be output.

Solution:

The structure chart in Figure 10–1 shows a modular design for this problem solution. The overall control module is shown in Figures 10–2 (flowchart) and 10–3 (pseudocode). As the program begins execution, A000 calls upon another module (B000) to input the table.

The program flowchart in Figure 10–4 and the pseudocode in Figure 10–5 show the processing steps for module B000. The name ITEM#/PRICE represents the table shown in Figure 10–6. This table stores the reference data of item numbers and unit prices. In this example, the fifth row, first column of the table [ITEM#/PRICE(5,1)] contains an item number of 54387. This item's unit price is $10.95, the amount located in the fifth row, second column of the table [ITEM#/PRICE(5,2)].

A DOUNTIL control structure in module B000 controls the loading of the table. Nested IFTHENELSE control structures are used because the number of items to be included in the table is not fixed. It is not known beforehand exactly how many times the DOUNTIL loop needs to be executed.

Since the pharmaceutical products are registered items, the designer of the solution algorithm has determined that not more than 200 items will have to be identified and priced. If fewer than 200 items are entered, a special input record (trailer record) with an item number of 99999 is to be entered to indicate that the table is complete. (Recall the discussion of trailer records in Chapter 5.) The inner IFTHENELSE checks the value of the subscript ROW, which is also used as a count of the number of table entries read into storage. If the maximum number of table entries (200) has been

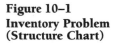

**Figure 10–1
Inventory Problem
(Structure Chart)**

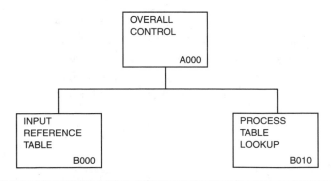

Figure 10–2
Inventory Problem—Overall
Control (Flowchart)

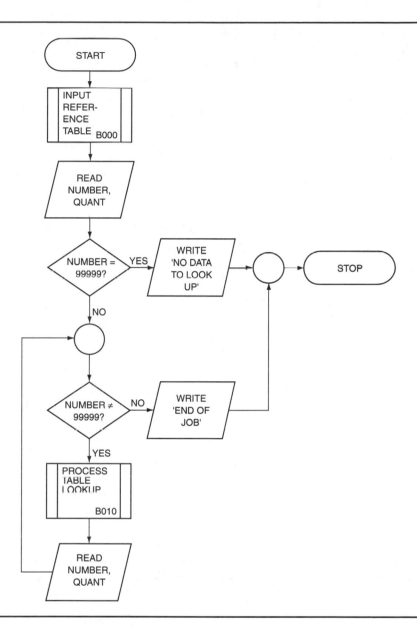

Figure 10–3
Inventory Problem—Overall
Control (Pseudocode)

```
Start
Input reference table (B000)
Read NUMBER, QUANT
IF NUMBER = 99999 THEN
    Write 'No data to look up'
ELSE
    DOWHILE NUMBER ≠ 99999
        Process table lookup (B010)
        Read NUMBER, QUANT
    ENDDO
    Write 'End of job'
ENDIF
Stop
```

Figure 10–4
Inventory Problem—Input
Reference Table (Flowchart)

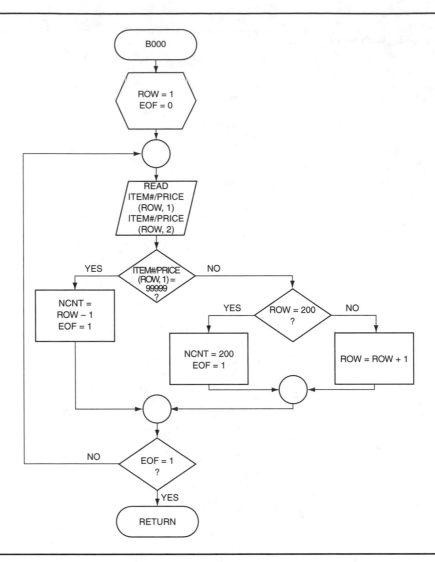

Figure 10–5
Inventory Problem—
Input Reference Table
(Pseudocode)

```
B000
Enter
ROW = 1
EOF = 0
DOUNTIL EOF = 1
   Read ITEM#/PRICE(ROW,1), ITEM#/PRICE(ROW,2)
   IF ITEM#/PRICE(ROW,1) = 99999 THEN
      NCNT = ROW - 1
      EOF = 1
   ELSE
      IF ROW = 200 THEN
         NCNT = 200
         EOF = 1
      ELSE
         ROW = ROW + 1
      ENDIF
   ENDIF
ENDDO
Return
```

Figure 10–6
Inventory Problem—
ITEM#/PRICE Reference
Table

ITEM#/PRICE TABLE

	COLUMNS	
	1	2
1	18337	50.85
2	35795	5.85
3	11427	1.50
4	98547	105.50
ROWS 5	54387	10.95
6	77378	3.50
7	48591	14.95
⋮	⋮	⋮
199	UNUSED	UNUSED
200	UNUSED	UNUSED

read, a special end-of-file indicator (EOF) is set to 1 and the number of table entries (NCNT) is set at 200. The outermost IFTHENELSE checks the item numbers of up to 200 entries to watch for the 99999 input record. If the 99999 record is detected, EOF is again set to 1. NCNT is set to ROW – 1 to prevent the 99999 record from being included in the table. Whichever of these tested conditions occurs first causes the DOUNTIL loop to be exited.

The DOUNTIL loop is controlled by the variable named EOF. The use of EOF is an example of how another important programming technique— the use of **program switches**—can be applied. In general, a program switch is used to set up the logic needed to deal with a special condition that may arise during processing. It may be implemented in any of several ways, depending on the hardware and software characteristics of the computer system in use. In this case, EOF is being used as a switch that contains either a value of 1 or a value of 0. When EOF contains a 1, the switch is ON; when EOF contains a 0, the switch is OFF. The switch EOF is set to 0 (OFF) in the preparation step in Figures 10–4 and 10–5. The switch EOF is set to 1 (ON) within the DOUNTIL loop when either of the two conditions indicating no more records are to be read occurs.

Note that in either case of loop termination, the number of table entries read into storage is placed in NCNT before EOF is set. NCNT can then be used as a loop control when the table is referred to in subsequent processing.

Now let's consider the logic in the overall control module (A000) (see Figures 10–2 and 10–3). After the values for the table have been input, module B000 returns control to A000 and another type of input is read: inquiries to be processed against the table. Each inquiry consists of an item number and a quantity. Because the number of inquiries to be processed will vary from one run of this program to another, a special input record containing 99999 as an item number is to be entered as an end-of-input record after all inquiries have been processed. An IFTHENELSE is used to make sure that there are, in fact, some inquiries to process. If not, a special "No data to look up" message is written as output. A DOWHILE structure is used to control the input of the rest of the inquiries. For each record that is input, the reference table is searched to determine if the item number that is currently input (NUMBER) is contained in the table. If so, the unit price corresponding to the item number (the second column in the current row of the table) is multiplied by the quantity entered as input (QUANT) to determine the total cost. The table is searched and the computation is done in a separate module (B010), shown in Figures 10–7 (flowchart) and 10–8 (pseudocode).

A DOWHILE loop controls the main processing in module B010. The loop is executed repeatedly until either one of two conditions exists:

■ The item number of the inquiry received as input in A000 (NUMBER) is matched with an item number in the reference table [ITEM#/PRICE(ROW,1)].

Figure 10–7
Inventory Problem—Process Table Lookup (Flowchart)

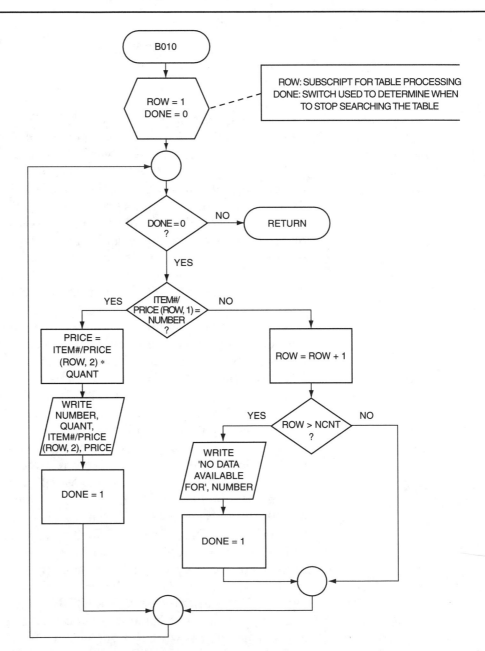

Figure 10–8
Inventory Problem—Process
Table Lookup (Pseudocode)

```
B010
Enter
ROW = 1
DONE = 0
DOWHILE DONE = 0
   IF ITEM#/PRICE(ROW,1) = NUMBER THEN
      PRICE = ITEM#/PRICE(ROW,2) * QUANT
      Write NUMBER, QUANT, ITEM#/PRICE(ROW,2), PRICE
      DONE = 1
   ELSE
      ROW = ROW + 1
      IF ROW > NCNT THEN
         Write 'No data available for', NUMBER
         DONE = 1
      (ELSE)
      ENDIF
   ENDIF
ENDDO
Return
```

- All item numbers in the table have been examined without finding an item number that matches the item number in the inquiry.

These conditions are tested for by the nested IFTHENELSE control structures within the DOWHILE. Whichever occurs first causes another switch, called DONE, to be set to 1. Note that DONE is initialized to 0 at the beginning of B010. When the DONE switch is tested and found to be 1, the DOWHILE loop is exited.

The THEN path of the outer IFTHENELSE shows the processing that occurs when an item-number match is found in the table. The DONE switch is set to 1 after this processing occurs. If a match is not found, then the next entry in the item-number table must be checked.

In the ELSE path of the outer IFTHENELSE, the subscript ROW is incremented and also checked to determine if ROW exceeds the number of entries (NCNT) in the table. If this is the case, no item number matching the input item number exists in the reference table. The THEN clause of the innermost IFTHENELSE is then executed to output the message "No data available for" followed by the unmatched item number. The DONE switch is set to 1.

In either case, the DOWHILE loop will be exited and control will return to A000. At this point another record will be read. After this record is tested, either module B010 will be executed again or the DOWHILE loop in A000 will be exited and an "End of job" message will be written.

What assumptions have you made about the ordering of entries within the item-number/unit-price reference table? Perhaps you think that the table entries are in ascending item-number sequence. This is not a requirement of the solution algorithm. The item numbers in the table may be in ascending sequence, or descending sequence, or no particular sequence at all (as is the case in Figure 10–6). Because the table-lookup module starts at the beginning of the table for each inquiry, it will work in any of these cases.

However, the sequence of entries in a table can affect the efficiency of table searching in terms of processing time. Because the table-lookup module in Figures 10–7 and 10–8 always starts with the first entry and proceeds toward the last, the most-used item number should be the first entry in the table, and the least-used item number should be the last. For example, if 60 percent of the inquiries involve item numbers 55040, 30456, and 32045, these item numbers should be the first ones in the table. The rest of the table should also be sequenced according to frequency of use. The total amount of time required for a run will be affected accordingly.

Binary Searches

A more sophisticated table-lookup routine should be considered in cases where (1) the frequency of use of table entries is evenly distributed over the table, (2) the number of entries in the table is very large, or (3) processing efficiency or high system performance is mandatory. The routine commonly employs a **binary search.** When this table-lookup technique is used, the entries in the table being searched must be in either ascending or descending sequence according to the values of a particular data item or items common to all entries. The portion of an entry that contains that data item or items is called the **key field.** The term *binary* is appropriate for this lookup technique because the portion of the table being searched is halved repeatedly. The search begins with an entry at or near the middle of the table. Based on a comparison, the search continues in either the first half or the second half of the table. The other half of the table is ignored. The next comparison is made against the value at or near the middle of the half just selected. The search continues by successively halving the portion of the table remaining. Eventually, a match occurs between the **search key** of the data being processed against the table and the key field of a table entry. Alternatively, it may be determined that no entry with a matching key field exists in the table. In such a case, an exception routine must be carried out.

Figure 10–9 illustrates how a table of 16 elements is accessed when a binary search is used. As you can see, five comparisons, at most, are needed to determine whether or not a match is found. As noted previously,

Figure 10–9
Binary Search

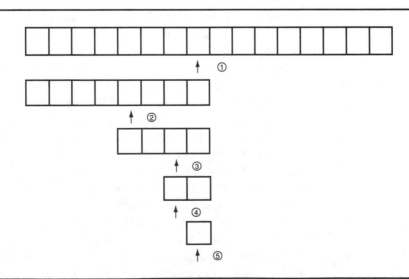

the binary search technique is particularly valuable when a table contains a large number of entries. For example, in a table with 1000 entries, the maximum number of comparisons that may be needed is only ten.

Sample Problem 10.2 (Binary Search Example)

Problem:

Assume that 70 company sales offices are identified by unique two-digit codes on a company's internal documents. When reports are printed for external use, however, the sales offices must be identified by location rather than by code number. Each program that provides a report for external use must have access to information associating the office code numbers with the actual office locations. The office codes and corresponding locations will be input in ascending order into two lists. These lists will then be used to locate a subsequent office code, also input. The office code list will be searched using the binary search technique, since the codes in the list are assumed to be in order.

Solution:

The structure chart in Figure 10–10 shows that this algorithm will be implemented as four modules. The overall control module (A000) will call upon module B000 to input the code numbers and corresponding locations into two tables. Another module (B010) will be used to search the code-numbers table, and a third module (B020) will handle the processing that must occur after the table has been searched.

Execution begins at the first step in the overall control module. The flowchart for this module is shown in Figure 10–11, and the corresponding pseudocode is shown in Figure 10–12.

A storage area set aside for a reason code (RC) is initialized to 0. This code will be checked in module B020 to determine how the processing should proceed. RC will be set to one of four values prior to the execution of module B020. These four values and their meanings are:

Code	Meaning
0	Office code input was found in the table.
1	No office code was specified for processing.
2	Code table was not in sequence.
3	Office code input was not in the table.

A second storage area used as a stop switch (STOPSW) is also set to 0. This switch will control a DOWHILE loop that causes the code table to be searched repeatedly for a specific input code later in module A000. This input code (INCOD) is read in the second step of A000. A check is made to determine whether or not the office code is 00, a special no-input code value indicating that no particular office code was specified for this processing run. If the office code is 00, both the reason code and the stop switch are set to 1; that is, the operations in the YES path from the first decision-making step are carried out. Execution of the program continues,

Figure 10–10
Binary Search
(Structure Chart)

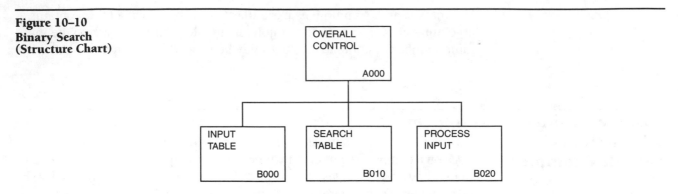

Figure 10–11
Binary Search—Overall
Control (Flowchart)

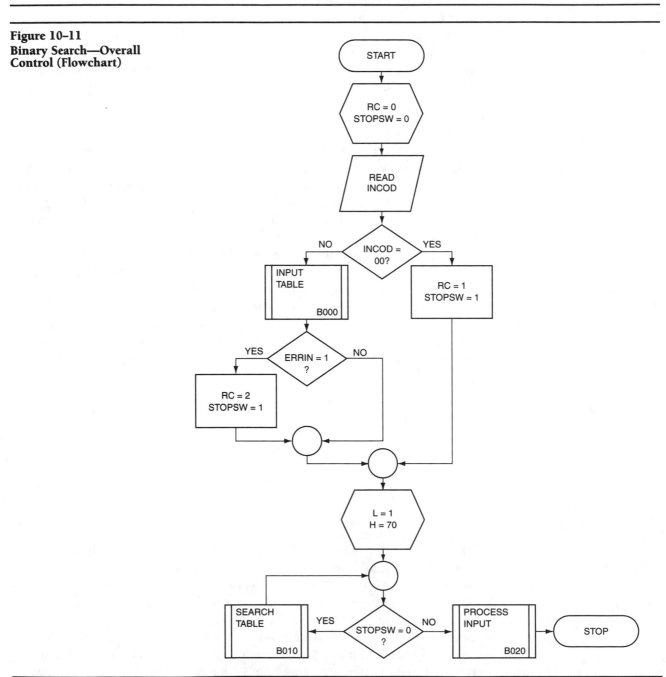

Figure 10–12
Binary Search—Overall
Control (Pseudocode)

```
A000
Start
RC = 0
STOPSW = 0
Read INCOD
IF INCOD = 00 THEN
    RC = 1
    STOPSW = 1
ELSE
    Input table (B000)
    IF ERRIN = 1 THEN
        RC = 2
        STOPSW = 1
    (ELSE)
    ENDIF
ENDIF
L = 1
H = 70
DOWHILE STOPSW = 0
    Search table (B010)
ENDDO
Process input (B020)
Stop
```

but we know that no association of office code to office location has to be made during this particular run.

If the office code is not 00, module B000 is executed (Figures 10–13 and 10–14). A variable SUB, to be used as a subscript, and an error indicator (ERRIN) are set to 0. Another program switch, in this case a first-time switch (FTSW), is set to 1. A DOUNTIL control structure is used to control the reading of the two-digit office codes and the corresponding office locations into storage as two one-dimensional arrays (COD and LOC). Together, the arrays form a reference table.

Because the office-code/office-location reference table is to be accessed using a binary search technique, the entries in the table must be ordered. A sequence check is performed to make certain that they are. This is where the first-time switch is used. To avoid sequence-checking the first code number against a preceding code number (because there is no code number preceding the first one), FTSW is initially set to 1. This causes the YES path (THEN clause of the first nested IFTHENELSE) to be executed the first time it is tested. Then the first-time switch is set to 0, or OFF; it remains OFF throughout program execution. The YES path of this decision-making step is not taken again because all succeeding code numbers must be sequence checked.

Each office code number must be greater than the one that precedes it. If it is not, the error indicator (ERRIN) is set to 1. The value of the error indicator should be checked by any routine that causes this input-table module to be executed. If ERRIN is 1, the reference table that the input-table module loads into storage should not be used in subsequent processing.

The DOUNTIL loop in Figures 10–13 and 10–14 is exited when all 70 table entries have been read into storage. Control is then returned to the overall control module (A000), where processing continues.

Figure 10–13
Binary Search—Input Table
(Flowchart)

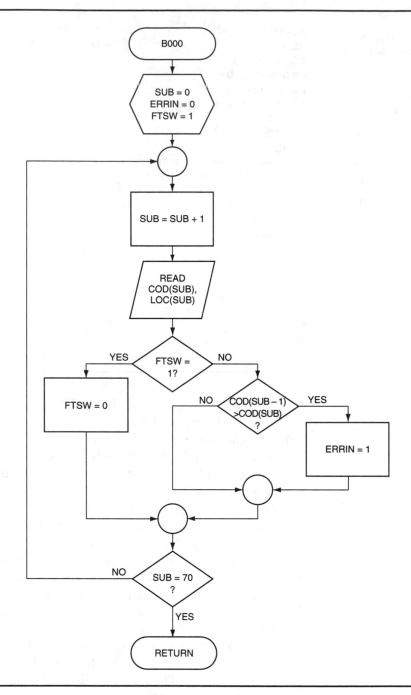

The next processing step in module A000 (see Figure 10–11 or 10–12) is a check of the value of the error indicator. If the value is 1, indicating a sequence error, the stop switch is set to 1 (thus ensuring that a certain DOWHILE loop later in the program will not be executed). The reason code is set to 2. It will be printed later (in module B020) to tell output recipients that a sequence error was detected when loading the reference table. Since something is wrong with the table, it is pointless to use the table until the errors have been identified and eliminated.

If the error indicator is not equal to 1, the reference table is assumed to be correct and available in storage. A variable L, used to store the

**Figure 10–14
Binary Search—Input Table
(Pseudocode)**

```
B000
Enter
SUB = 0
ERRIN = 0
FTSW = 1
DOUNTIL SUB = 70
   SUB = SUB + 1
   Read COD(SUB), LOC(SUB)
   IF FTSW = 1 THEN
      FTSW = 0
   ELSE
      IF COD(SUB-1) > COD(SUB) THEN
         ERRIN = 1
      (ELSE)
      ENDIF
   ENDIF
ENDDO
Return
```

lower bound of the reference table, is set to 1. A variable H, used to store the upper bound of the table, is set to 70 (because there are 70 entries). Then a DOWHILE loop is entered the first time. If the stop switch is not equal to 0, the DOWHILE loop is exited immediately, because either INCOD contains the special no-input code value of 00 or the reference table is bad. In either case, the reference table should not be used in processing.

If the stop switch is equal to 0, a module (B010) is called to perform a binary search on the reference table. The flowchart and corresponding pseudocode for module B010 are shown in Figures 10–15 and 10–16.

First, the current upper bound of the table, H, is compared against the current lower bound, L, to determine if H is less than L. The first time, the answer is obvious, but the values of H and L will change, as we shall see. This time the NO path (ELSE clause) of the outermost IFTHENELSE in the module is executed.

The midpoint of the office-code/office-location reference table is computed by adding the lower bound L and the upper bound H and then dividing their sum by 2. A special built-in function (INT) is then called upon to **truncate** (cut off or delete) the decimal portion of the result of the division and assign the truncated result to SUB. SUB is then used as a subscript during table processing. INT is a keyword that we have used to identify the function that truncates a value to integer form. (The programming language later used when writing the program may use that term or a different one.) The input to the INT function is a single-decimal number, and the output is the same number with the decimal portion truncated. For example, $INT(5.3) = 5$; $INT(7.9) = 7$; $INT(6.0) = 6$.

Next, the current value of INCOD (the office code number read as input) is compared to the midpoint value of the code-number portion of the reference table—COD(SUB). [SUB = INT$((1 + 70)/2)$ the first time through, so we know that SUB is equal to 35.]

Figure 10–15
Binary Search—Search
Table (Flowchart)

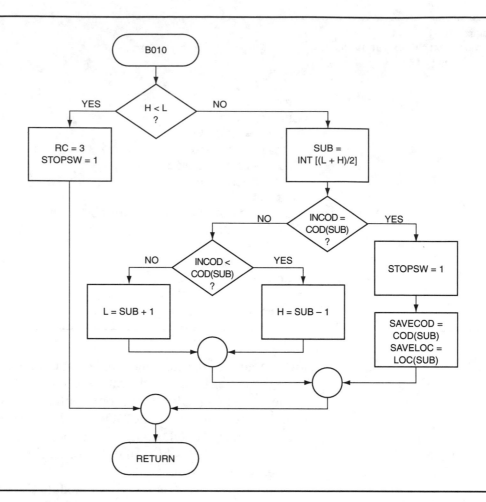

Figure 10–16
Binary Search—Search
Table (Pseudocode)

```
B010
Enter
IF H < L THEN
    RC = 3
    STOPSW = 1
ELSE
    SUB = INT((L + H)/2)
    IF INCOD = COD(SUB) THEN
        STOPSW = 1
        SAVECOD = COD(SUB)
        SAVELOC = LOC(SUB)
    ELSE
        IF INCOD < COD(SUB) THEN
            H = SUB - 1
        ELSE
            L = SUB + 1
        ENDIF
    ENDIF
ENDIF
Return
```

The program execution then proceeds as follows:

- If the value of INCOD is equal to the value of COD(SUB), the table search is ended because the code numbers match.
- If the value of INCOD is less than the value of COD(SUB), the lower half of the reference table is searched.
- If the value of INCOD is greater than the value of COD(SUB), the upper half of the reference table is searched.

These tests are set up in a structured manner as nested IFTHENELSE patterns.

If INCOD is not equal to COD(SUB), the DOWHILE loop in A000 will be executed again. The value of INCOD is tested against the midpoint value of the half of the table that contains the code number, as indicated by previous algorithmic steps. As before, if the compared values are equal, the search is ended. If not, then the appropriate half of the divided table (i.e., the quarter of the table the value may be in) is specified. Halving continues in this manner until the search is successful, or until it is proved that the code number cannot be found in the table. If it is found, the code number and the corresponding office location are saved for subsequent processing in module B020.

If adjustments to the original lower and upper bounds of the table cause them to overlap, it is assumed that the code number input has not been found in the table. The reason code (RC) is set to 3, and the stop switch is set to 1, which causes the DOWHILE loop in A000 to be exited. At this point, module B020 will be executed. This module will handle the processing of the office code and location, as well as alternative action if the reason code is equal to a value other than 0. We will not concern ourselves with the details of this module in this chapter.

Since the binary search algorithm can be somewhat complex, it may be useful to illustrate the details of each step with an example. Figure 10–17 shows a simulation or trace of this algorithm with some typical input values. First, a set of arbitrary values is read into the COD array. Figure 10–17 then illustrates the values of L, H, SUB, and COD(SUB) for a value of INCOD, say 21, that will eventually be found in the array, and for another value of INCOD, say 30, that will not be found in the array. The search will end when the lower bound L is found to be greater than the upper bound H (22 is greater than 21).

The algorithm in Figures 10–11 and 10–12 explains how to search the reference table to find a match to one office code received as input. With slight modification, the algorithm could be structured to process not just one office code but a variable number of office codes. The input-table module in Figures 10–13 and 10–14 would not have to be changed, and it should not be executed more than once. Some modifications to the program logic in Figures 10–11 and 10–12 would be required (see Exercise 10).

Sorting Lists

In the previous example, the office codes that were input into the list were checked to ensure that they were in ascending order. What if, however, the

Figure 10–17
Binary Search—Simulation

	COD			COD
1	01	25		34
2	02	26		35
3	04	27		36
4	05	28		37
5	06	29		40
6	09	30		41
7	10	31		42
8	11	32		44
9	12	33		45
10	13	34		46
11	15	35		47
12	17	36		48
13	20	37		50
14	21	38		52
15	22	39		53
16	23	40		54
17	25	41		55
18	26	42		58
19	27	43		59
20	28	44		60
21	29	45		61
22	31	•		•
23	32	•		•
24	33	•		•
		70		99

INPUT INCOD = 21

L	H	SUB	INCOD: COD(SUB)	
1	70	35	21 : 47	(<)
1	34	17	21 : 25	(<)
1	16	8	21 : 11	(>)
9	16	12	21 : 17	(>)
13	16	14	21 : 21	(=)

INCOD = COD (14)   INCOD FOUND

INPUT INCOD = 30

L	H	SUB	INCOD: COD(SUB)	
1	70	35	30 : 47	(<)
1	34	17	30 : 25	(>)
18	34	26	30 : 35	(<)
18	25	21	30 : 29	(>)
22	25	23	30 : 32	(<)
22	22	22	30 : 31	(<)
22	21			

H < L   INCOD NOT FOUND

office codes to be input were not in ascending order? We could still input them into the office-code list and then use another algorithm to sort the list. Before we look at a sorting algorithm, we need to discuss how to exchange two values within the computer's memory. This process is necessary in the sort procedure that follows.

Exchanging Values

Suppose that the memory location NUM1 was defined to be 5 and the memory location NUM2 was defined to be 3. Let us look at how we could exchange the values in NUM1 and NUM2. Your first attempt to exchange these two values might be to simply use two assignment statements, as shown in Figure 10–18. This approach will produce an incorrect result, since the old value for NUM1 is erased in Step 1 before it can be assigned to NUM2.

The correct procedure for exchanging values is shown in Figure 10–19. One additional storage location, TEMP, is required for use as a temporary storage area. TEMP is used to temporarily hold the value of NUM2 (Step 1), since a new value (NUM1) will replace the old value of NUM2 (Step 2). Once that happens, TEMP (the old value of NUM2) can replace the old value of NUM1 (Step 3).

The previous example illustrated the exchange with simple variables. Figure 10–20 shows the same logical process, used this time with a list of five elements. In this example, the third and fourth elements of the one-dimensional array LIST are exchanged.

Figure 10–18
Exchanging Values
Incorrectly

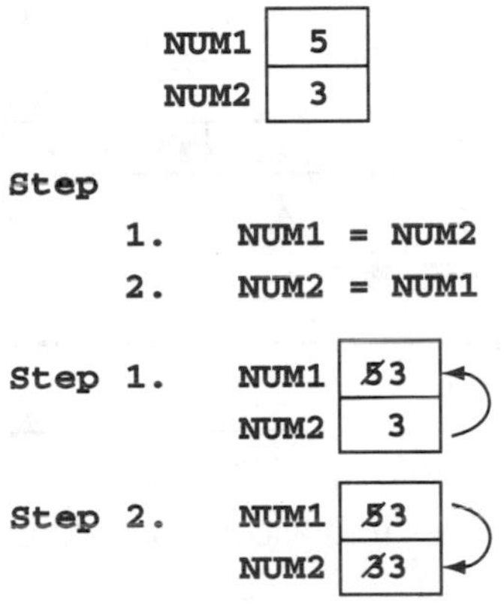

NUM1 ☐ 5
NUM2 ☐ 3

Step

1.   NUM1 = NUM2
2.   NUM2 = NUM1

Step 1.   NUM1 ☐ 5̸3
         NUM2 ☐ 3

Step 2.   NUM1 ☐ 5̸3
         NUM2 ☐ 3̸3

Figure 10–19
Exchanging Values Without
Arrays

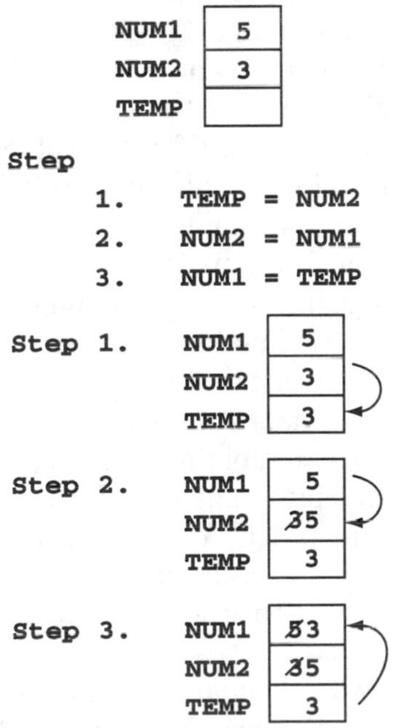

NUM1 ☐ 5
NUM2 ☐ 3
TEMP ☐

Step

1.   TEMP = NUM2
2.   NUM2 = NUM1
3.   NUM1 = TEMP

Step 1.   NUM1 ☐ 5
         NUM2 ☐ 3
         TEMP ☐ 3

Step 2.   NUM1 ☐ 5
         NUM2 ☐ 3̸5
         TEMP ☐ 3

Step 3.   NUM1 ☐ 5̸3
         NUM2 ☐ 3̸5
         TEMP ☐ 3

**Figure 10–20
Exchanging Values with
Arrays**

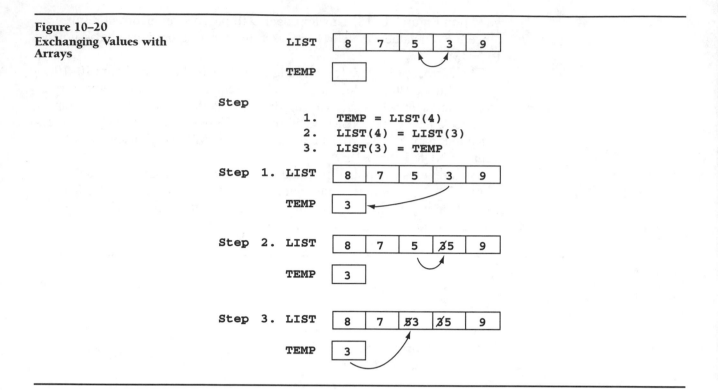

Step

1. TEMP = LIST(4)
2. LIST(4) = LIST(3)
3. LIST(3) = TEMP

Sample Problem 10.3 (Sort Example)

Problem:

Sort a list of four values into ascending order, and output the sorted list.

Solution:

A common method of sorting data into a required sequence is to read the values to be sorted into storage as a group of data items. The value in the first position in the group is compared with the value in the next position of the group. If the value in the first position is larger than the value in the second, they are interchanged. After the values in positions 2, 3, 4, . . . , n have been compared with the value currently in the first position, the **first pass** through the values is complete. The first position in the group is definitely known to contain the smallest value.

The first position is then temporarily ignored. The value in the second position of the group is compared with the values in position 3, 4, 5, . . . , n in a **second pass.** At the end of this pass, the second position is known to contain the second-to-smallest value.

The execution of passes continues, each pass requiring one less comparison operation than the preceding pass. After n – 1 passes, the values in the group are in ascending order. This is illustrated using a list of four values, as shown in Figure 10–21. As initially read into the computer, the values are 493, .06, 5, and .015. To arrange these values in ascending order, 4 – 1, or 3, passes are required.

Figure 10–22 shows a structure chart indicating the modules required to perform the actions diagrammed in Figure 10–21. Figure 10–23 shows the logic within the overall control module. This module calls upon three lower-level modules to input the array elements (B000), sort the array elements

**Figure 10–21
Sorting Four Numbers**

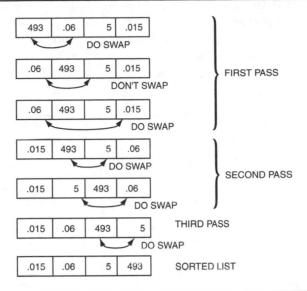

**Figure 10–22
Sorting Four Numbers
(Structure Chart)**

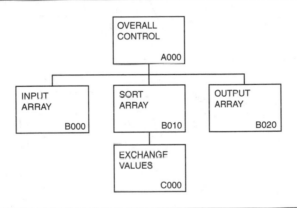

**Figure 10–23
Sorting Four Numbers—
Overall Control**

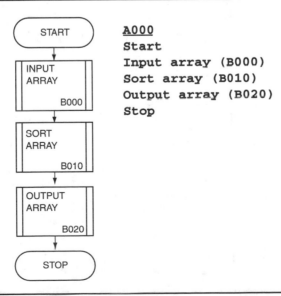

```
A000
Start
Input array (B000)
Sort array (B010)
Output array (B020)
Stop
```

(B010), and output the sorted array (B020). The logic required in B000 and B020 is nearly identical to the algorithms used to input and output array values in Chapter 8. To review those algorithms, see Figures 8–3 and 8–4.

Figure 10–24 shows the flowchart and Figure 10–25 the corresponding pseudocode for module B010, which actually sorts the list. This

Figure 10–24
Sorting Four Numbers—
Sort Array (Flowchart)

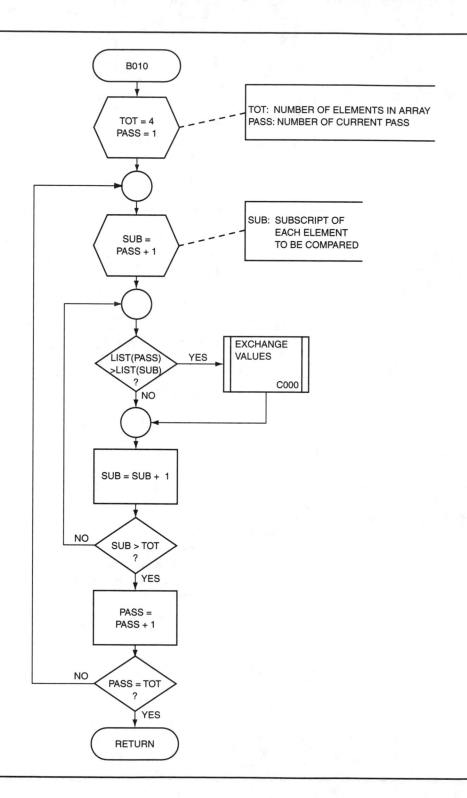

module utilizes a nested DOUNTIL loop. The outer DOUNTIL loop controls the number of passes, and the inner (nested) DOUNTIL loop controls the number of comparisons done in a single pass. An IFTHENELSE nested inside the inner DOUNTIL loop actually compares the appropriate elements in each pass, causing their values to be exchanged if the current value being compared is larger than the next value. The actual exchange is done in the third-level module C000, which is shown in Figure 10–26.

Figure 10–25
Sorting Four Numbers—
Sort Array (Pseudocode)

```
B010
Enter
TOT = 4
PASS = 1
DOUNTIL PASS = TOT
   SUB = PASS + 1
   DOUNTIL SUB > TOT
      IF LIST(PASS) > LIST(SUB) THEN
         Exchange values (C000)
      (ELSE)
      ENDIF
      SUB = SUB + 1
   ENDDO
   PASS = PASS + 1
ENDDO
Return
```

Figure 10–26
Sorting Four Numbers—
Exchange Values

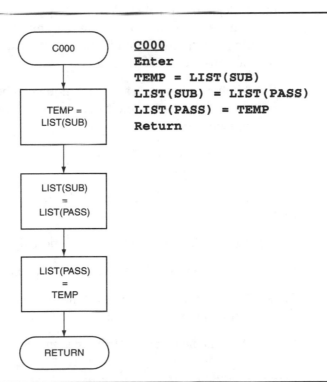

```
C000
Enter
TEMP = LIST(SUB)
LIST(SUB) = LIST(PASS)
LIST(PASS) = TEMP
Return
```

This algorithm sorts only four values, but it demonstrates a technique that can be used to sort any number of values (see Exercise 15).

Key Terms

loading a table	key field	second pass
table lookup	search key	(in sorting)
program switch	truncate	
binary search	first pass (in sorting)	

Exercises

1. (a) What is a table-lookup operation?
   (b) Give some examples (other than those in this book) of common situations where table-lookup operations can be used in problem solving.

2. The table-lookup module in Figures 10–7 and 10–8 is effective, but not particularly efficient. The module always begins searching for a new item number at the beginning of the table. Modify the solution algorithm in Figures 10–2, 10–3, 10–4, 10–5, 10–7, and 10–8 as follows: Assume that the input used to construct the table and the input referring to the table are to be processed in item-number sequence. Include sequence checks in the solution algorithm for verification. Terminate execution if (a) an item number equal to or lower than the preceding item number is provided as table input, or (b) an item number lower than the preceding item number is provided as input referring to the table. Begin each table search at the point in the item-number portion of the table where the preceding item number was found. Express the solution algorithm in both flowchart and pseudocode forms. Be sure to plan a well-structured program.

3. Explain how a binary search technique can be applied in searching a table of U.S. cities and their populations to find the population of the city of Chicago.

4. For what kinds of problem situations is use of a binary search apt to be especially appropriate?

Refer to Figures 10–11 through 10–17 to complete Exercises 5 through 9.

5. What search key is used in this solution algorithm?

6. What is the key field of a reference table entry?

7. (a) Identify three program switches used in this solution algorithm.
   (b) Explain how each of the switches is used.

8. (a) What is the purpose of the reason code used in this algorithm?
   (b) List and explain the values that the reason code may be assigned.

9. (a) Assume the value 11 is submitted as input and assigned to INCOD. Perform a simulation (trace) using the COD array values specified in Figure 10–17. Use the following table to record.

INCOD = 11

L	H	SUB	INCOD : COD(SUB)

(b) Assume INCOD is equal to 38 and redo part (a).

10. Modify the portion of the solution algorithm shown in Figures 10–11 and 10–12 to provide for the processing of a variable number of office codes received as input. You may assume that one input is fully processed (and the corresponding office location printed on an output report) before another office code is read as input.

11. Use program flowcharting or pseudocode to plan a well-structured, modular program that reads N and an N-member list called A. Include checks to make certain that the members of A are unique and in ascending order. Program execution should terminate if they are not. If they are, the program should read ARG, an input value to be processed against the list, in subsequent processing steps.

   ■ If ARG is less than A(1), set CODE equal to 0. Print out ARG, A(1), and CODE.
   ■ If ARG is equal to some member of A, set CODE equal to 1. Print out ARG and CODE.
   ■ If ARG is between A(1) and A(N), but there is no member of A equal to ARG, set CODE equal to 2. Print out ARG, CODE, and the member of A that is closest to but not greater than ARG.
   ■ If ARG is greater than A(N), set CODE equal to 3. Print out ARG, A(N), and CODE.

12. Repeat Exercise 11, but allow for a variable number of inputs to be processed against the table. An input value of 999 for ARG should be recognized as an end-of-file indicator. The program should print an end-of-job message as verification that all input has been processed.

13. The program logic in Figures 10–24 and 10–25 causes a list of four values to be arranged in ascending sequence. To sort these same values into descending sequence, only one processing step must be modified.

Identify this step by redoing that portion of the program logic in Figures 10–24 and 10–25.

14. The algorithm that you created in response to Exercise 13 should show how to perform a descending sort. Assume the following data items are provided as input to the program that you have planned: 52, .091, 708, 10.
    (a) What output should be provided by the program?
    (b) Perform a simulation (trace) to verify that the program will perform as you intend.
    (c) If the results of your simulation in (b) do not match the results you specified in (a), examine both your solution algorithm and your simulation to determine where errors have occurred. Make changes to eliminate the errors.

15. Consider modules B000 and B010 in the sort algorithm in this chapter. Modify its program flowcharts and pseudocode representations to show how to place any number of values in ascending sequence. An input value of 0 should be recognized as a dummy indicator, signaling that all values to be sorted have been read. When the sort operation is finished, the message "SORT COMPLETED" should be printed for control purposes.

16. Construct a program flowchart and corresponding pseudocode to solve the following problem. Assume there are ten records, each containing two temperature values. The first temperature value on each record represents a high temperature from a weather station, and the second temperature on each record represents a low temperature from a weather station. Input these temperatures into a table TEMP(10,2) with the high temperatures from the ten stations in column 1 of the table, and the low temperatures from the ten stations in column 2 of the table. After reading in all the temperatures, find and output the average high temperature and the average low temperature for the ten weather stations. Be sure to plan a well-structured, modular program.

17. Construct a program flowchart and corresponding pseudocode to solve the following problem. Read a series of numbers, one number per record, into a one-dimensional array called X. The number of input values will be specified by a number on the first input record. This first number should not be included in the array. Your algorithm is to compute the mean and the standard deviation of the values in array X. The mean can be computed according to the following formula:

$$\overline{X} = \sum_{i=1}^{N} X_i / N$$

The symbol Σ means the summation of; the mean is represented by the symbol $\overline{X}$. Thus, the formula says that the mean is equal to the summation of the array elements, X_i, where i goes from 1 to N, divided by N.

The standard deviation can be computed according to the following formula:

$$\sigma = \sqrt{\frac{\sum\limits_{i=1}^{N}(X_i - \overline{X})^2}{N-1}}$$

First, square each of the differences between each element in the array (i.e., X_i) and the computed mean. Each of these differences squared is added to a variable to accumulate their sum. Then divide this summation by the number of items (N) minus 1. Finally, take the square root of the results to find the standard deviation (σ). After the computations are complete, output the array X, the computed mean, and the computed standard deviation.

11 Master File Update Processing

Objectives	*Upon completion of this chapter you should be able to*

- Distinguish between online processing and batch processing.
- Define the terms *file maintenance* and *file maintenance run*.
- Explain the purpose of a turnaround file.
- Distinguish between sequential and direct processing.
- Design an algorithm that updates a sequential master file.
- Explain how CASE tools are helping to promote code reusability and thereby increasing programmer productivity.

Introduction

The programmer directs a great deal of attention to the logic within a program, but he or she must also be conscious of the environment in which the program will operate. If the execution of a program is initiated by a user at a terminal (or personal computer or workstation) to meet the user's problem-solving needs, the program is said to operate in an **online-processing environment.** Such a program is often an independent entity. It generates its own input or accepts input directly from the user, without that input being operated on beforehand by another program. It provides output that is routed directly to the user or to other users at terminals (or personal computers or workstations): The output is not used as input to another program.

Any program designed to solve one specific problem is apt to operate in this fashion. For example, a single program may plot the path of an object fired vertically from the Earth's surface as a function of time, according to a ballistics formula. Another single program may determine when return on investment will begin in a business venture, given principal, rate of interest to be compounded annually, and an accumulated sum to be attained. In effect, such a program is a system in itself.

In a typical business organization, many computer programs are run on a regularly scheduled basis. Large volumes of input are collected and processed as sets, or **batches,** by the first of a series of interrelated programs, during a single processing run. Each complete series of programs is designed to meet the information-processing requirements of one organizational function—payroll, accounts receivable, billing, or inventory control, for example. The complete series of programs forms a system. Source documents

Figure 11–1
Monthly Billing Program
(System Flowchart)

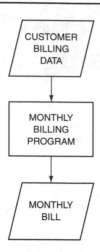

within the system may be used to create inputs for one or more programs, and outputs generated by one program may serve as inputs for one or more other programs. The programs are said to operate in a **batch-processing environment.**

Whether a system comprises one program or several, it can be described by a system flowchart. The simplest type of system flowchart was introduced in Chapter 2 of this book. It represents one computer program that accepts one form of input and provides one form of output. One of the system flowcharts we discussed in Chapter 2 is shown again in Figure 11–1. Numerous CASE tools support methodologies and tools for describing existing and planned systems in terms of their inputs, outputs, and involved programs or modules. Such information is valuable to people who want to understand the "big picture" of a system.

File Maintenance

Figure 11–2 shows a system flowchart for a system that performs master-file updating at a large publishing company. As we learned in Chapter 6, a master file is a collection of related records containing relatively permanent data essential to system processing. However, even permanent data must be changed occasionally; updating of master files for one or more systems is required at almost all information-processing installations. Updating a master file is called **file maintenance;** execution of a program that performs file maintenance is referred to as a **file maintenance run.**

The publishing company using the system described in Figure 11–2 stores the names, addresses, and other pertinent information about all its magazine subscribers in a master name and address file (master N/A file). The file is processed weekly to perform operations such as:

- Add names and addresses of new subscribers.

- Delete names and addresses of subscribers for whom subscriptions have expired.

- Modify records of current subscribers who have renewed their subscriptions or changed their addresses.

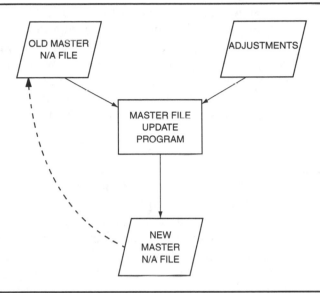

Figure 11–2
Master File Update Program
(System Flowchart)

This system flowchart indicates that master-file updating is performed by a master file update program. There are two inputs to the program. One is the current N/A file, called the old master N/A file to distinguish it from the new master N/A file, which will be created by the program. The second input is another file containing adjustments to be made to the master N/A file. This file is the transaction, or detail, file.

The master file update program provides an updated (or new) master N/A file, which will be used as a current (or old) master N/A file the next time this program is executed. Programmers often use broken lines, as shown in Figure 11–2, to indicate a **turnaround file.** The new master N/A file may also be used by other programs (e.g., by a print program that prepares address labels for use in mailing).

Sequential Processing

A major consideration when processing records is to determine the sequence in which they are processed. If a file is stored on magnetic tape, for example, the records must be accessed in the order in which they are stored on the tape. It would take far too long to spin a tape backward or forward looking for a particular record. Instead, a particular record can be accessed only after all preceding records in the file have been accessed. We say that **sequential processing** of the records is required.

So that sequential processing can be performed in an efficient, effective manner, the records in a magnetic-tape master file are arranged in sequence according to a particular data item or items common to all records in the file. The portion of the record that contains this data is called the **key field.** For example, the key field of records in a master payroll file may contain employee number; the key field of records in a master inventory file may contain part number; and so on. All records to be included in the file must have the required key field, and the field must contain valid data.

An additional requirement of sequential processing is that any transaction records to be processed against a sequential master file must be in the same sequence as the master file records. During program execution, the key field value of a transaction record is compared with the key field values of successive master records until an equal comparison or match results. If transaction records and master records were not arranged in the same sequence before the comparisons were made, some master file records would be read long before their matching transaction records were accessed. It is likely that few, if any, matches would occur.

Direct Processing

Master files can be stored on tape, but they can also be stored on disks. Records stored on a magnetic disk can be accessed sequentially or directly. If they are accessed directly, they do not have to be processed in order. This type of processing is called **direct,** or **random, processing.** If records are processed directly, they do not need to be sorted first. There is also no requirement to sequence transaction records in the same order as master records. In this case, a **random update procedure** can be used.

Sequential Master File Update Example

Let's direct our attention now to the processing steps within a large program that performs a **sequential update procedure.** Any of several programming techniques can be used to match transaction records with corresponding master records for updating. The remainder of this chapter illustrates one such approach. Before we discuss the problem, it is important to emphasize the assumptions being made, and to stress that these assumptions are basic to the successful execution of this program. The assumptions to be made are:

- The master file and the transaction file are assumed to be in the same sequence according to the key fields ID#-M and ID#-T, respectively.
- ID#s read from either file must be in the range from 1 through 10,000.
- Automatic end-of-file processing logic will be used in conjunction with both files.

All such assumptions made during the design stage of program development must be recognized and verified before the design plan is accepted. These assumptions should be stated clearly in the program documentation and pointed out whenever changes to the program or its inputs are discussed.

A structure chart outlining the modular design of a sequential master file update program is shown in Figure 11–3. As you can see, the design is not a simple one. This program consists of many modules, some of which appear in multiple locations on the structure chart. For example, module B020 is called by three different modules (A000, C000, and C010) during program execution. Reuse of a module is far preferable to writing similar code two or even three or more times to implement the same logic. In the past, such duplication of effort occurred often, usually because programmers had no way of knowing what potentially usable code, routines, and modules already existed, or where to find them. Well-designed CASE tools now provide ways to catalog and manage these components in online libraries. The tools promote code reusability and help to increase programmer productivity.

We will now discuss how the program shown in Figure 11–3 will operate in a general manner. Then we will take a look at the specific steps in each module.

After the appropriate initialization is completed, one record is read from the master file and one record is read from the transaction file. The update procedure is begun by comparing the key field from the transaction record to the key field from the master record. Three possibilities exist:

- If the transaction record key is *less than* the master record key, the transaction record is added to the master file and the next transaction is read.

- If the transaction record key is *equal to* the master record key, the master record is either deleted or updated with the information from the transaction record. In this case the next transaction record also needs to be read.

- If the transaction record key is *greater than* the master record key, there are no more transaction records that affect the current master record. Therefore, that master record is output to a new master file and the next master record is read.

Figure 11–3
Sequential Master File
Update Problem (SMFUP)
(Structure Chart)

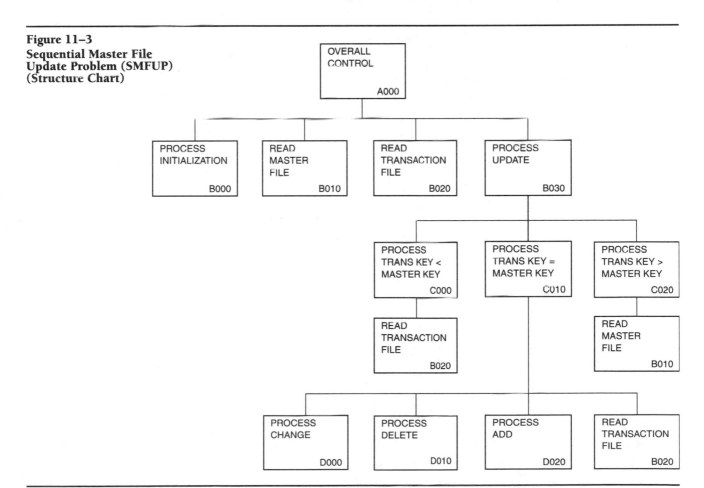

This overview of the processing involved in updating a master file is helpful, but many additional details must be taken into account. For example, how do we handle end-of-file processing when we are reading from two separate files and either one may end before the other? What types of errors can occur during the processing? These questions and others are answered in the detailed discussion of each module.

The flowchart and pseudocode for the overall control module (A000) are shown in Figures 11–4 and 11–5.

The first module called is B000, which handles all the initialization. The flowchart and pseudocode for B000 are shown in Figure 11–6.

Four flags are used in this program, and they are all initially set to 0. Since we are reading from two separate files, each file will reach end-of-file independently of the other. EOF-M will be set to 1 in module B010 when end-of-file has been reached in the master file. Similarly, EOF-T will be set to 1 in module B020 when end-of-file has been reached in the transaction file. This logic is important, because we need to continue to process

Figure 11–4
SMFUP—Overall Control
(Flowchart)

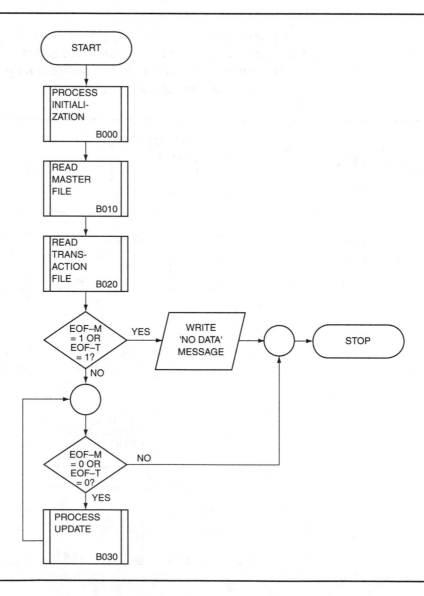

**Figure 11–5
SMFUP—Overall Control
(Pseudocode)**

```
A000
Start
Process initialization (B000)
Read master file (B010)
Read transaction file (B020)
IF EOF-M = 1 OR EOF-T = 1 THEN
   Write 'No data' message
ELSE
   DOWHILE EOF-M = 0 OR EOF-T = 0
      Process update (B030)
   ENDDO
ENDIF
Stop
```

**Figure 11–6
SMFUP—Process
Initialization**

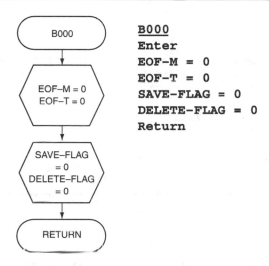

```
B000
Enter
EOF-M = 0
EOF-T = 0
SAVE-FLAG = 0
DELETE-FLAG = 0
Return
```

the remaining transaction records (valid transactions can only be adds at this point) if we reach end-of-file in the master file first. Similarly, if we reach end-of-file in the transaction file first, we need to read the rest of the master file and copy these records (unchanged) to the new master file. The flowchart and pseudocode for the modules that read the master file and transaction file are shown, respectively, in Figures 11–7 and 11–8.

These two modules are exactly the same, except that one reads the master file (B010) and the other reads the transaction file (B020). Each master record contains an identification number (ID#-M), name, and address of a person subscribing to a magazine. Also included in the record are a magazine code (MAGZ-M) and the expiration date of the magazine (EXPDT-M). Recall from our earlier discussion that the key field being used in this program is ID#-M. Each transaction record contains the same information as the master record, with the addition of a special code field (CODE) specifying the type of transaction. Valid codes are "A" (add), "C" (change), and "D" (delete).

Remember also that the key field for the transaction record is ID#-T. When end-of-file is reached in one of the files (automatically, not trailer record), the EOF flag is set to 1 and the ID# for that file is set to 99999.

Figure 11–7
SMFUP—Read Master File

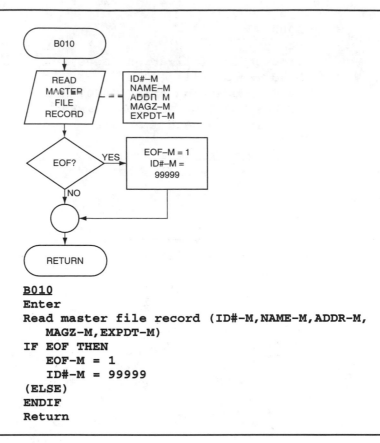

```
B010
Enter
Read master file record (ID#-M,NAME-M,ADDR-M,
    MAGZ-M,EXPDT-M)
IF EOF THEN
    EOF-M = 1
    ID#-M = 99999
(ELSE)
ENDIF
Return
```

Figure 11–8
SMFUP—Read
Transaction File

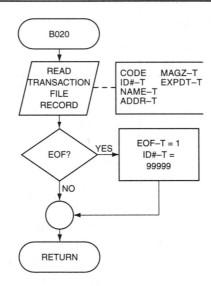

```
B020
Enter
Read transaction file record (CODE,ID#-T,NAME-T,ADDR-T,
    MAGZ-T,EXPDT-T)
IF EOF THEN
    EOF-T = 1
    ID#-T = 99999
(ELSE)
ENDIF
Return
```

Remember the assumption that any ID#s read from either file must be in the range 1 through 10,000.

When end-of-file is finally reached in one of the files, the remaining records in the other file must still be processed. Since this processing involves the comparison of key fields from both the transaction and master files, the ID# from the file that has reached end-of-file no longer exists. If this file is the master file, a key of 99999 in the master file will guarantee that any subsequent transaction key will be less than the master key, and the add operation will be done for each remaining transaction record. If the transaction record reaches end-of-file first, a key of 99999 in the transaction file will guarantee that the transaction key will be greater than any subsequent master key. This will cause the remaining master records to be output unchanged to the new master file.

Two other flags are initialized in B000, SAVE-FLAG and DELETE-FLAG. DELETE-FLAG is used to indicate whether the current master record is to be deleted. If DELETE-FLAG is set to 1, the master record will not be output to the new master file. In other words, deleting a record is the act of not writing it to a new master file. SAVE-FLAG is used to indicate whether or not the current master record has been copied to a separate area in memory (save area). This will be done whenever a transaction record needs to be added to the master file. The current master record will be saved in another area and SAVE-FLAG will be set to 1.

The transaction record to be added will then be copied to the area formerly used for the current master record. This is necessary because only a record in the current master record area of memory can be output to the new master file. After this transaction record is actually added to the new master file, the saved master record must be copied back to the current master record area so that it can be processed.

After both files have been read for the first time, a test is made in A000 to determine if the main processing should even be attempted (Figures 11–4 and 11–5). The first decision step in this module makes sure that neither of the files is empty (end-of-file reached on the first read attempt). If there are no transaction records, the master file does not need to be updated. If there are no master records, the master file does not exist but needs to be created. The creation of a master file should be done in another program. In either case, a "No data" message will be output. (Consider how you might change this module to output either of two messages, depending on which file was empty. See Exercise 5.)

If both files contain at least one record, then the update processing (module B030) will be done inside a DOWHILE loop, as long as either of the files contains records to be processed. Remember, processing must continue with one file even when the other file reaches end-of-file. When end-of-file is finally reached in both files, program execution will terminate.

The flowchart and pseudocode for the process update module (B030) are shown in Figure 11–9. B030 calls three modules to do the actual processing. The first module (C000) gets control if the transaction record key is *less than* the master record key. Module C010 gets control if the transaction record key is *equal to* the master record key. Module C020 handles the writing of a new master record, which will occur when the transaction record key is *greater than* the master record key.

Figure 11–9
SMFUP—Process Update

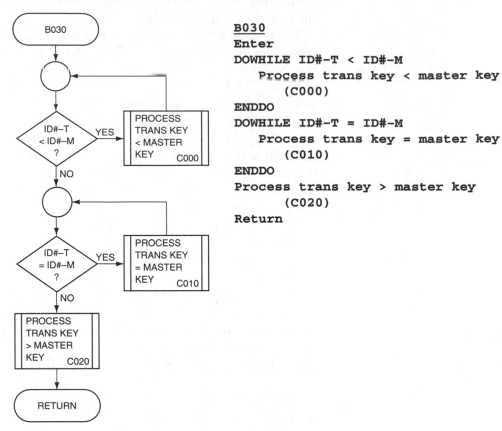

```
B030
Enter
DOWHILE ID#-T < ID#-M
    Process trans key < master key
        (C000)
ENDDO
DOWHILE ID#-T = ID#-M
    Process trans key = master key
        (C010)
ENDDO
Process trans key > master key
        (C020)
Return
```

The flowchart and pseudocode for module C000 are shown in Figures 11–10 and 11–11. A test is made to determine if the transaction code (CODE) is an "A." This is the only valid possibility. If the code is an "A," the current master record will be saved in another area to be processed at a later time, and the save flag will be set to 1. The transaction record to be added will then be copied into the current master record area (see Figure 11–12). If the code is not an "A," either it was invalid or an attempt was made to delete or change a record that does not exist in the current master file. In either case, an error message will be output. (Consider how you might change this module to output one of three specific error messages denoting a bad delete attempt, a bad change attempt, or an invalid code. See Exercise 6.)

After the current transaction record is either copied or determined to be in error, a new transaction record is read and control is returned to B030. The new transaction record's key is then tested against the current master record key. You might wonder why we make this test again. It seems unlikely that a subsequent transaction record key could be less than the master record key, because the current master record key is the previous transaction key. Remember, the keys are assumed to be in sequence. The only time this will occur is if the previous transaction was in error or our assumption is wrong. In either case, the master record key remained unchanged. The new transaction key may still be less than the master record key at this point. Consider the case when a transaction record with

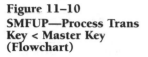

Figure 11–10
SMFUP—Process Trans
Key < Master Key
(Flowchart)

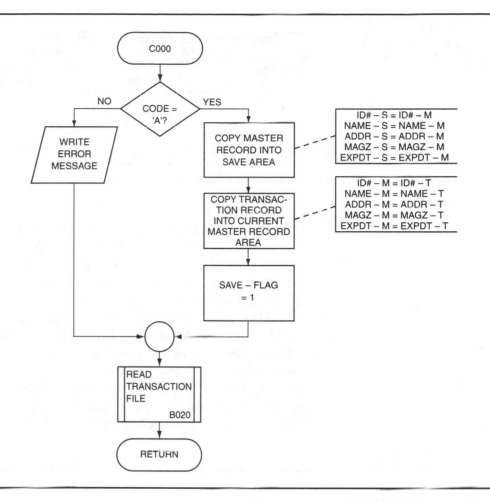

Figure 11–11
SMFUP—Process Trans
Key < Master Key
(Pseudocode)

```
C000
Enter
IF CODE = 'A' THEN
     ID#-S = ID#-M
     NAME-S = NAME-M
     ADDR-S = ADDR-M          Copy master record
     MAGZ-S = MAGZ-M          into save area
     EXPDT-S = EXPDT-M
     ID#-M = ID#-T
     NAME-M = NAME-T          Copy transaction record
     ADDR-M = ADDR-T          into current master
     MAGZ-M = MAGZ-T          record area
     EXPDT-M = EXPDT-T
     SAVE-FLAG = 1
ELSE
     Write error message (deleting or changing
          a record that doesn't exist or
          invalid transaction code)
ENDIF
Read transaction file (B020)
Return
```

Figure 11–12
Adding a Master Record
(Code = "A" and ID#-T <
ID#-M)

	CURRENT TRANSACTION RECORD			CURRENT MASTER RECORD		SAVE AREA	
	CODE	ID#–T	OTHER FIELDS	ID#–M	OTHER FIELDS	ID#–S	OTHER FIELDS
①	A	000123		000586			
②	A	000123		000586 ⟶		000586	
③	A	000123 ⟶		000123		000586	

an invalid code is immediately followed by a valid transaction record with a code of "A." Eventually, the transaction record key will no longer be less than the master record key and the second DOWHILE loop test (ID#-T = ID#-M) in B030 is made. If this condition is true, module C010 will be executed. Again, a loop is used, because a single master record may have several transactions associated with it.

The flowchart and pseudocode for module C010 are shown in Figures 11–13 and 11–14. A CASE control structure is used to determine the type of transaction. One of three modules is called if the transaction code is valid, and an error message is output if the transaction code is not valid. In any case, another transaction is read after the previous one is processed, and control is returned to B030. The keys are tested again, and if they are no longer equal, module C020 gets control.

Figure 11–13
SMFUP—Process Trans
Key = Master Key
(Flowchart)

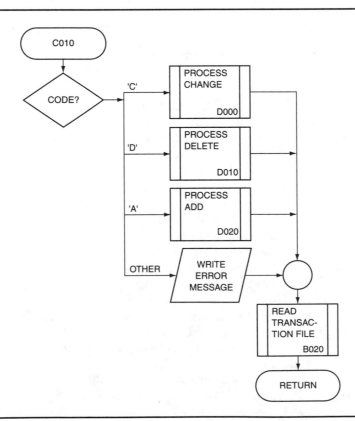

Figure 11–14
SMFUP—Process Trans
Key = Master Key
(Pseudocode)

```
C010
Enter
CASENTRY CODE
    CASE 'C'
        Process change (D000)
    CASE 'D'
        Process delete (D010)
    CASE 'A'
        Process add (D020)
    CASE other
        Write error message (invalid transaction
          code)
ENDCASE
Read transaction file (B020)
Return
```

The flowchart and pseudocode for module C020 are shown in Figures 11–15 and 11–16. This module will be called by B030 only when the transaction record key is greater than the master record key. This indicates that there are no more transactions to be processed against the current master record. At this point the current master record can be written to a new

Figure 11–15
SMFUP—Process Trans
Key > Master Key
(Flowchart)

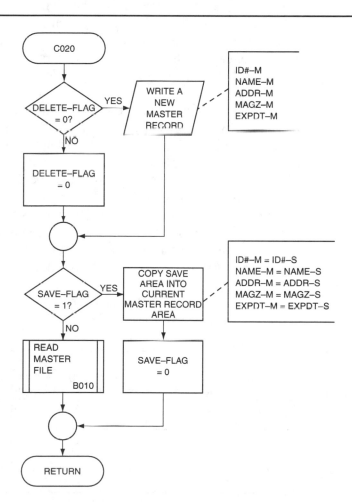

Figure 11-16
SMFUP—Process Trans Key
> Master Key (Pseudocode)

```
C020
Enter
IF DELETE-FLAG = 0 THEN
    Write a new master record (ID=-M,NAME-M,ADDR-M,MAGZ-M,
        EXPDT-M)
ELSE
    DELETE-FLAG = 0
ENDIF
IF SAVE-FLAG = 1 THEN
    ID#-M = ID#-S
    NAME-M = NAME-S          Copy save area
    ADDR-M = ADDR-S          into current master
    MAGZ-M = MAGZ-S          record area
    EXPDT-M = EXPDT-S
    SAVE-FLAG = 0
ELSE
    Read master file (B010)
ENDIF
Return
```

master file (another actual file, as shown in the system flowchart in Figure 11-2), unless the delete flag has been set to 1. If a previous transaction specified that this master record was to be deleted, the delete flag was set to 1 (see module D010). In this case, the current master record will simply not be copied to the new master file. The delete flag will then be reset to 0 so it does not cause subsequent master records to be deleted.

Since the current master record was either deleted or copied to the new master file, it would seem appropriate to read another record from the master file. Module C020 *may* read a record next, but first it checks the save flag. If the save flag is a 0, a master record is read. If the save flag is a 1, we know that a master record that has not yet been processed is stored in a save area. (Remember module C000.) In such a case, it is inappropriate to read a new master record, because one exists in the save area and has not yet been processed. This master record in the save area is then copied back into the current master record area, and the save flag is reset to 0 (see Figure 11-17). Control is then returned to B030. B030 returns control to A000 and the end-of-file flags are checked prior to reentering the main loop.

Recall that module C010 calls upon one of three modules to process a transaction with a valid code. If the code is a "C," module D000 (Figure 11-18)

Figure 11-17
Copying Save Area into
Current Master Record

	CURRENT TRANSACTION RECORD			CURRENT MASTER RECORD		SAVE AREA	
	CODE	ID#-T	OTHER FIELDS	ID#-M	OTHER FIELDS	ID#-S	OTHER FIELDS
①	C	01234		000123		000586	
②	C	01234		000586 ←		000586	

handles the processing. First, the delete flag is checked to make sure that the current master record is not marked for deletion. If it is, an error message is output because it makes no sense to change a deleted record. If the record has not been marked for deletion, the transaction record data is copied into the current master record area, replacing what was there before (see Figure 11–19). Control is then returned to module C010.

If the code is a "D," module D010 (Figure 11–20) handles the processing. Again, the delete flag is checked to determine if the current master record has been marked for deletion. If it has, an error message will be output indicating an attempt has been made to delete an already-deleted record. Although it would not hurt to "delete again" (since we would simply be setting a flag to 1 that was already 1), this action is probably not the intent of the person creating the transaction file. It is more likely a data entry error, so by providing an error message we alert someone to a potential problem. If the current master record has not been marked for deletion, the delete flag is set to 1 and control is returned to module C010.

Figure 11–18
SMFUP—Process Change

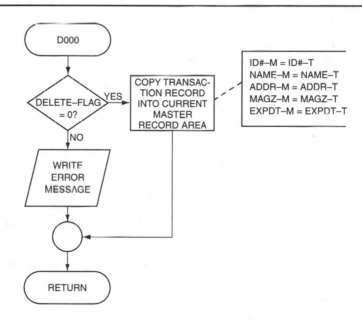

```
D000
Enter
IF DELETE-FLAG = 0 THEN
    ID#-M = ID#-T
    NAME-M = NAME-T        Copy transaction record
    ADDR-M = ADDR-T        into current master
    MAGZ-M = MAGZ-T        record area
    EXPDT-M = EXPDT-T
ELSE
    Write error message (changing a deleted record)
ENDIF
Return
```

Figure 11–19
Changing a Master Record (CODE = "C" and ID#-T = ID#-M)

	CURRENT TRANSACTION RECORD			CURRENT MASTER RECORD		SAVE AREA	
	CODE	ID#–T	OTHER FIELDS	ID#–M	OTHER FIELDS	ID#–S	OTHER FIELDS
①	C	01234		01234		00586	
②	C	01234 ⟶		01234	one or more of the fields in the current master record will be replaced with data from the current transaction record	00586	

Figure 11–20
SMFUP—Process Delete

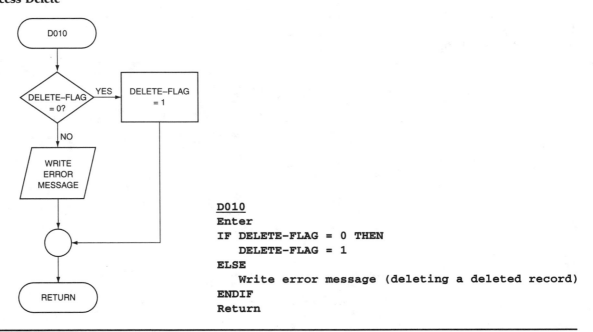

```
D010
Enter
IF DELETE-FLAG = 0 THEN
    DELETE-FLAG = 1
ELSE
    Write error message (deleting a deleted record)
ENDIF
Return
```

If the code is an "A," module D020 (Figure 11–21) handles the processing. In most cases, this module will be called when an attempt to add a record is made and that record already exists. In this case, an error message will be output. It is possible, however, to add a record that has just been deleted. If this happens, ID#-T will be equal to ID#-M and module C010 will be called—not C000, which does the normal add. Therefore, if the delete flag is 1, the current transaction record can be copied right over the current master record (since it was previously deleted) (see Figure 11–22). Do you see why we do not have to save the master record first? The delete flag must be reset to 0, because the current master record should no longer be marked for deletion. An add transaction that immediately follows a delete transaction has the same effect as a single-change transaction.

Figure 11–21
SMFUP—Process Add

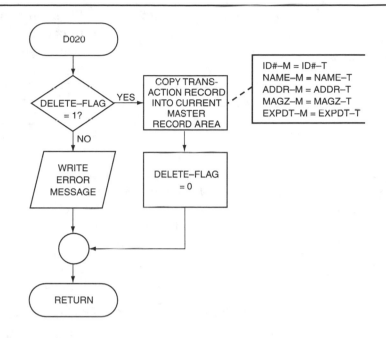

```
D020
Enter
IF DELETE-FLAG = 1 THEN
    ID#-M = ID#-T
    NAME-M = NAME-T       ⎫  Copy transaction record
    ADDR-M = ADDR-T       ⎬  into current master
    MAGZ-M = MAGZ-T       ⎭  record area
    EXPDT-M = EXPDT-T
    DELETE-FLAG = 0
ELSE
    Write error message (adding a record that already exists)
ENDIF
Return
```

Figure 11–22
Adding a Master Record (CODE = "A" and ID#-T = ID#-M and DELETE-FLAG = 1)

	CURRENT TRANSACTION RECORD			CURRENT MASTER RECORD		SAVE AREA	
	CODE	ID#–T	OTHER FIELDS	ID#–M	OTHER FIELDS	ID#–S	OTHER FIELDS
①	A	01534		01534		00586	
②	A	01534	⟶	01534	one or more of the fields in the current master record will be replaced with data from the current transaction record	00586	

Key Terms	online-processing environment	file maintenance run	random update procedure
	batch	turnaround file	
	batch-processing environment	sequential processing	sequential update procedure
		key field	
	file maintenance	direct (random) processing	

Exercises

1. Define the following terms:
   (a) online-processing environment
   (b) batch-processing environment
   (c) file maintenance run

2. What is the most significant characteristic of a magnetic-tape file in determining how records in the file must be processed?

3. Explain the purpose of each program switch initialized in Figure 11–6.

4. Modify the solution algorithm presented in this chapter to compute and output a count of the number of master records processed. The count should be (1) initialized to 0, (2) increased by 1 whenever a master record is written as output, and (3) output with an appropriate message before processing is terminated.

5. Redo the flowchart and/or pseudocode in Figures 11–4 and 11–5 to output one of two specific messages, depending on which file contained no data.

6. Redo the flowchart and/or pseudocode in Figures 11–10 and 11–11 to output one of three specific error messages denoting a bad delete attempt, a bad change attempt, or an invalid transaction code.

7. (a) Simulate the execution of the algorithm presented in this chapter using the following input records (make up values for the other fields):

Transaction File		Master File
CODE	ID#-T	ID#-M
C	00002	00002
D	00003	00003
C	00007	00006
C	00007	00007
A	00008	00009
		00010
		00012
		00014

   (b) Show the contents of the new master file when processing is completed.
   (c) List all the error messages that will be output (if any).

8. (a) Simulate the execution of the algorithm presented in this chapter using the following input records (make up values for the other fields):

Transaction File		Master File
CODE	ID#-T	ID#-M
A	00001	00003
C	00002	00004
A	00002	00005
C	00003	00006
B	00004	00007
C	00005	00008
D	00007	00010
D	00009	
D	00010	
C	00010	

(b) Show the contents of the new master file when processing is completed.

(c) List all the error messages that will be output (if any).

9. (a) Simulate the execution of the algorithm presented in this chapter using the following input records (make up values for the other fields):

Transaction File		Master File
CODE	ID#-T	ID#-M
D	00003	00001
A	00003	00002
C	00005	00003
D	00006	00004
D	00006	00006
C	00007	00007
A	00008	00008
A	00009	
A	00011	
D	00012	
A	00013	

(b) Show the contents of the new master file when processing is completed.

(c) List all the error messages that will be output (if any).

Objectives

Upon completion of this chapter you should be able to

- Define the terms *control break* and *control field (key)*.
- Distinguish among a detail-printed report, a group-printed report, and a group-indicated report.
- Design an algorithm that handles single-level control-break processing.
- Design an algorithm that handles multiple-level control-break processing.

Introduction

In most of the problems and solutions discussed in this book, the output contains detail lines, total lines, or both. Recall our discussion of these different types of output lines in Chapter 5. It is sometimes necessary to output intermediate total lines as well as final totals. For example, a sales report may need to show individual employee sales (detail lines), department total sales (intermediate total lines), and accumulated sales from all departments (final total line).

We have already seen many examples of algorithms that output detail lines and/or final total lines. An intermediate total line can also be output; it's normally written when a control break occurs. A **control break** is an interruption of the normal detail processing when the value in a designated key, or control field, of the input records changes.

For example, look at Figure 12–1. Assume all records for department 1000 are read first. When the first record for department 2000 is input, an intermediate total line containing accumulated totals for department 1000 can be output. Similarly, when the first record for department 3000 is input, an intermediate total line containing totals for department 2000 can be output. Do you see the pattern? When the department number changes, normal processing is interrupted and total information for the previous group of departments is output.

In this example, department number is defined to be the **key,** or control field. The **control field** is the field that determines when a control break is to occur. In control-break processing, we make one very important assumption: The input must be in sequence according to the values in the control field. When a record with department number 2000 is first input, we assume that all records for department number 1000 have been input. Only in this way can we be sure that the total information for department 1000 is complete.

In a control-break program, it is possible to output detail lines, intermediate total lines, and final total lines. If the report includes detail lines, it is called a **detail-printed report.** This is a report where one line is printed for every input record processed. If the report does not include detail lines, it is called a **group-printed report.** This type of report prints one line of output for every group of input records processed (intermediate total lines), but does not output the detailed information about each input record (see Exercise 10). A group-printed report may be output when only summary information is needed. It is not always necessary or even desirable to output a highly detailed document. Sometimes "less is better," depending on the information in the report and who will be reading it. As discussed previously, the use of CASE tools allows users to review and approve sample outputs early in the program development cycle.

The following problem illustrates the logic behind a control-break algorithm. As you will see, this algorithm produces a detail-printed report.

Sample Problem 12.1 (Single-Level Control Break)

Problem:

The ABC Corporation needs a program to produce a weekly sales report. The input to the program consists of department number, salesperson name, number, and weekly sales, as illustrated in Figure 12–1. The input can be assumed to be in ascending order by department number. The report should contain both a report heading and column headings at the top of

Figure 12–1
Control-Break Processing Problem (CBPP)—Sample Input

DEPARTMENT NUMBER	SALESPERSON NAME	SALESPERSON NUMBER	WEEKLY SALES
1000	JOHN WEAVER	3498	5003.00
1000	NANCY SMITH	2281	6154.00
1000	JAMES JOHNSON	3098	4234.50
2000	MARY STEVENS	1154	2213.80
2000	PAUL PRATT	7638	8874.40
3000	THEODORE JONES	5540	9832.30
.	.	.	.
.	.	.	.
.	.	.	.
7000	STEVE BLACK	4554	2394.80
7000	LAURA CUNNINGHAM	1092	5541.70
.	.	.	.
.	.	.	.
.	.	.	.

every page, and each page should be numbered. No more than 50 detail lines should be output on a single page. Each detail line should contain department number, salesperson name, salesperson number, and weekly sales. There should also be one line showing accumulated sales information for each department. A final total line indicating the total sales volume for all departments should be output at the end of the report. The format of the output is illustrated in Figure 12–2.

Solution:

A structure chart illustrating the modular design of this algorithm is shown in Figure 12–3. All the module names and functions should be familiar to you, with the exception of module B020 (process department change). This module will handle the processing necessary when a control break occurs.

The program flowchart and pseudocode representations of the overall control module (A000) are shown in Figures 12–4 and 12–5.

After the necessary initialization is done, the first record is input. As usual, this record is tested to determine if end-of-file (automatic, not trailer record) has been reached on the first read attempt. If so, a "No data" message is output and processing terminates. If end-of-file has not been

Figure 12–2
CBPP—Sample Output

```
                         ABC CORPORATION
                       WEEKLY SALES REPORT

    DEPARTMENT          SALESPERSON      SALESPERSON       WEEKLY
      NUMBER               NAME             NUMBER          SALES

      1000            JOHN  WEAVER          3498          5,003.30
      1000            NANCY  SMITH          2281          6,154.00
      1000            JAMES  JOHNSON        3098          4,234.50

                  TOTAL  SALES--DEPARTMENT 1000:         15,391.80


      2000            MARY  STEVENS         1154          2,213.80
       .                   .                  .              .
       .                   .                  .              .
       .                   .                  .              .

                  TOTAL  SALES--DEPARTMENT 2000:        120,681.30


      3000            THEODORE  JONES       5540          9,832.30
       .                   .                  .              .
       .                   .                  .              .
       .                   .                  .              .

                     TOTAL  WEEKLY  SALES:              443,952.90
```

Figure 12–3
CBPP (Structure Chart)

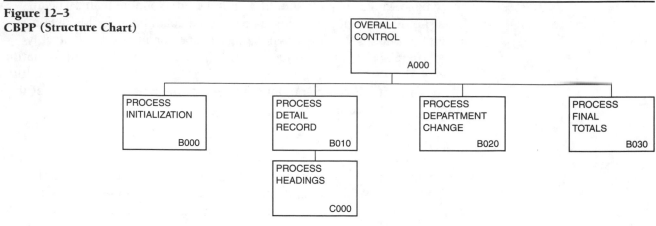

Figure 12–4
CBPP—Overall Control
(Flowchart)

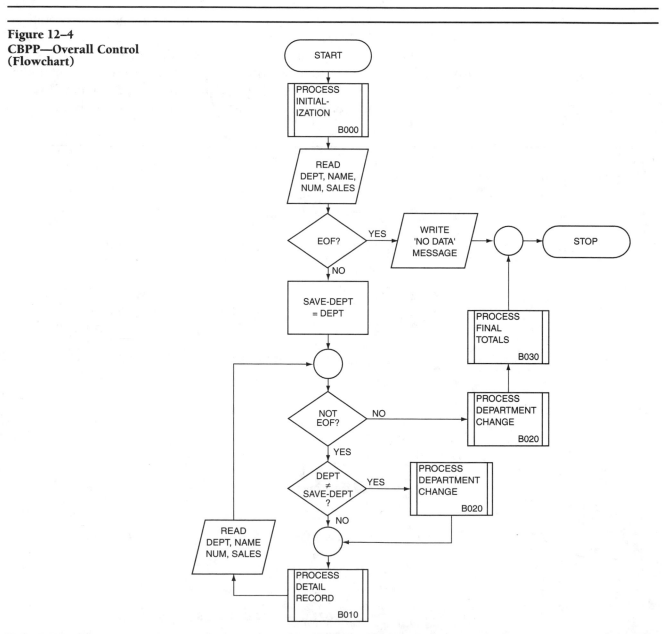

Figure 12–5
CBPP—Overall Control
(Pseudocode)

```
A000
Start
Process initialization (B000)
Read DEPT, NAME, NUM, SALES
IF EOF THEN
   Write 'No data' message
ELSE
   SAVE-DEPT = DEPT
   DOWHILE not EOF
      IF DEPT ≠ SAVE-DEPT THEN
         Process department change (B020)
      (ELSE)
      ENDIF
      Process detail record (B010)
      Read DEPT, NAME, NUM, SALES
   ENDDO
   Process department change (B020)
   Process final totals (B030)
ENDIF
Stop
```

reached, the control field (DEPT) is copied into another area (SAVE-DEPT) before the DOWHILE loop is begun.

You might wonder why. Each time a new record is read, we need to determine if the department number just input is different from the previous department number. It is therefore necessary to save the value of the first department number and check that value against each subsequent department number input. As you can see, this test is the first step that is done in the main processing loop. If the department number just input (DEPT) is not equal to the department number in the save area (SAVE-DEPT), a control break has occurred and module B020 must be executed. If the two department numbers are, in fact, equal, the normal detail processing (module B010) is executed. Then another record is read.

It is important to see why a null ELSE was used here. If a control break has not occurred, only module B010 is executed—because there are no steps to be done in the NO path of the IFTHENELSE. If a control break has occurred—that is, if the YES path of the IFTHENELSE is taken—module B020 is executed. When module B020 completes its processing, module B010 is then executed. Can you see why?

After the intermediate total line for department number 1000 is output (module B020), the detail processing still must be done for the current record that was input. Remember, a control break for department 1000 was detected because a record for department 2000 was read. That record (for department 2000) must be processed before a new record can be read. This repetitive kind of processing continues until end-of-file is reached. When the end-of-file is finally reached, module B020 is executed one last time; then the final total line is output (module B030).

You might wonder why module B020 is executed again. When end-of-file is reached, the intermediate total for the last group of department numbers has not yet been output. Remember, this is done only when a control break occurs, and a control break can be detected only when the control field in the input changes. An end-of-file is, in effect, a change in the control field. (In this case, it contains a nonexistent department number.)

A program flowchart and corresponding pseudocode for module B000 (process initialization) are shown in Figure 12–6. Two accumulators are set to 0. DEPT-ACCUM is used to keep track of the total weekly sales within one department. FINAL-ACCUM keeps track of the total weekly sales for all departments. The page count (PAGECNT) is set to 1, and the line count (LINECNT) is set to 50. LINECNT indicates how many detail lines are currently printed on a page of the report. Obviously, no lines have been printed yet, but initializing the line count to 50 makes the computer think it's already at the bottom of a page. Do you remember why this is done?

A program flowchart and corresponding pseudocode for module B010 (process detail report) are shown in Figure 12–7. The first processing step is an IFTHENELSE that determines if headings need to be printed. Remember, when LINECNT reaches 50 or greater, a new page is started and the headings must be printed first. The detail processing in this algorithm is quite simple: The detail line contains information, all of which has been input, so no calculations are necessary. The line is printed and LINECNT is incremented. Finally, the weekly sales amount from the input (SALES) is added to the department accumulator (DEPT-ACCUM) before control is returned to A000.

A program flowchart and corresponding pseudocode for module B020 (process department change) are shown in Figure 12–8. When this module gets control, a control break has occurred and a department total line must be output. Although the actual spacing of output lines is not always a consideration in the design phase, it may help to visualize the final report if we indicate when spacing is to occur. Prior to printing the department total line, a blank line is output; after the total line is printed, two blank lines are output. This will help to distinguish the intermediate total line from the detail lines. The department number (SAVE-DEPT) and the accumulated sales for that department (DEPT-ACCUM), as well as identifying text, are output.

**Figure 12–6
CBPP—Process
Initialization**

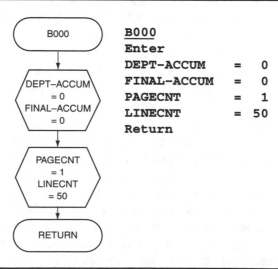

```
B000
Enter
DEPT-ACCUM    =    0
FINAL-ACCUM   =    0
PAGECNT       =    1
LINECNT       =   50
Return
```

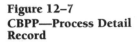

Figure 12-7
CBPP—Process Detail
Record

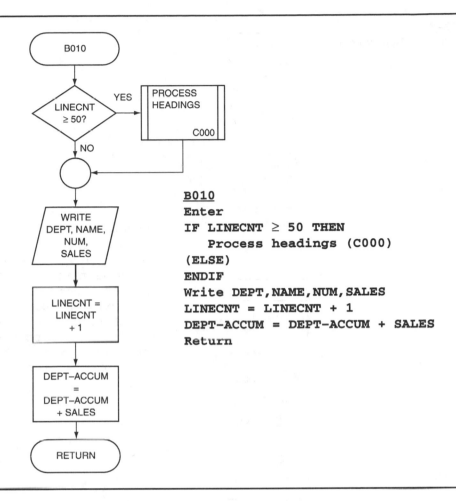

```
B010
Enter
IF LINECNT ≥ 50 THEN
    Process headings (C000)
(ELSE)
ENDIF
Write DEPT,NAME,NUM,SALES
LINECNT = LINECNT + 1
DEPT-ACCUM = DEPT-ACCUM + SALES
Return
```

Why is SAVE-DEPT output and not DEPT? Remember, DEPT contains information from the current input record. Since four physical lines have been printed (three blank lines and one total line), the line count is incremented by 4. The department accumulator is added to the final accumulator and then reset to 0. Do you see why? When the next group of department numbers are processed, we do not want the previous department's total sales to be included in the current department's totals.

Finally, because we are getting ready to process a new group of department numbers, the save area (SAVE-DEPT) needs to be updated. Remember, this area is used to hold the value of the current department being processed. For example, when a control break occurs the first time, the current department number must be changed from 1000 to 2000.

A program flowchart and corresponding pseudocode for module B030 (process final totals) are shown in Figure 12–9. This module simply writes out the value of the final accumulator (FINAL-ACCUM) with an identifying message. Remember, FINAL-ACCUM represents the total weekly sales for all departments.

A program flowchart and corresponding pseudocode for module C000 (process headings) are shown in Figure 12–10. In this module, we are again trying to indicate some degree of spacing. The report heading is followed by one blank line, and the column headings are followed by one blank line.

**Figure 12–8
CBPP—Process Department
Change**

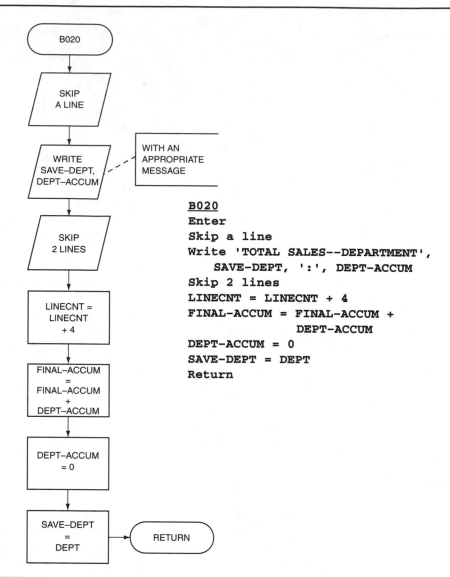

```
B020
Enter
Skip a line
Write 'TOTAL SALES--DEPARTMENT',
     SAVE-DEPT, ':', DEPT-ACCUM
Skip 2 lines
LINECNT = LINECNT + 4
FINAL-ACCUM = FINAL-ACCUM +
                    DEPT-ACCUM
DEPT-ACCUM = 0
SAVE-DEPT = DEPT
Return
```

**Figure 12–9
CBPP—Process Final Totals**

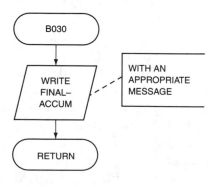

```
B030
Enter
Write 'TOTAL WEEKLY SALES:', FINAL-ACCUM
Return
```

The spacing is primarily for readability; it may or may not be specified by the user. In either case, the programmer must include an indication of spacing requirements somewhere in the documentation.

You might wonder why the line count is not checked prior to writing out either the intermediate total line in B020 or the final total line in B030. It is entirely possible that the line count could be equal to 50 prior to writing out the total lines. Because module B020 does not check the line count, a department total line is always output on the same page where the detail lines for that same department are printed. This enhances the readability of the report; it would be very confusing to see a department total at the top of a new page without the detail lines preceding it. Similarly, the final total line is always output on the same page where the last department total line is printed.

With some quick computations, we can figure the maximum number of lines that could be output on a page. Each time B010 is called, the line count is checked. If no intermediate total lines are output, the line count will be incremented by 1 each time B010 executes—until it gets to 50. Then a new page will be started and the line count will be reset to 0. If

Figure 12–10
CBPP—Process Headings

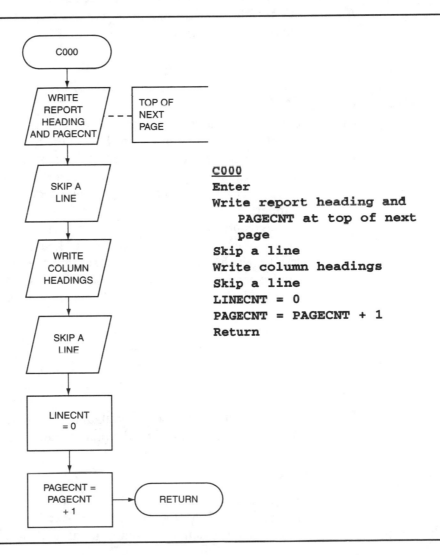

```
C000
Enter
Write report heading and
    PAGECNT at top of next
    page
Skip a line
Write column headings
Skip a line
LINECNT = 0
PAGECNT = PAGECNT + 1
Return
```

B020 is called, let's say midpage (LINECNT about 30), the four intermediate total lines (blank line, actual total line, and two blank lines) are output on the current page and the line count is incremented to 34.

The maximum number of lines would be printed only if the following sequence of steps were executed: LINECNT is 49 on entry to B010 (no new page would be started yet); B010 executes, incrementing LINECNT to 50; B010 returns control to A000 and a new record is read; a control break occurs, so B020 executes next, incrementing LINECNT to 54; B020 returns control to A000, which immediately gives control to B010; B010 checks LINECNT and calls C000, which starts a new page and resets LINECNT to 0. The only time B010 is not executed immediately after B020 is when end-of-file is reached. At this point B030 executes and outputs one last line, the final total line. Since the line count was previously 54, we now know that 55 lines (excluding headings) have been output. If module C000 outputs six lines (two report heading lines, one blank line, two column heading lines, and one blank line), the total number of printed lines on one page would be 61. Since most printers can print 66 physical lines on a page, this should not present a problem. It is important to interpret the specifications properly. The results would have been entirely different if the problem statement had said that a maximum of 50 lines (any type) could be output.

Sample Problem 12.2 (Multiple-Level Control Break)

Problem:

The XYZ Computer Company needs a program to produce a weekly sales report. As illustrated in Figure 12–11, the input to the program consists of branch number, salesperson number, customer number, item description, and sales amount of item. The input can be assumed to be in ascending order by customer number, within salesperson number, within branch number.

The report should contain both a report heading and column headings at the top of every page. Each page should be numbered. No more than 40 detail lines should be output on a single page. Each detail line should contain branch number, salesperson number, customer number, description of item, and sales amount of item. There should also be one line showing accumulated sales information for each customer, for each salesperson, and for each branch. A final total line indicating the total sales volume for all branches should be output at the end of the report. The format of the output is illustrated in Figure 12–12. Note that the customer number is only printed next to the first item purchased by each customer. This is an example of a **group-indicated report.** Group-indicated reports generally appear less cluttered and easier to read than detail-printed reports. Note that both the salesperson number and the branch number are also group indicated.

Solution:

A structure chart illustrating the modular design of this algorithm is shown in Figure 12–13. All the module names and functions should be familiar to you. In this example, a control break will occur whenever a customer

Figure 12–11
Multiple-Level
Control–Break–Processing
Problem (MLCBPP)—
Sample Input

BRANCH NUMBER	SALESPERSON NUMBER	CUSTOMER NUMBER	ITEM DESCRIPTION	SALES AMOUNT
10	1122	345	Monitor	400.00
10	1122	345	Printer	200.00
10	1122	345	Modem	100.00
10	1122	412	Copier	500.00
10	1122	412	Printer	600.00
10	1122	567	Keyboard	100.00
10	2334	123	Modem	100.00
10	2334	123	Computer	1000.00
10	2334	246	Hard Drive	350.00
20	1111	137	Hard Drive	350.00
20	1111	137	Monitor	400.00
20	2222	387	Computer	1000.00
20	3333	190	Copier	500.00
20	3333	190	Modem	100.00
20	3333	224	Hard Drive	350.00
20	3333	367	Keyboard	100.00
20	3333	367	Fax Machine	500.00
30	1479	108	Computer	1000.00
.	.	.	.	.
.	.	.	.	.
.	.	.	.	.

number, salesperson number, or branch number changes. Note that we have included three separate modules (B020, B030, and B040) to handle this processing.

The program flowchart and pseudocode representations of the overall control module (A000) are shown in Figures 12–14 and 12–15.

After the necessary initialization is done, the first record is input. As usual, this record is tested to determine if end-of-file (automatic, not trailer record) has been reached on the first read attempt. If so, a "No data" message is output and processing terminates. If end-of-file has not been reached, then each control field (CUST#, SALES#, and BRANCH#) is copied into another area (SAVE-CUST#, SAVE-SALES#, and SAVE-BRANCH#) before the DOWHILE loop is begun. You probably remember using the same step in the previous problem. Once again, each time a new record is read, we need to determine if any of the control fields just input (CUST#, SALES#, or BRANCH#) is different from the previous values. It is therefore necessary to save the value of the first customer number, salesperson number, and branch number, and to check those values against each subsequent customer number, salesperson number, and branch number input.

The first processing step within the DOWHILE loop blanks out three areas: CUST#-OUT, SALES#-OUT, and BRANCH#-OUT. These variable names represent the customer number, salesperson number, and branch

Figure 12–12
MLCBPP—Sample Output

```
                      XYZ  COMPUTER  COMPANY
                      WEEKLY  SALES  REPORT

   BRANCH        SALESPERSON      CUSTOMER         ITEM            SALES
   NUMBER          NUMBER          NUMBER       DESCRIPTION        AMOUNT

     10            1122             345         Monitor           400.00
                                                Printer           200.00
                                                Modem             100.00

                   TOTAL CUSTOMER 345 SALES:                      700.00

                                    412         Copier            500.00
                                                Printer           600.00

                   TOTAL CUSTOMER 412 SALES:                     1100.00

                                    567         Keyboard          100.00

                   TOTAL CUSTOMER 567 SALES:                      100.00

                   TOTAL SALESPERSON 1122 SALES:                 1900.00

                   2334             123         Modem             100.00
                                                Computer         1000.00

                   TOTAL CUSTOMER 123 SALES:                     1100.00

                                    246         Hard Drive        350.00

                   TOTAL CUSTOMER 246 SALES:                      350.00

                   TOTAL SALESPERSON 2334 SALES:                 1450.00

                   TOTAL BRANCH 10 SALES:                        3350.00

     20            1111             137         Hard Drive        350.00
                                                Monitor           400.00
                                      .
                                      .
                                      .
                   TOTAL BRANCH 20 SALES:                        3300.00

     30            1479             108         Computer         1000.00
                                      .
                                      .
                                      .
                   TOTAL BRANCH 30 SALES:                        5000.00


                   TOTAL ACCUMULATED SALES:                     78950.00
```

Figure 12–13
MLCBPP (Structure Chart)

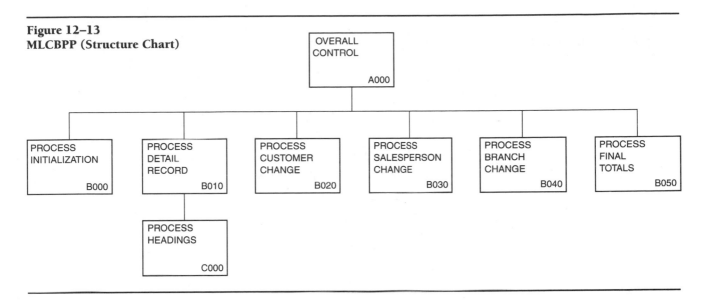

number fields that will be output. This step is necessary because the report is to be group indicated. The only time that the actual customer number, salesperson number, and branch number will be placed in these fields for output will be at the start of a new page (done in the headings module) and when one of the control fields changes (done in the appropriate control-break module).

This step is then followed by three nested IFTHENELSE statements, which determine if one of the control fields has changed. It is very important to notice the order in which these tests are made. A branch number change implies both a salesperson number change and a customer number change. When there is a change in branch number, the module that processes a customer change will be executed first, followed by the module that processes a salesperson change, and then the module that processes the branch change. When there is a change in branch number, the customer total line will be output first, followed by the salesperson total line, and finally the branch total line. Similarly, a salesperson number change implies a customer number change. When there is a change in salesperson number, the module that processes a customer change will be executed first, followed by the module that processes a salesperson change. Again, the customer total line will be output first, followed by the salesperson total line. Lastly, when there is a change in customer number, only the module that processes a customer number change will be executed and a customer total line will be output. If none of the control fields has changed, the normal detail processing (module B010) is executed. Then another record is read. It is important to see that module B010 is also executed when modules B020, B030, and/or B040 complete their processing. Do you remember why?

After one or more total lines are output, the detail processing still must be done for the current record that was input. Remember, a control break was detected as a result of a change in one or more control fields based on information input from a new record. This new record must be processed before another new record can be read. This repetitive kind of processing continues until end-of-file is reached. When the end-of-file is finally

**Figure 12–14
MLCBPP—Overall Control
(Flowchart)**

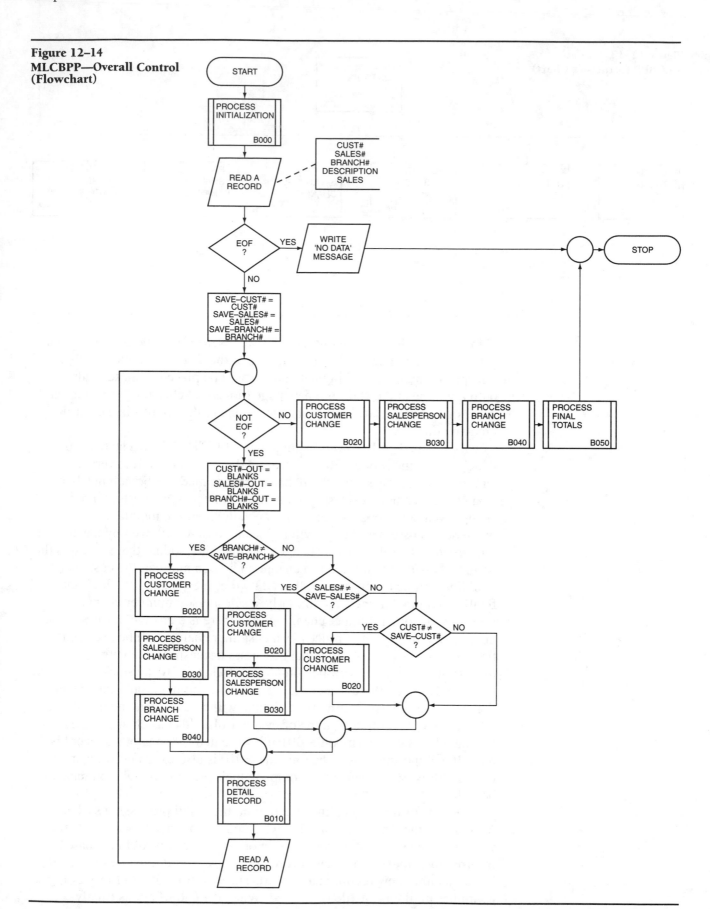

Figure 12–15
MLCBPP—Overall Control
(Pseudocode)

```
A000
Start
Process initialization (B000)
Read CUST#, SALES#, BRANCH#, DESCRIPTION, SALES
IF EOF THEN
    Write 'No Data' message
ELSE
    SAVE-CUST# = CUST#
    SAVE-SALES# = SALES#
    SAVE-BRANCH# = BRANCH#
    DOWHILE not EOF
        CUST#-OUT = Blanks
        SALES#-OUT = Blanks
        BRANCH#-OUT = Blanks
        IF BRANCH# ≠ SAVE-BRANCH# THEN
            Process customer change (B020)
            Process salesperson change (B030)
            Process branch change (B040)
        ELSE
            IF SALES# ≠ SAVE-SALES# THEN
                Process customer change (B020)
                Process salesperson change (B030)
            ELSE
                IF CUST# ≠ SAVE-CUST# THEN
                    Process customer change (B020)
                (ELSE)
                ENDIF
            ENDIF
        ENDIF
        Process detail record (B010)
        Read CUST#, SALES#, BRANCH#, DESCRIPTION, SALES
    ENDDO
    Process customer change (B020)
    Process salesperson change (B030)
    Process branch change (B040)
    Process final totals (B050)
ENDIF
Stop
```

reached, modules B020, B030, and B040 are executed one last time, and the final total line is output (module B050).

You might wonder why modules B020, B030, and B040 are executed again. When end-of-file is reached, the intermediate totals for the last group of customer numbers, salesperson numbers, and branch numbers have not yet been output. Remember, this is done only when a control break occurs—and a control break can be detected only when a control field in the input changes. An end-of-file is, in effect, a change in a control field.

A program flowchart and corresponding pseudocode for module B000 (process initialization) are shown in Figures 12–16 and 12–17. The page count (PAGECNT) is set to 1 and the line count (LINECNT) is set to 40.

Four accumulators are set to 0. CUST-ACCUM is used to keep track of the total sales amount for one customer. SALES-ACCUM is used to keep track of the total sales for one salesperson. BRANCH-ACCUM is used to keep track of the total sales for one branch. FINAL-ACCUM keeps track of the total sales for all branches.

A program flowchart and corresponding pseudocode for module B010 (process detail record) are shown in Figures 12–18 and 12–19. The first processing step is an IFTHENELSE that checks to see if headings need to be printed. Remember, when LINECNT reaches 40 or greater, a new page is started and the headings must be printed first. The detail processing in this algorithm is quite simple. The detail line contains information—all of which has been input—so no calculations are necessary. The line is printed and LINECNT is incremented. Note that we are printing the fields BRANCH#-OUT, SALES#-OUT, and CUST#-OUT and not the fields BRANCH#, SALES#, and CUST#. BRANCH#-OUT, SALES#-OUT, and CUST#-OUT will either contain the actual branch number, salesperson number, and customer number or contain blanks—depending on whether or not the current record contains information on the first branch number, salesperson number, or customer number in a group. This is necessary

Figure 12–16
MLCBPP—Process
Initialization (Flowchart)

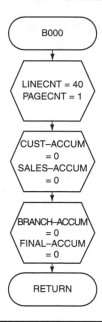

Figure 12–17
MLCBPP—Process
Initialization (Pseudocode)

```
B000
Enter
LINECNT = 40
PAGECNT = 1
CUST-ACCUM = 0
SALES-ACCUM = 0
BRANCH-ACCUM = 0
FINAL-ACCUM = 0
Return
```

because the report is to be group indicated. Finally, the sales amount for one customer from the input (SALES) is added to the customer number accumulator (CUST-ACCUM) before control is returned to A000.

A program flowchart and corresponding pseudocode for module B020 (process customer change) are shown in Figures 12–20 and 12–21. When this module gets control, a control break has occurred and a customer total line must be output. Prior to printing the customer total line, a blank line is output; after the total line is printed, another blank line is output. This will

Figure 12–18
MLCBPP—Process Detail
Record (Flowchart)

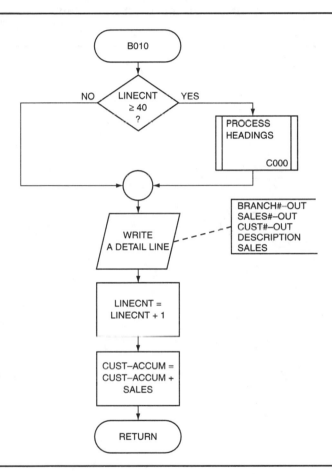

Figure 12–19
MLCBPP—Process Detail
Record (Pseudocode)

```
B010
Enter
IF LINECNT ≥ 40 THEN
    Process headings (C000)
(ELSE)
ENDIF
Write BRANCH#-OUT, SALES#-OUT, CUST#-OUT, DESCRIPTION, SALES
LINECNT = LINECNT + 1
CUST-ACCUM = CUST-ACCUM + SALES
Return
```

help to set the customer total line apart from the other lines in the report. The customer number (SAVE-CUST#) and the accumulated sales amount for that customer (CUST-ACCUM), as well as identifying text, are output.

Remember, CUST# contains information from the current input record; therefore, we need to output SAVE-CUST#. Because three physical lines have been printed (two blank lines and one total line), the line count is incremented by 3. The customer accumulator is added to the salesperson accumulator and then reset to 0. Do you see why? When the next customer is processed, we do not want the previous customer's total sales to be included in the current customer's totals.

Figure 12–20
MLCBPP—Process Customer Change (Flowchart)

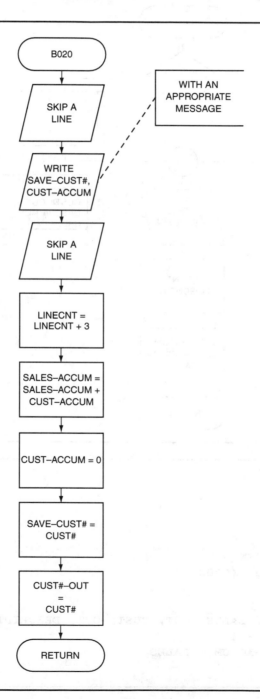

**Figure 12–21
MLCBPP—Process
Customer Change
(Pseudocode)**

```
B020
Enter
Skip a line
Write 'TOTAL CUSTOMER', SAVE-CUST#, 'SALES:',
  CUST-ACCUM
Skip a line
LINECNT = LINECNT + 3
SALES-ACCUM = SALES-ACCUM + CUST-ACCUM
CUST-ACCUM = 0
SAVE-CUST# = CUST#
CUST#-OUT = CUST#
Return
```

Finally, because we are getting ready to process a new customer, the save area (SAVE-CUST#) needs to be updated. Remember, this area is used to hold the value of the current customer number being processed. For example, when a control break occurs the first time, the current customer number must be changed from 345 to 412. CUST#-OUT must also be reset to the new customer number so that the actual number—not a blank field—will be output the next time a detail line is written.

A program flowchart and corresponding pseudocode for module B030 (process salesperson change) are shown in Figures 12–22 and 12–23. When this module gets control, a control break has occurred and a salesperson total line must be output. After the total line is printed, a blank line is output. This will help to set the salesperson total line apart from the other lines in the report. The salesperson number (SAVE-SALES#) and the accumulated sales for that salesperson (SALES-ACCUM), as well as identifying text, are output.

Remember again that SALES# contains information from the current input record; therefore, we need to output SAVE-SALES#. The line count is then incremented by 2. The salesperson accumulator is added to the branch accumulator and then reset to 0. This is the same step we used in the previous module. When the next salesperson is processed, we do not want the previous salesperson's total sales to be included in the current salesperson's totals.

Finally, because we are getting ready to process a new salesperson, the save area (SAVE-SALES#) needs to be updated. Remember, this area is used to hold the value of the current salesperson number being processed. For example, when this control break occurs the first time, the current salesperson number must be changed from 1122 to 2334. SALES#-OUT must also be reset to the new salesperson number, so that the actual number will be output the next time a detail line is written.

A program flowchart and corresponding pseudocode for module B040 (process branch change) are shown in Figures 12–24 and 12–25. When this module gets control, a control break has occurred and a branch total line must be output. After the total line is printed, a blank line is output. This will help to set the branch total line apart from the other lines in the report. The branch number (SAVE-BRANCH#) and the accumulated sales for that branch (BRANCH-ACCUM), as well as identifying text, are output.

Figure 12–22
MLCBPP—Process
Salesperson Change
(Flowchart)

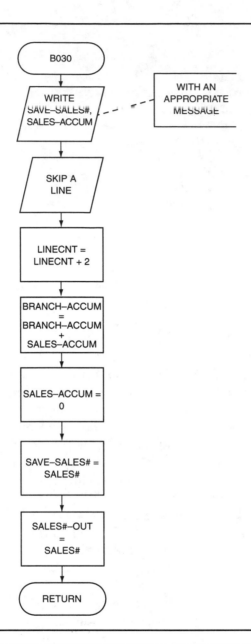

Figure 12–23
MLCBPP—Process
Salesperson Change
(Pseudocode)

```
B030
Enter
Write 'TOTAL SALESPERSON', SAVE-SALES#, 'SALES:', SALES-ACCUM
Skip a line
LINECNT = LINECNT + 2
BRANCH-ACCUM = BRANCH-ACCUM + SALES-ACCUM
SALES-ACCUM = 0
SAVE-SALES# = SALES#
SALES#-OUT = SALES#
Return
```

Figure 12–24
MLCBPP—Process Branch
Change (Flowchart)

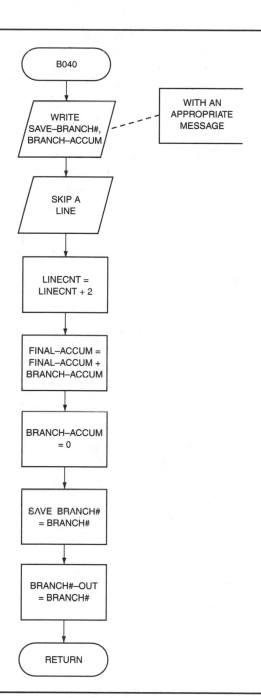

Figure 12–25
MLCBPP—Process Branch
Change (Pseudocode)

```
B040
Enter
Write 'TOTAL BRANCH', SAVE-BRANCH#, 'SALES:', BRANCH-ACCUM
Skip a line
LINECNT = LINECNT + 2
FINAL-ACCUM = FINAL-ACCUM + BRANCH-ACCUM
BRANCH-ACCUM = 0
SAVE-BRANCH# = BRANCH#
BRANCH#-OUT = BRANCH#
Return
```

Remember again that BRANCH# contains information from the current input record; therefore, we need to output SAVE-BRANCH#. The line count is then incremented by 2. The branch accumulator is added to the final accumulator and then reset to 0. When the next branch is processed, we do not want the previous branch's total sales to be included in the current branch's totals.

Finally, because we are getting ready to process a new branch, the save area (SAVE-BRANCH#) needs to be updated. Remember, this area is used to hold the value of the current branch number being processed. For example, when this control break occurs the first time, the current branch number must be changed from 10 to 20. BRANCH#-OUT must also be reset to the new branch number, so that the actual number will be output the next time a detail line is written.

A program flowchart and corresponding pseudocode for module B050 (process final totals) are shown in Figures 12–26 and 12–27. This module simply writes out the value of the final accumulator (FINAL-ACCUM) with an identifying message. Remember, FINAL-ACCUM represents the total sales for all branches.

A program flowchart and corresponding pseudocode for module C000 (process headings) are shown in Figures 12–28 and 12–29. In this module, we are again trying to indicate some degree of spacing. The report heading is followed by one blank line, and the column headings are followed by one blank line. The spacing is primarily for readability; it may or may not be specified by the user. In either case, the programmer must include an indication of spacing requirements somewhere in the documentation. Notice also that the three output fields (CUST#-OUT, SALES#-OUT, and BRANCH#-OUT) are set to their corresponding input values (CUST#,

Figure 12–26
MLCBPP—Process Final Totals (Flowchart)

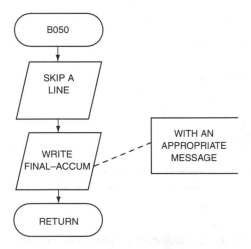

Figure 12–27
MLCBPP—Process Final Totals (Pseudocode)

```
B050
Enter
Skip a line
Write 'TOTAL ACCUMULATED SALES:', FINAL-ACCUM
Return
```

SALES#, and BRANCH#). Can you see why this is necessary? Whenever a new page is started, the actual branch number, salesperson number, and customer number should be output—not blank fields. This step likewise improves the readability of the report.

Figure 12–28
MLCBPP—Process Headings
(Flowchart)

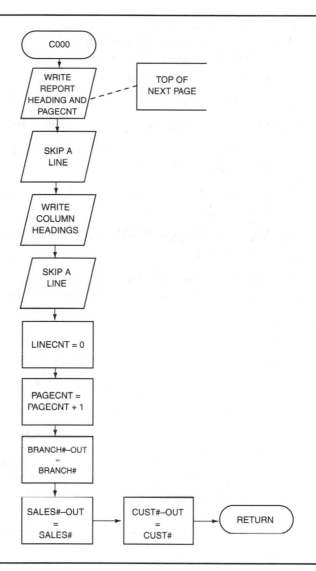

Figure 12–29
MLCBPP—Process Headings
(Pseudocode)

```
C000
Enter
Write report heading and PAGECNT
    at top of next page
Skip a line
Write column headings
Skip a line
LINECNT = 0
PAGECNT = PAGECNT + 1
BRANCH#-OUT = BRANCH#
SALES#-OUT = SALES#
CUST#-OUT = CUST#
Return
```

Key Terms

control break   detail-printed report   group-indicated report
control field (key)   group-printed report

Exercises

1. (a) What is a detail-printed report?
   (b) What is a group-printed report?
   (c) What is a group-indicated report?

2. What is a control field?

3. What does it mean to say that a "control break" has occurred?

4. What would happen if SAVE-DEPT were not reset to DEPT in Figure 12–8 (module B020)?

5. What would happen if DEPT-ACCUM were not reset to 0 in Figure 12–8 (module B020)?

6. What would happen if FINAL-ACCUM were also reset to 0 in Figure 12–8 (module B020)?

7. Explain what would happen if the processing steps inside the DOWHILE loop in Figure 12–4 (module A000) had been written as follows.

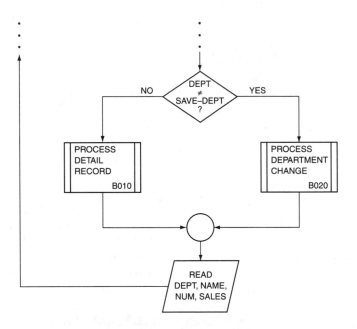

8. Harris Wholesale Distributors maintains comprehensive records of the type, volume, and sales price of all merchandise dispatched from its warehouse locations. These records are updated daily with computer help. They provide the basis for numerous management inquiries, as well as for weekly sales reports. As a part of year-end processing, a summary report showing monthly sales volume—the total dollar value of all merchandise dispatched from the warehouses each month—is needed.

   The input to the program that will generate the summary report comprises one record for each warehouse that reported activity during a month. The record tells the name and location of the warehouse, its total sales volume for the month (in dollars), and a numerical indicator of the month: 1 for January, 2 for February, and so on (see the following illustration). Because the input records are to be read from a distribution master file, they can be assumed to be in ascending order by month (all January records first, then all February records, etc.). There will be at least one warehouse record for each month. A special end-of-file record containing 0 in the month-indicator field, 0s in the sales volume field, and no data in the other fields will be provided as the last input record. If the input fields are being edited by a smart terminal, the name and location fields may need to include at least one blank.

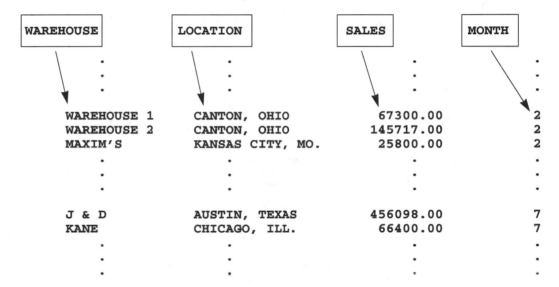

The summary report is to contain one print line (detail line) for each warehouse record—that is, for each warehouse from which merchandise was dispatched during a particular month. When all the records for a month have been read and printed, a total sales volume for the month is to be printed. A grand total indicating the sales volume for the year is to be printed at the end of the report.

```
                    HARRIS WHOLESALE DISTRIBUTORS
                     YEAR-END TOTAL SALES REPORT

MONTH           WAREHOUSE            LOCATION                        SALES

January         Tompkin's            Aberdeen, Maryland          45,069.00
January         Warehouse A          Des Moines, Iowa            44,036.00

   .                 .                    .                          .
   .                 .                    .                          .
   .                 .                    .                          .

                JANUARY TOTAL SALES VOLUME                  $3,846,077.00

   .                 .                    .                          .
   .                 .                    .                          .
   .                 .                    .                          .

                YEAR-END TOTAL SALES VOLUME               $51,994,223.00
```

Construct a flowchart and corresponding pseudocode to solve this problem, but consider the following: The illustration shows that the name of the month is to be output—not the number of the month as shown in the input. For example, "January" will be output, not the number 1. This is clearly more descriptive to anyone reading the report. To make this task easier, assume that you have available a one-dimensional array called MONTHNAME as follows:

MONTHNAME

JANUARY
FEBRUARY
MARCH
APRIL
MAY
JUNE
JULY
AUGUST
SEPTEMBER
OCTOBER
NOVEMBER
DECEMBER

In this case, MONTHNAME(1) = JANUARY, MONTHNAME(2) = FEBRUARY, and so on.

9. Redo Exercise 8 so that the output will contain the name of the month only on the first detail line printed for a particular month, as follows:

```
                    HARRIS WHOLESALE DISTRIBUTORS
                    YEAR-END TOTAL SALES REPORT

MONTH           WAREHOUSE           LOCATION                      SALES

January         Tompkin's           Aberdeen, Maryland          45,069.00
                Warehouse A         Des Moines, Iowa            44,036.00

   .               .                   .                           .
   .               .                   .                           .
   .               .                   .                           .
                JANUARY TOTAL SALES VOLUME                  $3,846,077.00

February        Warehouse B         Washington, D.C.            35,072.00
                Warehouse C         Chicago, Illinois           37,345.00
                Warehouse D         Boston, Mass.               42,128.00

   .               .                   .                           .
   .               .                   .                           .
                FEBRUARY TOTAL SALES VOLUME                 $8,723,119.00

   .               .                   .                           .
   .               .                   .                           .
   .               .                   .                           .
```

10. Student records are input, each containing student id, student name, and one test score. There may be several scores for one student, but each score will be input on a separate record, as follows:

STUDENT ID	STUDENT NAME	TEST SCORE
111111111	Mary Davidson	80
111111111	Mary Davidson	90
111111111	Mary Davidson	100
222222222	Dean Black	70
222222222	Dean Black	60
333333333	Ginny Smith	85
.	.	.
.	.	.
.	.	.

Assume the records are in ascending order by student id. Construct a flowchart and corresponding pseudocode to compute and output the average for each student. Each line of output should contain the student id, student name, and average. Note that no detail lines or final total line are required.

11. Redo Exercise 10 to compute two control totals: the number of students for whom averages are computed and the total number of test scores processed for all students. Output these two control totals at the end of the report in a final total line.

12. A rebate report is to be prepared for a major department store. Design an algorithm to produce the required report. The input consists of customer records that contain the customer number, item number purchased, type of purchase code, and amount of purchase. The type of purchase code indicates whether the purchase was made on a sale item (code of 1) or a non-sale item (code of 2). The output consists of a rebate report containing the customer number, item number purchased, type of purchase (ON SALE or REGULAR), and amount of purchase. The message "ON SALE" and "REGULAR" should be extracted from an array SALETYPE (see below) based upon the value in the "type of purchase" code field in the input record.

SALETYPE

1	ON SALE
2	REGULAR

In addition, total number of sale items, total number of non-sale items, total amount of sale purchases, total amount of non-sale purchases, total credits issued, and rebate earned are to be printed for each customer.

Total credits for each customer are calculated in the following manner: 0 credits for each regular purchase below $100; 1 credit for each regular purchase between $100 and $500; 2 credits for each regular purchase over $500 but under $1,000; 3 credits for each regular purchase of $1,000 or more. Purchases made on sale items do not count in the credit calculation. Based on the total credits, one of the following messages should be printed:

		Rebate Earned Message
	0	NO REBATE
Credits Issued	1–5	$20 REBATE
	6–20	$50 REBATE
	Over 20	$100 REBATE

After all records are processed, final totals should be printed on a separate page. Final totals should include: total number of sale items, total number of non-sale items, total amount of sale purchases, total amount of non-sale purchases, total number of $20 rebates earned, total number of $50 rebates earned, and total number of $100 rebates earned.

A sample of the output follows.

```
                        DEPARTMENT STORE REBATE REPORT                Page 1

CUSTOMER          ITEM              TYPE OF              AMOUNT
NUMBER            NUMBER            PURCHASE             OF PURCHASE

1111              123               ON SALE              $ 150.00
                  234               REGULAR              $ 300.00
                  364               REGULAR              $ 200.00
                  334               ON SALE              $ 950.00

SALE ITEMS      - TOTAL 2         SALE PURCHASES      - TOTAL $1100.00
NON-SALE ITEMS  - TOTAL 2         NON-SALE PURCHASES  - TOTAL $ 500.00

TOTAL CREDITS ISSUED  - 2         REBATE EARNED - $20 REBATE


2222              456               REGULAR              $1750.00
                  249               REGULAR              $  80.00
                  987               REGULAR              $1650.00

SALE ITEMS      - TOTAL 0         SALE PURCHASES      - TOTAL $   0.00
NON-SALE ITEMS  - TOTAL 3         NON-SALE PURCHASES  - TOTAL $3480.00

TOTAL CREDITS ISSUED  - 6         REBATE EARNED -  $50 REBATE

                           (Separate Page)

                        DEPARTMENT STORE                     Page X
                          FINAL TOTALS

TOTAL NUMBER OF SALE ITEMS        -        125
TOTAL NUMBER OF NON-SALE ITEMS    -        300
TOTAL SALE PURCHASES              -     $ 50,925
TOTAL NON-SALE PURCHASES          -     $142,855

TOTAL REBATES EARNED
        $ 20 REBATES EARNED       -         20
        $ 50 REBATES EARNED       -         10
        $100 REBATES EARNED       -          6
```

This report is to be group indicated, that is, the customer number is, to be printed only for the first record in the group. Include the "No data" message, report headings, and column headings on every page. Use automatic end-of-file to indicate the end of the input. Records are assumed to be in ascending order by customer number.

13. A sales report is to be prepared for the appliance department in a major department store. Design an algorithm to produce the required report. The input consists of salesperson records that contain the salesperson number, salesperson name, type of appliance code, color code, and sales price. The output consists of a kitchen appliance sales report containing the salesperson number, salesperson name, appliance sold, color, and sales price. Assume that you have available two one-dimensional arrays called TYPE and COLOR as follows:

TYPE

1	REFRIGERATOR
2	DISHWASHER
3	COMPACTOR
4	STOVE

COLOR

1	WHITE
2	GOLD
3	AVOCADO

In addition, subtotals and final totals for three control-break levels—salesperson, appliance, and color—are to be output. Design the output as a group-indicated report. A sample of the output follows on the next page.

```
                      KITCHEN APPLIANCE SALES INC.                Page 1

      SALESPERSON     SALESPERSON    APPLIANCE      COLOR        SALES
      NUMBER          NAME           SOLD                        PRICE

         10           John Black     Refrigerator   Avocado      700.00
                                                                 600.00
                                                                 500.00

                                     COLOR Avocado SALES        1800.00
                                                UNITS SOLD             3

                                                   Gold          500.00
                                                                 600.00

                                     COLOR Gold     SALES       1100.00
                                                UNITS SOLD             2

                                     TOTAL Refrigerator SALES   2900.00
                                                UNITS SOLD             5

                                     Dishwasher      White       500.00
                                                                 400.00

                                     COLOR White     SALES       900.00
                                                UNITS SOLD             2

                                     TOTAL Dishwasher  SALES     900.00
                                                UNITS SOLD             2

                          TOTAL FOR SALESPERSON NUMBER   10     3800.00
                                                UNITS SOLD             7
                                                   .
                                                   .
                                                   .
                                     GRAND TOTAL SALES       150560.00
                                        TOTAL UNITS SOLD           300
```

Assume that the input data is properly sequenced, and include the "No data" message. Include report headings and column headings on every page, as well as page numbers, with 30 detail lines per page. Use automatic end-of-file to indicate the end of the input.

14. Redo Exercise 13 to include an additional report (on a new page) as follows:

```
      SUMMARY OF SALES BY APPLIANCE SOLD              Page X


APPLIANCE                    NO. OF UNITS              SALES PRICE
                             SOLD

Refrigerator                     XXX                  XXXXXXXXX.XX
Dishwasher                       XXX                  XXXXXXXXX.XX
Compactor                        XXX                  XXXXXXXXX.XX
Stove                            XXX                  XXXXXXXXX.XX


              *** GRAND TOTALS ***                  XXXXXXXXXXXX.XX
```

15. Redo Exercise 14 to include an additional report (on a new page) as follows:

```
        SUMMARY OF SALES BY COLOR                     Page X


COLOR OF                     NO. OF UNITS              SALES PRICE
APPLIANCE                    SOLD

White                            XXX                  XXXXXXXXX.XX
Gold                             XXX                  XXXXXXXXX.XX
Avocado                          XXX                  XXXXXXXXX.XX


              *** GRAND TOTALS ***                  XXXXXXXXXXXX.XX
```

American National Standards Institute (ANSI) recommendations for use of symbols on program flowcharts are presented in this appendix. The shape of each recommended symbol, its meaning, and one or more examples are given. The symbols that you are most apt to find useful in your design work are explained in greater detail in one or more chapters in this book. The chapter in which each symbol is introduced is given in parentheses following the explanation of the symbol below.

Input/Output Symbol

Generalized input/output function; reading data from an input medium or writing data to an output medium (Chapter 2)

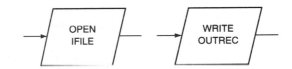

Process Symbol

Any processing step; an operation or group of operations causing change in value, form, or location of data (Chapter 2)

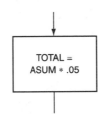

Flowline Symbol

Sequence of operations and direction of data flow; arrowheads are required if linkage is not top-to-bottom or left-to-right (Chapter 2)

Annotation Symbol

Additional explanation; comments (Chapter 4)

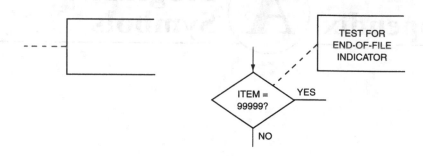

Connector Symbol

Exit to, or entry from, another part of the flowchart; if the *to* or *from* step is on another page, a page reference should be stated (Chapter 3)

Terminal Interrupt Symbol

Terminal point in a flowchart—start, stop, or break in the line of flow (Chapter 2)

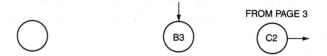

Decision Symbol

Decision-making operation, usually based on a comparison, that determines which of two or more alternative paths should be followed (Chapter 3)

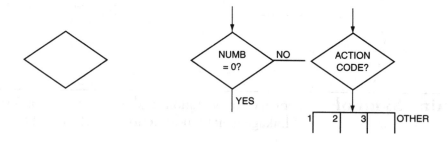

Preparation Symbol

An operation performed on the program itself for control, initialization, overhead, or cleanup; examples are to set a switch, to place a limit value in a loop-control variable, and to initialize an accumulator (Chapter 4)

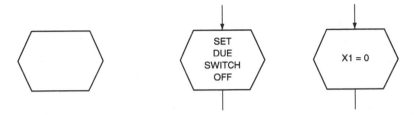

Predefined-Process Symbol

One or more operations specified in detail elsewhere, such as in a reference manual or on a different flowchart, but not on another part of the flowchart where this symbol appears (Chapter 4)

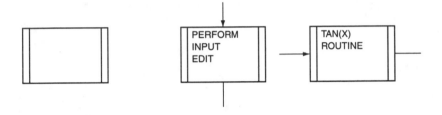

Appendix B Structured-Programming Control Structures

The three basic patterns of structured programming—SIMPLE SEQUENCE, IFTHENELSE, and DOWHILE—are summarized in this appendix. Two additional control structures, CASE and DOUNTIL, which represent frequently used combinations of these basic patterns, are also summarized. First, the general form of the control structure is given. Then an example is expressed in both flowchart and pseudocode forms. The chapter in which each structure is introduced is given in parentheses following the explanation.

SIMPLE SEQUENCE

The execution of one processing step after another, in normal execution sequence (Chapter 2)

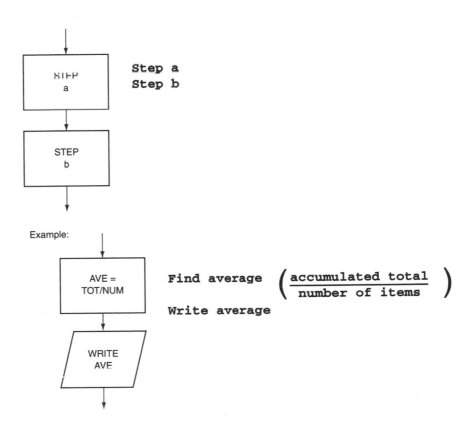

Step a
Step b

Example:

Find average $\left(\dfrac{\text{accumulated total}}{\text{number of items}} \right)$

Write average

IFTHENELSE The selection of one of two alternatives (Chapter 3)

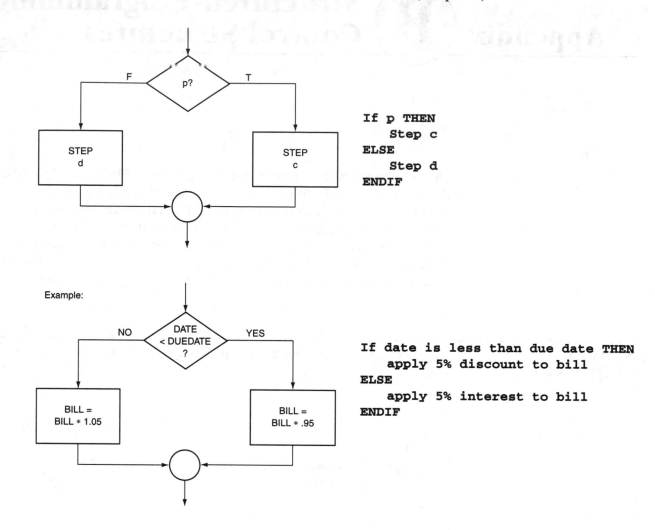

```
If p THEN
    Step c
ELSE
    Step d
ENDIF
```

Example:

```
If date is less than due date THEN
    apply 5% discount to bill
ELSE
    apply 5% interest to bill
ENDIF
```

DOWHILE

The execution of processing steps within a program loop as long as a specified condition is true; a leading-decision loop (Chapter 4)

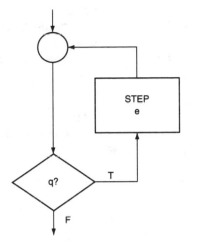

```
DOWHILE q is true
    Step e
ENDDO
```

Example:

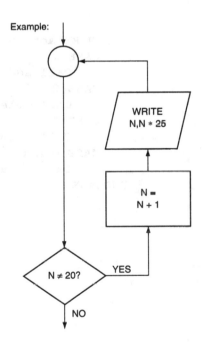

```
DOWHILE counter N is not equal to 20
    N = N + 1
    Write N, N*25
ENDDO
```

CASE

The selection of one of more than two alternatives (Chapter 6)

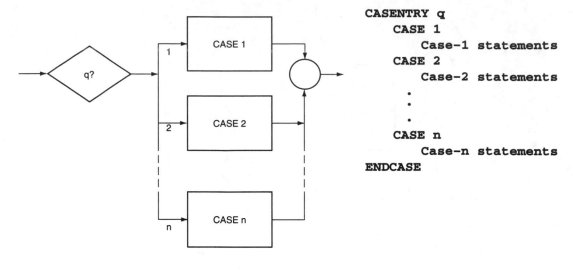

```
CASENTRY q
   CASE 1
      Case-1 statements
   CASE 2
      Case-2 statements
       .
       .
       .
   CASE n
      Case-n statements
ENDCASE
```

Example:

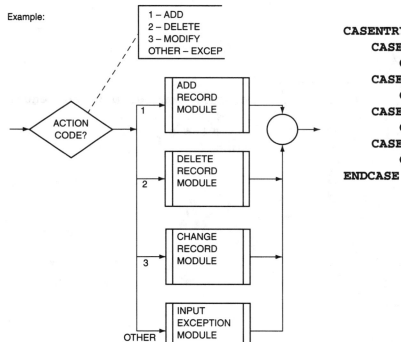

```
CASENTRY action code
   CASE 1
      Call add record module
   CASE 2
      Call delete record module
   CASE 3
      Call change record module
   CASE other
      Call input exception module
ENDCASE
```

DOUNTIL   The execution of processing steps within a program loop until a specified condition is true; a trailing-decision loop (Chapter 7)

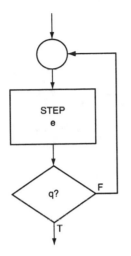

```
DOUNTIL q is true
    Step e
ENDDO
```

Example:

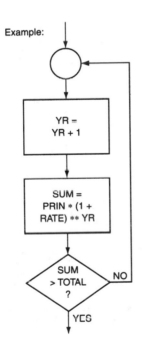

```
DOUNTIL sum of principal and interest (SUM)
    is greater than limit value (TOTAL)
    Add 1 to number of years
    SUM = principal * (1 + rate) ** number of years
ENDDO
```

Appendix C Answers to Selected Exercises

Responses to selected exercises from each of the chapters in this book are given in this appendix. For some of these exercises, there is no one correct answer. In such cases, the responses are representative answers to the problems.

Chapter 1

1. The steps in the system development life cycle are:
   - Analyze the current system.
   - Define the new system requirements.
   - Design a new system.
   - Develop a new system.
   - Implement the new system.
   - Evaluate the new system.

2. The steps in the program development cycle are:
   - Review the program requirements.
   - Develop the program logic.
   - Write the program.
   - Test and debug the program.
   - Complete the program documentation.

Chapter 2

1. An algorithm is a step-by-step procedure to solve a problem.

4. **(a)** file, record, field, character

6. A system flowchart shows very general information about an application. The information shown includes the major inputs, processes, and outputs for each program in the application. A program flowchart shows the specific details of how one program works. Both types of flowcharts give us information graphically: The system flowchart gives general information and can involve several programs; the program flowchart gives specific information about only one program.

7. (a) The normal direction of flow on both system and program flow-charts is top-to-bottom and left-to-right.

9. (a) −49

10. 310.40

Chapter 3

1. A decision-making step provides for a choice among alternative paths, which is a variation in processing sequence dependent on the data entering the system or situations that arise during processing.

3. (a) Pseudocode is an English-like description of an algorithm that uses indentation to more clearly identify the three basic control structures.

5. (a) A null ELSE indicates that no processing steps are to occur within the false path of an IFTHENELSE statement.

7. In a sequential IFTHENELSE pattern, all the tests are executed regardless of the outcome of previous tests. In a nested IFTHENELSE pattern, a test is either executed or not executed depending upon the results of the previous test.

Chapter 4

1. A program loop permits a sequence of processing steps to be done repeatedly (i.e., reexecuted or reused) during processing.

5. Because each basic pattern has only one entry point and one exit point, it can be treated as a SIMPLE SEQUENCE pattern. Further, a series of these basic patterns can be treated as a SIMPLE SEQUENCE. (We say that the contained patterns are nested.) The combining of patterns and building up of logic can continue until a complete program is constructed. A program containing only basic patterns and combinations thereof can have only one entry point and one exit point. It can itself be thought of as a SIMPLE SEQUENCE, or basic building block.

7. The three basic patterns are SIMPLE SEQUENCE, IFTHENELSE, and DOWHILE.

9. **(a)** Each time the loop is executed, COUNT will be reset to 0. Since the last step in the loop adds 1 to COUNT, the value of COUNT will continue to be equal to 1, never reaching the maximum value of 6. When the test (COUNT < 6) is made to determine if the loop should be executed, the answer will always be yes, thus creating an infinite loop.

15.

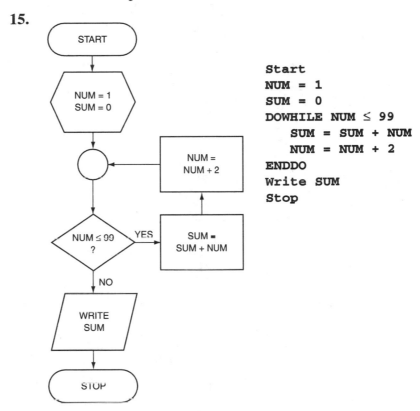

```
Start
NUM = 1
SUM = 0
DOWHILE NUM ≤ 99
    SUM = SUM + NUM
    NUM = NUM + 2
ENDDO
Write SUM
Stop
```

Chapter 5

1. In header record logic, the first record in the input specifies how many records will follow. The loop must be controlled by a counter that gets its initial value from the first record (header record). In trailer record logic, the last record in the input specifies that no more records will follow. The loop is not controlled by a counter. A test is made, following each read statement, to determine whether or not the last record (trailer record) has been read.

5.

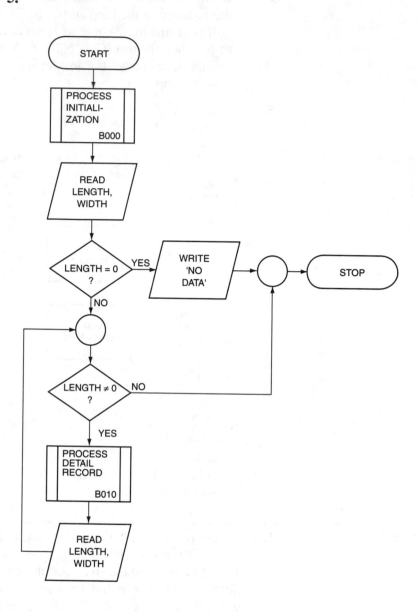

5. (continued)

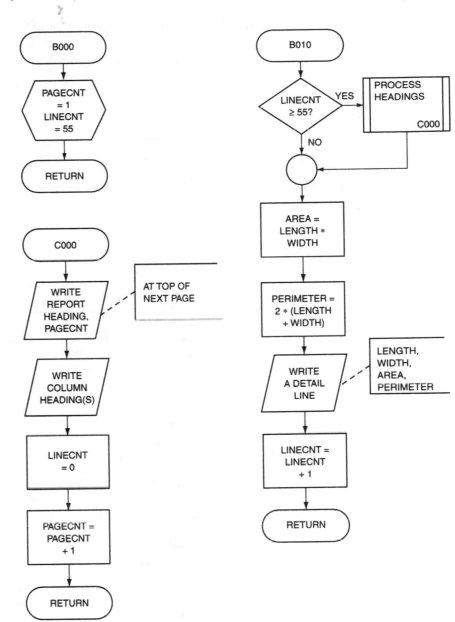

Chapter 6

1. (a) A master file contains a large volume of relatively permanent data kept for reference purposes. A transaction file contains current activities, or transactions, that will be used to update a master file.

5. (a)

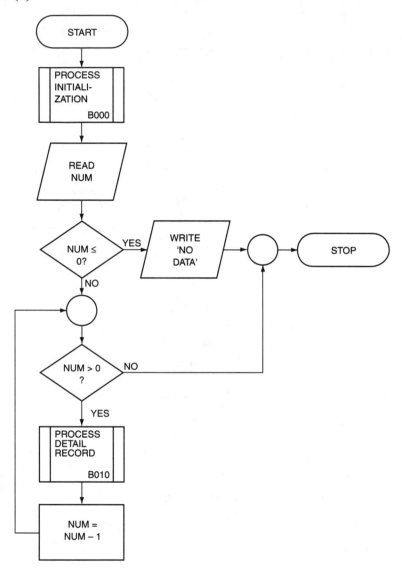

5. (a) (continued)

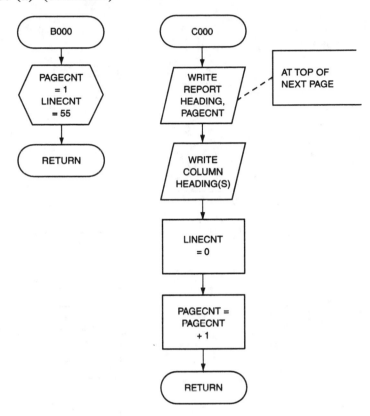

5. (a) (continued)

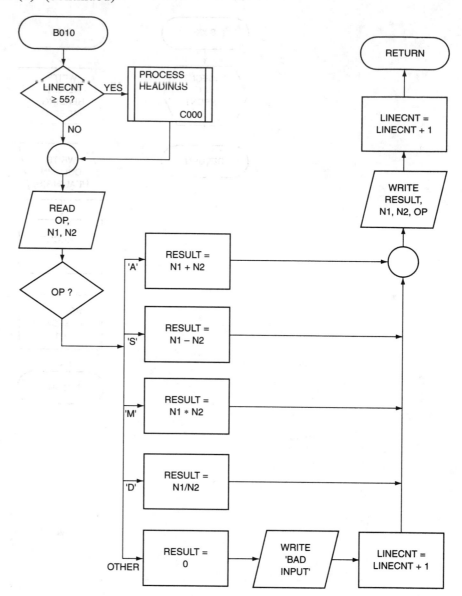

Chapter 7

1. (a) A leading-decision loop is formed in a DOWHILE pattern.

6.

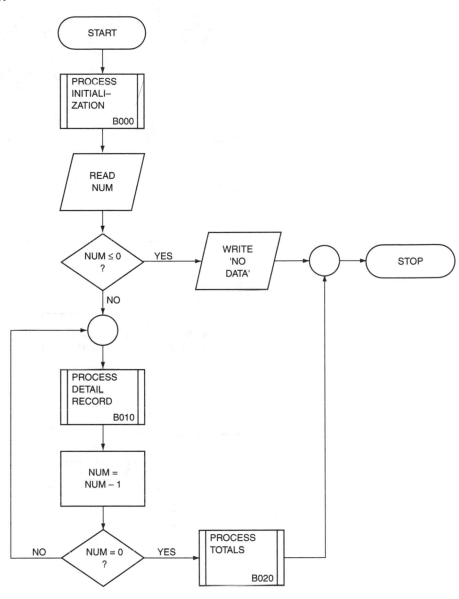

6. (continued)

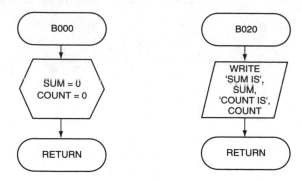

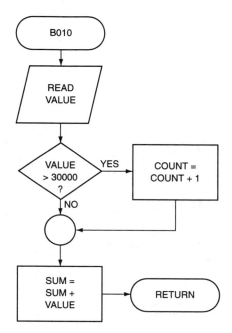

Chapter 8	**1. (a)** A data group is a collection of similar data items for which a single storage area large enough for all the items is reserved. The individual items are not assigned names; instead, one name is assigned to the entire group of items.
	3. (a) E(4) contains 48.
	(b) E(1)
	(c) E(R)
	(d) 1 and 8

Chapter 9	**1.** In procedure-oriented design of programs, the emphasis is on doing things; that is, on performing actions and on the sequence of those actions—the data is secondary. In object-oriented design of programs, the emphasis is on the data to be manipulated and the operations to be performed on the data.
	3. A class definition contains both data and behavior. The data describes what an object looks like and the behavior describes what an object does. The data that defines a class can also be referred to as properties, data members (of the class), or instance variables. The behaviors can also be referred to as methods or member functions.
	7. Overloading is the ability to use the same method to invoke different methods that perform different actions based on the number or type of arguments in the method invocation.
	11. Inheritance is a mechanism by which one class acquires the data and methods of another class.
	13. Overriding is the process of reimplementing a method inherited from a base class.

Chapter 10	**1. (a)** A table-lookup operation is a search of the entries in a table to find a table entry applicable to the value being processed against the table.
	5. The office code read as input and assigned to INCOD is the search key.
	7. (a) Three program switches used in this solution algorithm are STOPSW, FTSW, and ERRIN.
	14. (a) 708 52 10 .091

Chapter 11

1. (a) In an online-processing environment, the execution of a program is initiated by a user at a terminal, personal computer, or workstation. The user is in direct communication with the computer.

5.

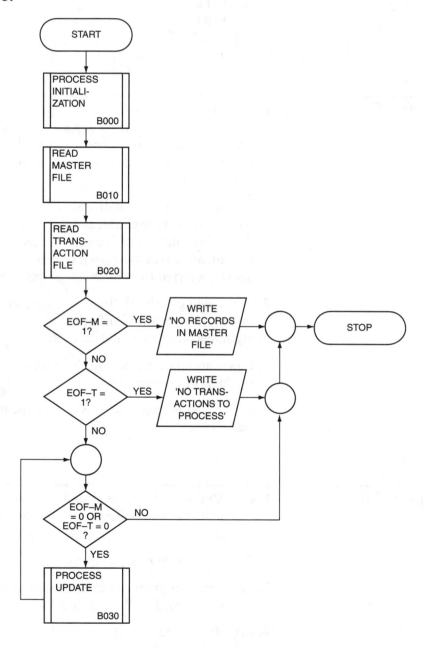

7. (b) The new master file contains the following records:

ID#-M	Status
00002	changed
00006	unchanged
00007	changed (2nd change)
00008	added
00009	unchanged
00010	unchanged
00012	unchanged
00014	unchanged

(c) No error messages will be output.

Chapter 12

1. (a) A detail-printed report is a report in which one line of output is printed for each input record processed.

3. A control break occurs when the value in a designated field in the input (the control field) changes. Normal processing is interrupted and control-break processing is begun.

5. Each subsequent department sales total would reflect the sales totals from all previous departments. DEPT-ACCUM would in effect be an accumulation of the sales from all the input records.

Index

A

Accumulator, 64
Algorithm, 15–17, 20
Alphabetic data, 132
American National Standards Institute (ANSI), 19, 29, 309
Annotation symbol, 72, 310
ANSI. *See* American National Standards Institute
Array processing, 181–211, 231–55
Assignment statement, 22, 61–62, 64
Assignment symbol, 22
Automatic end-of-file facility, 102–103, 114, 169–171, 263–265, 279–281

B

Basic, 8, 30–31, 50–51, 84–85, 115–117, 146–147, 172, 181, 194, 203–204
  blank space, 30–31
  Data statement, 115–116
  Dim statement, 203–204
  double quotes, 30
  DOUNTIL loop, 172
  End statement, 30
  Input statement, 30
  Print statement, 30
  program loop, 84–85
  Read statement, 115–116
  Rem statement, 115–116
  SELECT CASE structure, 146–147
  Shared statement, 115–116
  Subprogram, 115–117
Batch-processing environment, 258
Binary search, 238–245
Block diagram, 16. *See also* Program flowchart
Bohm, C., 11, 84
Bug, 8. *See also* Logic error *and* Syntax error
Building-block concept, 84

C

C/C++, 7–8, 181, 194, 203, 229
Called module, 72

Calling module (callee), 72
CASE. *See* CASE control structure *and* Computer-assisted software engineering
CASE control structure, 127–158, 159, 268–269, 316
Case tools, 4, 8, 30, 41
Character, 17–18
Character string, 132
Character-string constant, 30, 47, 188–190
Class, 214
  Base (parent, super), 221
  Data member (instance variable, property), 214
  Derived (child, subclass), 221
  Method (member function), 214
COBOL, 7, 181, 182, 194, 203
Collector, 40, 66. *See also* Connector symbol
Column (in table), 194
  Column-major order, 202–203
Computer-assisted software engineering (CASE), 4, 130
Computer-based information system, 1
Conditional branch, 38
Connector symbol, 40, 66, 132, 310
Constant, 22
  character-string, 30, 47, 188–190
Constructor, 217–218
  arguments, 218
  parameters, 218
Control break, 277
Control break processing, 277–307
Control field, 277–278. *See also* Key field
Control structure, 10–11, 313–317
Counter, 64–65, 67–69
Counter-controlled program loop, 61–91, 93, 114, 161–163, 195–197, 198–201

D

Data hiding, 214
Data hierarchy, 17–18
Data independent, 21

333